the PROPERTY HANDBOOK

the PROPERTY

HANDBOOK

complete guide to:

- BUYING
- SELLING
- FINANCING
- RENTING
- PLANNING
- IMPROVING . . .

. . . everything you need to know
about your house and home

Sphere
Reference

SPHERE BOOKS LTD
Published by the Penguin Group
27 Wrights Lane, London W8 5TZ, England
Viking Penguin Inc., 40 West 23rd Street, New York, New York 10010, USA
Penguin Books Australia Ltd, Ringwood, Victoria, Australia
Penguin Books Canada Ltd, 2801 John Street, Markham, Ontario, Canada L3R 1B4
Penguin Books (NZ) Ltd, 182–190 Wairau Road, Auckland 10, New Zealand

Penguin Books Ltd, Registered Offices: Harmondsworth, Middlesex, England

First published in Great Britain by Sphere Books Ltd, 1988
Copyright © Shepherds Keep Studio Ltd, 1988
All rights reserved

TRADE
MARK

Designed and produced by The Pen and Ink Book Company Ltd
Illustrations by Richard Bonson and DMD Ltd
Cartoons by Nigel Paige
Photography by Chris Perrett
Printed and bound in Great Britain by Scotprint Ltd, Musselburgh, Scotland

CONTENTS

Authors' notes

Throughout this book, wherever it has been necessary for us to consider legal matters, our reference point has been English Law, which applies to all property in England and Wales. However, Scottish Law does differ considerably in a number of respects and therefore we have included a separate section on the subject on page 142.

Please regard all references to *he* as meaning *he* or *she*. We recognize that bank managers/estate agents/solicitors etc, etc can be as easily female as male, but we have tried not to make the text too cumbersome by quoting either/or throughout.

What do we all have in common? What is the most dominant factor likely to influence our sense of wellbeing, security and happiness? What shapes our lifestyle and demonstrates our financial standing? What most affects our self-image and the image other people have of us? What offers the greatest degree of comfort or causes the greatest degree of stress? It is the place we like to call *home*.

Tragically, *home* to the underprivileged could mean a park bench or a railway arch, but for the vast majority of us, it means a property, and whether it is a castle or a bedsit, it is likely to represent the focal point in our lives. Yet we tend to treat the subject so casually. Have you ever bought or sold a house? If so, you will know the decision to buy takes place after one or two brief visits to the property, and usually in stage whispers conducted barely out of the earshot of both vendor and estate agent. Would you make such a hasty decision about the purchase of a new car, a new cooker, even a new item of clothing? As a nation, our ignorance on the subject is staggering, which is why this book is such vital reading if you have a property in your life – whether it is your own or someone else's.

In recent years, no one can have been unaware of the extraordinary upsurge in property values. Prices in many areas of the country have become unreal – monopoly money – and this tends to heighten our sense of disorientation and increase the feeling that we are generally out of our depth. This book will give you a thorough understanding of the property market and demonstrate how to get the best out of it, whatever your personal circumstances. This is not a book about how to do your own conveyancing, nor do we intend to turn you into a DIY expert, nor indeed a property tycoon. However the biggest, most materially, important aspect of your life is almost certainly your home and so it is vital you know just what goes on in the property world. You owe it to yourself.

ALAN AND DEBORAH FOWLER

Houses

What is a house? A house is a dwelling which stands on its own ground, has its own four walls and its own roof. It can be a palace, a semi-detached, a terraced house, a bungalow, a cottage – you can buy it or you can lease it. By and large, it is most people's ambition to own a house – what type of house, of course, depends entirely on the individual. An Englishman's home is still his castle and while some castles may be more modest than others, it is a marvellous feeling to be in possession of a piece of land which is yours, upon which sit bricks and mortar which are yours, also.

In the last ten years it has been possible for an increasing number of people to buy their own home and when it comes to making an outright purchase, it is a house people tend to want rather than a flat. In recent years there have been far more funds available for house purchase and it is this very availability of money which has created, in a way, its own market. Attitudes

to lending have changed, too – banks and building societies are quite literally falling over themselves to provide mortgages. Ten years ago the rules were very strict. You could borrow twice, or very occasionally two and a half times, your annual earning capacity, and amazing as it seems now, wife's earnings were rarely taken into account as they were considered of a temporary and inferior nature. The concept of a couple who were unmarried, or of the same sex, making a joint purchase of a property was heavily frowned upon. Today, you will find you can borrow up to four times your annual wage, and if you are making a joint purchase, both salaries will be taken into account. Also available are improvement grants, instant credit and long term loans for house improvements. Indeed, provided you have an income – even a fairly low one – there is little to stop you acquiring a house of your own. As one bank manager said to us during the research for this book, in his view, today, the easiest part of buying a house is finding the money. It is the

Today, the average house price in the north-east of England is less than £35,000. In the Greater London area, the average house price is £85,000 plus – it is important to stress here that this is for *exactly the same type of house*. Not only that, but houses in the south of England are increasing in value faster than those in the north. Let us look at a hypothetical example. You get offered a job in Bradford which is too good to turn down. You sell your house in Middlesex for £85,000 and buy a lovely four-bedroomed house on the edge of the Yorkshire Moors for £32,000. You cannot believe your luck: you have a property to be proud of and cash in the bank. Careful – supposing the job in Yorkshire does not work out and you have to return to the south of England. To buy a house equivalent to your old home may now cost £95,000 whereas all you can get for your house on the Yorkshire Moors is £35,000 – assuming that you can sell it at all. Low house prices mean poor demand. While you will have people falling over themselves to buy your property in Middlesex, in the north-east, houses can sit on the market for months.

Of course, houses can be rented, as well as purchased, but given the choice and the circumstances, you should buy. If you are renting a house, rather than a flat, presumably it is because you require the advantages a house has to offer – i.e. better facilities, more privacy. This in turn suggests that where you live is very important to you. If this is the case, unless your requirement is short term, why throw money down the drain on a rental when the same money applied to a mortgage will build you an asset for the future?

surveys, the solicitors, the gazumping and the emotional trauma of it all which cause the main headaches.

So, buying a house is easy, but is it a sensible thing to do? Yes, most certainly, provided you use commonsense. In the next section of this book we will look in more detail at the important safeguards necessary to ensure you buy the right house for the right money, but there is another aspect to consider. How long are you intending to own this house? It really is not worthwhile owning a house for less than two years, for the buying and selling costs involved are likely to absorb any increase in value, and that applies even with today's escalating prices. However if you intend staying more than two years and have properly surveyed the property and conducted the necessary searches, and paid the right price, it should be a gilt-edged investment and, in theory at any rate, you cannot lose money. What remains currently the biggest stumbling block to safe house purchase, however, is the north/south divide.

Flats and bedsits

A flat, by definition, is part of a house or a larger building. The property is divided into separate dwelling units which are either let or sold.

Whereas our advice so far as houses are concerned is to buy wherever you can, this

is not necessarily the case with flats, for two main reasons:

◆ By the very nature of the beast, a flat tends to attract people at a transient stage in their lives. In other words, it is the very young and the very old who tend to occupy flats – at any rate where they have a choice in the matter. The young leave home, either to go to a job, college or university and usually share a flat with a number of others. They marry and for a few years, before they start a family, a flat proves an ideal home. When they settle down to a family life, however, they want a house. At the other end of the scale, when the children have flown the nest and perhaps one partner has died, the elderly seek a flat rather than a house for completely different reasons – reduced cost, greater security, less demanding. In other words a flat is often used, not as a lifetime's home but as a staging post. If you do not see a requirement for a flat long term it may not be worth buying.

◆ If you have a short lease on a flat then your responsibilities, under the terms of the lease, tend to be with regard to the decorations and furnishings and fittings (if any) of the flat you have rented. If you purchase the flat, then suddenly the whole property in which it is situated is of very real concern. Supposing you buy a flat in a house, apparently in good condition. Supposing the other tenants do not undertake their share of maintenance. You could find your investment rapidly declining. You may have checked out your neighbours very carefully before purchasing the flat but what if a load of trouble-makers take on the flat across the hall? As well as wrecking their own flat, they could seriously undermine the value of the whole property. In other words, you are far more vulnerable buying a flat than buying a house which is why, of course, there are so many residents' associations created – particularly in new apartment buildings – to ensure that standards are maintained.

Of course, for a great many people, living in a flat is the right long-term answer, in which case, as with houses, it's far better to put your money into paying off a mortgage than throwing it down the drain paying rent. Most flat purchases involve buying a long lease subject to a small ground rent payable to the freeholder or head leaseholder. In major cities, the freehold often belongs to one of the major landowners in the country. For example, the Duke of Westminster owns most of Mayfair and Belgravia, and Prince Charles wearing his Duchy of Cornwall hat, owns a sizeable piece of Central London as well. In these instances, when you acquire a flat, you may find that your ground rent is payable direct to the relevant estate, as the freeholder. It is more likely, however, that your landlord will merely own the long leasehold of the building. Ideally, your lease should be sufficiently long to ensure that continuing inflation of the property value will outweigh the gradual reduction of the asset, by virtue of the reducing length of lease.

Many modern flat developments tend to operate through a tenants' association; and frequently, the freehold or headlease of the property is owned by a management company in which all of the tenants are shareholders. This is a good idea since it tends to help the residents to look at the building concerned as a cohesive whole and tackle such problem areas as roof repairs, security, parking and communal gardens. If there is no association, then the rule of 'I'm all right, Jack' tends to apply. The message, therefore, is do be particularly careful when buying a flat to look at the whole building and its circumstances.

Some flats, mostly shorter leaseholds, are what are best described as service flats. A service flat can be almost like living in a hotel. You can take a short lease on what is little more than one room, and have the facilities of a porter, cleaning and laundry, and perhaps within the block of flats, a restaurant and bar. Other service flats offer virtually no facilities other than a porter, but are still so described. What you do have to watch is the ratio of service to service charges. Some charges are unacceptably high for flats offering virtually no facilities,

while others could, perhaps, include hot water and heating and therefore amply justify themselves.

Certainly for the right person, a flat can make an excellent long term home. If you have no children and a busy working life, then it is bliss not to have the responsibilities of a garden. In fact before contemplating a move from a flat to a house, you need to consider very seriously whether you have the time to devote to the requirements of a house – with tiles coming off the roof, leaky guttering, a lawn which needs mowing, etc., etc. By contrast, flat life can seem very attractive.

You might consider, in addition to your own home, a holiday flat, either in this country or abroad and we will be dealing with the purchase of properties other than your main home on page 34 of this book. Suffice to say here that while you can reasonably safely invest in a holiday house, we are somewhat dubious about buying a flat as an investment if you are not going to live in it yourself. When you live on the premises, up to a point you have the ability to police the whole building. If your flat is situated some distance from your main place of residence – perhaps even in a different country – it is very difficult to keep tabs on the property when you only see it every few months.

It all comes down to the same thing – renting a flat as a short term requirement is fair enough. However, if you are considering buying one, then you do need to be very sure of the long-term future of the entire building, the attitude of co-tenants and the likely prosperity, or otherwise, of the district as a whole.

THE FREEHOLDER WROTE, "STORAGE OF HIS WINDSURFER" INTO MY LEASE

Mobile homes/caravans

A mobile home, in theory at any rate, is a very good idea if you have limited resources and want a property of your own. Acquiring a reasonably priced, well-equipped mobile home is not difficult – it is the availability of the site which is all important. In rare instances, and we would stress *rare*, it may be possible to buy a plot of land to site your mobile home, but planning permission, in these circumstances, is very difficult and certainly you would be most unwise to buy a mobile home without first having found and secured a suitable site.

While individual sites are rare, sometimes planning permission can be obtained if you have existing land and the addition of a mobile home is required for a quite specific purpose. For example, it may be possible to obtain planning permission to put elderly parents in a mobile home, in your garden.

Alternatively, if you run a business such as a farm, a riding stables or a market garden and require staff accommodation, here again, planning permission may well be given for you to house them in a mobile home on your existing land.

This rather sticky attitude to mobile homes on the part of the planning authorities is not unreasonable. While internally mobile homes are often very comfortable and extremely well designed, it has to be said they are not things of beauty, and the concept of them springing up all over the country – everywhere there is a piece of free land – is not an attractive one.

Given the problems of planning, most mobile homes are to be found on a park, and before you throw up your hands in horror and say – *I wouldn't live on a caravan site –*

some mobile home parks are really very pleasant places in which to live. Recently it has been recognized that park homes can provide excellent homes for the elderly. They are all on one level, are very easy to run and because they are considerably cheaper than bricks and mortar, the elderly person can trade down, by disposing of a house or flat, and end up with a new home and some surplus cash. These new parks, aimed principally at the elderly, are in many instances beautifully landscaped and offer extremely good facilities. All mobile home parks offer the basic services of drainage, water, electricity and sometimes gas, but the sites do vary enormously in quality and it is here you have to be very careful.

Costs

The price range of mobile homes is quite extensive. You can pay as little as £18,000 for a small second-hand unit or up to £60,000 for a new large home. There is very little maintenance and mobile homes have a useful life of between twenty and thirty years. However it is important to recognize that if you are buying a mobile home on an existing site, it is likely that at least 50% of the cost will relate, not to the home itself, but to the site. In 1983, the Mobile Homes Act gave owners the right to sell their park homes to include, not only the home itself, but also the right to the site. If you are buying a mobile home on an attractive, well-run, secure site, then inevitably the vendor can charge a premium for that, which again emphasizes that the site itself is more important than the home.

There is very little differential in site rentals. You will be asked to pay between £10–£15 per week on the average park which includes water rates. General rates, although extra, are not high. It is not the rental which should concern you but the difference in *standards* of parks. Bearing in mind how much of what you pay for a home will relate to the site, you need to recognize what may happen if the site operator goes out of business. The likely outcome is that your mobile home has to be re-sited and not only that – in all probability, it will instantly become worth half the price you paid for it.

Financing a mobile home

Traditionally, so far as the banks and finance companies are concerned, financing the purchase of a mobile home is a bad credit risk. Banks generally find that there is a very high default rate and it is easy to see why. The typical buyer is a young couple, with or without children, who have been living with parents. The parents put up the deposit to get the young family out of their home but then the couple are unable to meet the repayment programme. Of course banks can repossess the home in these circumstances, but particularly where children are involved, it is not something they like doing. Despite this poor track record, however, finance is available, but your likelihood of obtaining it depends as much on the status and reputation of the park operator as your own personal credit standing. Up to 80% of the purchase price should be available from a finance company and usually can be borrowed over a maximum of five years. The interest rates are higher than a standard mortgage but definitely a lot lower than HP – something in the region of between 3%–5% over base rate. It is the short-term repayment programme which causes most of the problems, although interest is tax deductable if the home is truly your main residence. Similarly, any profit you make on the sale of your mobile home should be free of Capital Gains Tax, but again, only if it can be demonstrated that it is your main residence.

Despite the obvious disadvantages, the fact remains that once you have bought and paid for your mobile home, if it is situated on a pleasant site, you will have many, many years ahead of very cheap and comfortable living.

Houseboats

A houseboat is a static object providing accommodation, which just happens to be floating on water. Yes, people do live in *proper* boats – narrow boats, cabin cruisers and yachts – but the true houseboat can be compared with a mobile home – in theory it can be moved about but, in practice, it never is.

It is a wonderfully romantic notion, living on the water. The concept of buying a boat, floating off into the sunset and living where one pleases, sounds wonderful. In practice it does not work unless you are going to be continually on the move – a floating gypsy – for whether you are thinking of living on the canal system, on a river or around the coast, there are very heavy restrictions in force to ensure that you simply cannot moor wherever you please on a permanent basis.

Take the canal system – British Waterways Board control virtually all of the canals and are responsible for issuing houseboat certificates. Staggeringly, on the entire canal system there are only 155 houseboat certificates issued, and BWB have no intention of increasing that number. They do not want people living on the canals and those

who do are mostly coralled into basins and backwaters off the main waterway system.

The picture is not so bleak on the country's rivers and coastal regions, but only if you play by the rules. Essentially, if you want to live on a boat on a permanent basis, you need a residential mooring in a yacht basin or marina. Such residential moorings are available on many of Britain's waterways. However, while on some rivers the private owning of banks enables individuals to secure a residential licence, on the whole the vast majority of these moorings are within the large marinas.

It is important to recognize that in order to secure a residential mooring, there are two pieces of legislation to overcome.
1 You need a licence from the authority appropriate to your chosen waterway, and
2 You need planning permission.
The latter, of course, will be automatic if you are moored in an established marina, but if you are hoping to moor your houseboat at the bottom of a friend's garden, in order to do it legally, you have to seek planning permission.

Costs

It is very difficult to give you a clear idea of just what you are likely to be charged in terms of licence and mooring fees, because so much depends on the part of the country in which you are based. However, as a rule of thumb, licence fees from whatever authority is applicable are likely to be somewhere in the region of £200–£300 per year – in other words, not a hefty sum. The difficulty lies in acquiring the licence at all.

So far as mooring is concerned, currently, the Chelsea Yacht Basin are charging £40 per foot, per year, for mooring, plus £11 per foot, per year, for services and maintenance. Looking at coastal moorings, at Chichester the current rate is £110 per metre (£34 per foot), per annum. This is not the highest on the South Coast but on the East Coast, say, it is considerably less.

The message here is that while the costs are not very high, availability is decidedly restricted. *Do not even contemplate purchasing any form of boat to live in unless you have found a permanent residential mooring on which to put it. Do not contemplate buying a houseboat unless you have had it properly surveyed.*

Finance

It is virtually impossible to obtain any finance at all for the purchase of a houseboat unless additional security can be provided. Sorry to sound defeatist, but this is the fact. Because of the problems with moorings, because houseboat owners have a reputation for default and because houseboats cannot be registered with the British Register of Shipping, they are not an attractive proposition. You may well be querying what the British Register of Shipping has to do with finance – because houseboats are not really craft, as such, they cannot be registered as a mobile object, and indeed for practical purposes most are not. This means their value is linked to their mooring, and should the houseboat lose its mooring, its value would drop substantially. In other words, houseboats have very little value in their own right.

However, if you are intending to purchase an ordinary boat in which to live – a boat capable of moving around the waterways and therefore able to be registered – then you can borrow money to purchase it, on the following terms:

- You can borrow up to 50% of value.
- You will be granted a five to ten year period of repayment – about one year for each £1,000 borrowed.
- The interest rate is likely to be 3% over finance house base rate for a small loan of, say, £5,000 to £10,000.

Interest can be tax deductable but only if your boat is truly your main residence.

Any profit you make on the sale of your boat should be free of CGT but again, only if it can be demonstrated that the boat is your main residence.

You may feel that the potential houseboat resident is being greatly penalised by not being able to raise finance and that banks and finance houses are being very short-sighted in refusing to fund their purchase. There is a reverse argument, however. Because finance is not available to purchase the traditional houseboat, it has kept prices low. As a spokesman for Chelsea Yacht Basin told us, 'Living on a houseboat in Chelsea has to be by far the cheapest way of living in that highly desirable part of London.' If finance was available, houseboats probably would be fetching not a great deal less than the bricks and mortar in the same area. You cannot have it both ways!

Commercial property

The object of this book is to explore property as it relates to you and your home. In other words, we are concentrating on all aspects of private residential property as opposed to industrial property. However, it would be wrong to ignore the fact that many people live and work under the same roof. During the course of this book, we will be dealing in detail with the problems and, indeed, the opportunities of combining home and workplace but, at this stage, we feel it is important to identify the type of property most likely to have a dual use.

There are several ways in which commercial and residential properties may overlap:

- You might acquire a commercial property such as a barn, an old mill or a former shop and wish to convert it into a residential property.
- You may have a residential property which you want to turn into a commercial one – perhaps into a hotel, a shop or restaurant.
- You may live, or are intending to live, 'over the shop' – in other words, you have living accommodation on the site of your workplace.
- Perhaps you work from home as we do – i.e. the home dominates the major part of the property, but it also contains an office or workshop, from which you earn your living.

Let us now look at the three main circumstances in which you may find yourself involved in a commercial property:

When buying

If you are buying a commercial property in which you intend to live – or indeed the reverse – you will require planning consent for *change of use*, irrespective of whether or not you are making any physical alterations/conversions. If you are not continuing to operate the property in the way it has been operated in the past, it is essential that you obtain permission for change of use. If you do not, the planning authorities may force you to stop your new activities – whether

commercial or residential – if they consider them inappropiate.

Undoubtedly you can acquire a property more cheaply if you do not expose your hand by seeking approval for change of use in advance of purchase. This is a fairly risky thing to do, though. There is very little point in having a property which you cannot use for the purpose for which you acquired it. If you are prepared to be a strategic gambler, a quiet word with the planning officer might elicit the response that, in his view, it is likely that an application for change of use would be granted. However, planning decisions are not made by the planning officer – they are made by the planning committee. While he will give you the benefit of his advice, he will also stress to you that his views are far from infallible and may well not reflect the ultimate decision of the planning committee. While there is almost certainly going to be a price advantage in not disclosing your plans, on balance we would always recommend you sign your contract subject to being able to obtain change of use – or indeed obtain change of use in advance of your acquisition.

When selling

If you feel the property you are selling has potential for development in an area so far not exploited by yourself, it is sometimes better to simply sell the property with potential, rather than first obtain the necessary planning permission and then sell. We would particularly stress this piece of advice if you know your local planning office is likely to be difficult about permission. Selling with potential passes on the headache to the buyer and is still likely to give your property an enhanced value. However, if you have once sought planning permission and been rejected, then any chance of selling at a premium is lost.

Case history

Some friends of ours, Bill and Jenny, decided to sell up their farm, in prime Warwickshire countryside, and move to a smaller, less demanding farm in Norfolk. Part of their Warwickshire farm butted right up to a nearby village and Bill and Jenny put in a planning application for a small estate of ten good quality houses to be built in the field nearest the village. Their application was turned down. So . . . they sold their farm as just that – farmland plus farmhouse – and moved to Norfolk. Imagine their indignation when, three months later, the new owner of the farm in Warwickshire put in a fresh application and was granted permission for part of the land to be developed, thus making an enormous profit. The lesson to be learnt here is that Bill and Jenny would have been better either to have taken their application further or not to have applied at all. In the latter case, they could probably have sold well over the normal price for their farm by convincing a potential purchaser of the *possibility* of developing the land.

When changing the use of your existing home

In the 'Property for Special Use' section we will be dealing, in detail, with the planning problems of working from home. Here, however, is a little food for thought for you to consider before reaching that section. In theory if you have a desk, a phone and a filing cabinet in the corner of your living room from which you work – occasionally, part-time or full-time, then you need planning permission. In practice, the planning authorities stress that they would be simply appalled if everyone in these circumstances did apply for change of use. The reverse of this situation is that there are many, many business being conducted from home, throughout the country, which clearly do need planning permission, but cheerfully operate without it. Why? It is all a question of good neighbourliness. In assessing whether you will need permission to conduct your busines from home, you should not so much be thinking of the planning authority rules (we probably will be locked up for saying this) but whether you are going to upset your neighbours. If what you are going to do is neither noisy, nor smelly, nor untidy, nor indeed outwardly noticeable, then frankly you should not be unduly concerned about applying for change of use. The simplest rule of thumb is to put yourself in your neighbours' position – would you like to be living next door to what you are doing? We are not trying to persuade you to actively flaunt the planning rules – certainly if you are going to start a business which will involve employing people and requires deliveries to the house etc, etc, you must apply for change of use, but if you are working for yourself and making the minimum of fuss and mess, then frankly just get on with it. It is an important point to remember that if you are forced to seek change of use and therefore designate part of your house for commercial purposes, when you come to sell your property that portion will not be exempt from Capital Gains Tax, as is the rest of your main residence.

Council houses

Over the last few years, there has been a considerable reduction in the number of council houses available, due mainly to tenants being encouraged to buy their own council property. There are some splendid council estates, and some truly terrible ones and all stations in between, but it has to be said that being a council tenant is vastly less fraught than renting in the private sector. On the whole, councils do look after their tenants and provide that much needed feeling of security of tenure which,

thanks to current legislation, cannot always be taken for granted in the private sector. There are other advantages, too, like relocation and tenant swaps if it is necessary for you to move to a new area. The ability to buy your house is, without doubt, the most significant step of all. Let us look at this in more detail.

Buying

If you are interested in the concept of buying your own council house, you should obtain a leaflet called *Your Right To Buy Your Home* which you will find at your local council offices. This leaflet will spell out all the circumstances in which you are entitled to buy, but here are some guidelines for you to consider:

◈ If you have been a council tenant for two years you are entitled to purchase your house at a discount of 32% on the current market value.

◈ If you have been a tenant for thirty years or more you are entitled to a discount of 60%

◈ To qualify for these discounts you do not even need to have lived in the same property, or in the same council district, and in fact there are certain circumstances where non-council property can be added to your qualifying period. If you have lived in some types of tied housing connected with your job or if you have spent time living in armed forces' married quarters, this will qualify. However it must be stressed that you can only buy your own council house if you are currently a tenant – you cannot apply to buy a council house in which you are not already living.

◈ If your application is accepted, then the council is under an obligation to offer you a mortgage – even up to 100%, if you so wish. However, do not simply accept the council mortgage because it is on offer, for you may well find that you can get a better rate from a building society. Certainly you should shop around before committing yourself.

◈ In doing your sums to see if you can afford to buy your council house, do remember that there are a great many costs involved in addition to the purchase of the house itself. There are the one-off costs which apply equally to council property or to a private house – valuation and survey charges, solicitor's fees and land registry fees. Also, of course, once you have purchased your house, you instantly become responsible for rates, insurance, repair and maintenance, which formerly would have been included in your rent.

◆ If you would like to buy your house but cannot afford the mortgage payments immediately, you have the right to apply and then ask that your purchase be delayed for two years from the date of your application. In this instance, the price and terms under which you can buy remain exactly the same as at the date of application.

◆ It is normal when you buy your house to share the ownership with your co-tenant, who is mostly likely to be your husband or wife. However, joint purchases are not restricted to families and any number of joint tenants can participate in the purchase if they so wish. However, if a joint tenant does not want to, his or her tenancy rights in the house will be lost when the sale takes place.

◆ If you are living in a council flat, while you are unable to purchase the freehold, you do have the right to purchase a long lease, which, to all intents and purposes, amounts to the same thing.

◆ There are certain properties which are exempt from the normal rights to purchase. These include special housing for handicapped or elderly people and housing pending redevelopment. Clearly, if you are squatting on council property, you will not be entitled to purchase.

◆ There are a number of housing associations connected with council property, and in some instances tenants of these houses will enjoy the same rights to purchase. However if the housing association is funded by public subscription, it is unlikely you will have the right to buy. Almshouses normally fall within that category.

Selling

◆ Having purchased your council house, if you sell within three years, you are likely to have to repay some of the discount received by you.

◆ Generally speaking you are entitled to sell your council house to anyone. In a very few instances, where your council house might be situated in an area of outstanding natural beauty – say on the edge of a park – then it is possible that the council may insist on having the right to veto any purchaser of your property whom they do not consider desirable. This is not, however, a particularly arbitrary rule – the only reason for making it is to ensure that you do not sell your property to a property developer.

◆ A word of caution on buying a council house, which is only relevant if you are considering ultimately selling it. While you may have put a great deal of time, trouble, thought and money into the house you have purchased from the council, the fact is, it is likely to be on a council estate and surrounded by a number of houses which are not privately owned. It therefore does need to be recognized that the house is unlikely to increase in value to the same extent as a property not on a council estate. We are not trying to undermine the enormous advantages of being able to buy your own council house, and provided you can afford the mortgage repayments, it is something you should seriously consider. All we would ask you to recognize is that your house may not be worth the same as a house on the high street, even though you have better accommodation and a garden etc, etc. Be aware also that your property is likely to increase in value at a slower rate because of its location.

Farms and agricultural property will generally attract three distinct types of people:

◆ The professional, established farmer who may own his own land or be a tenant, who is likely to spend his life working the same acres. In all probability his father worked them before him.

◆ Those who wish to buy farm property for non-agricultural use – i.e. converting an old farmhouse, barn or cottage as an attractive home in the country but with no aspirations towards working on the land.

◆ The aspiring smallholder – who could be a couple retiring early to the country to pursue a lifetime's ambition, or perhaps younger people in a bid for self-sufficiency.

Let us look in general terms at the pros and cons of living in the country. Moving to a cottage in a cornfield has to be many people's pipe dream. In reality, just how idyllic is it? On a warm summer's day it may seem like heaven on earth, but what about the winter months? Between November and March most of Britain's truly rural areas disappear under a sea of mud. Venturing outside the back door without wellington boots is out of the question. Add to that our usual quota of ice/snow/fog, and suddenly living in the country can make one feel extremely isolated. It may sound romantic but what about access to schools and shops? In many areas the rural bus system has almost collapsed. The isolation may be all quite an adventure while you are young and healthy, but as you get older it can make life very difficult. Services, too, are often not very efficient – water/gas/ electricity/sewage – in a city one takes these all for granted. In the country they are often non-existent or unreliable. The postman, bless him, will usually get through but you are unlikely to receive milk every day, nor have rubbish collected every week and as for the papers being delivered . . . well, forget it.

Assuming it is an agricultural property you are converting or are planning to live in, there is a strong possibility that it may be adjacent to a working farm. This can be a far from romantic experience. Farms are noisy and smelly – tractors thunder past, cows separated from their calves bellow half the night . . . Farmers are subject to very little planning control when it comes to constructing farm buildings. You could find your picturesque cottage literally surrounded by modern, concrete barns if your farmer neighbour decides to expand.

If this seems all a rather pessimistic view of country life then we, the authors, can counter-balance this by saying that we live in a totally rural area, in a cottage adjacent to a working farm and we adore it. Our neighbours are wonderful people and life is enriched by being a part of their daily working routine; there is no way we will ever move again. The point we are making is that it is very important to differentiate between living in a village – which after all is just a town on a smaller scale – and living 'out in the sticks'.

Land

If you are buying land in the country, do look very carefully at the following:

◆ Rights of way – footpaths, bridleways, rights to hunt, shoot or fish over your land. These may not represent a problem at all if you are prepared for them, but you do need to know exactly what is involved and how often these rights are exercised.

◆ Boundaries – do make sure you are aware who is responsible for maintaining the fencing around your land. If your local farmer's cattle break through the fencing and destroy your newly landscaped garden, is it his fault or yours? If your local farmer's cattle break through the fencing and injure themselves on your land and the boundary is your responsibility, will you be liable?

◆ Domestic animals/livestock – boundaries need to be effective not only to keep farm animals out of your land but to keep in domestic animals. Your dog worrying sheep, particularly around lambing, is asking to be shot and probably will be – and you will be liable for the damage he has caused.

◆ If you are intending to embark on a smallholding and perhaps have very little agricultural experience, do not rely on estate agents to tell you the worth of the land. You need a farmer to tell you what will grow and what livestock is suitable.

Planning

It goes without saying that you will need planning permission for any major alteration to an agricultural property. You may also need change of use. This is obvious if you are taking the basic shell of a barn and turning it into a home, but change of use may be necessary if you are buying a farm cottage or even a farmhouse. You may find that when planning permission was originally granted for the house or cottage, the planning authority imposed a condition upon that permission restricting the occupation of the dwelling to a member of the agricultural population or to people employed by the farm – i.e. a tied cottage. It is possible to get this condition removed and it certainly is difficult to imagine a planning authority allowing a perfectly good cottage or house to fall into disrepair if it is no longer relevant for a member of the farming community to live in it. However, it is very important that if you are buying a farmhouse or cottage you make sure that you have the right to live in it.

As a general rule, planning authorities, these days, are not terribly enthusiastic about cottages being built on farmland – they prefer them in villages. If, as a farmer, you wish to build a cottage, you are more likely to obtain planning permission if the cottage is located close to other farm buildings. In addition, you are most likely to obtain permission if you can show a genuine requirement to have a worker living on the premises. However, your application is likely to be turned down if you are thinking of building a cottage for your retirement. For this reason, if you would like to live on your land when the farm has been passed on to your son or daughter, you should apply for permission to build your cottage while you are still working on the farm, not when you retire.

In conclusion, therefore, if you are buying an agricultural property you do need to be a little more cautious than if you were buying a straight forward residential home. It is so easy to wander across the fields and see only one side of the story. Make sure you have considered carefully all of the implications of rural living.

Freehold

The term *freehold* denotes the absolute ownership of property. Another word for freehold, which you may see appear occasionally on legal documents, is fee simple. If you own the freehold of a property what it means is that the land is yours and all the buildings on it are yours – absolutely. However property, like life, is not always as simple as it seems and the description 'absolutely' is in reality quite often 'subject to'. Subject to what? There are four main situations which could undermine your absolute ownership of your property. They are as follows:

Possession

In order for a property to be 100% yours, so far as possession is concerned, you must have what is known as vacant possession. This means that once you own the property, no one else does, or can, live on your property – legally or illegally. There are various circumstances in which you may be denied *vacant possession*:

◈ You could own a property which has a sitting tenant. We will be discussing the legal implications of tenancy agreements on page 30, but if you are buying a property where a tenant is in occupation, you need to recognize that he or she may have security of tenure, even without a tenancy agreement.

◈ A house or cottage left empty for any length of time – particularly in an urban area – runs the risk of being taken over by squatters. Squatters can be evicted but it takes time and money and there is likely to be enormous damage done to your property.

◈ You may have bought a house which has been divided into flats, with all or some of the tenants having a number of years to run on their leases.

◈ You may buy a shop with a vacant showroom but the living accommodation is sub-let, or vice versa.

◈ You may buy a farmhouse with land but that land may well be let out to a local farmer.

In all these circumstances, therefore, although the property is yours in name, your access and use are restricted.

Covenants

A freehold property may be 100% yours but can you do with it what you want? You may have entered into covenants with the vendor which in some way restrict what you can actually do, or you may purchase a property and with it take over covenants imposed by previous vendors. What is a covenant? It is a condition which can be either negative or positive, which is attached to the conveyance indicating that the property is yours, provided you undertake to do, or not do, one or more things. Let us look at some of the typical covenants you might be asked to enter into:

◈ To erect and maintain walls, fences, hedges or ditches.

◈ Not to fell trees.

◈ Not to carry on any business.

◈ Not to alter, build or demolish any part of the building without consent of neighbours.

◈ To maintain or share responsibility for roads and paths.

◈ Not to build more than one house on the site or perhaps one house per acre or whatever.

There can be more than one charge on a property and occasionally, people tend to borrow against their house rather more money than it is strictly speaking worth – a dangerous situation.

A note of caution – If you inherit a property, do not assume that there are no charges against it, just because there is no evidence of bank or building society lending. Perhaps Auntie Maude – who has left you her country cottage – was really a secret gambler or boozer and had the house charged against outstanding debts to either betting shop or off-licence. A bit far fetched? Certainly not, it happens all the time. Before you make any decisions about your inherited property, you need to be aware of all the liabilities attached to it.

We will be dealing with covenants in considerable detail in the 'Insurance' section of this book but it is important to say here that you must be aware of all covenants into which you might enter, but at the same time not be too alarmed by them. Solicitors do tend to over-react - very often covenants have lapsed or are no longer even relevant to the property and certainly it is unlikely that a covenant alone, unless very restrictive, would deter you from going ahead with the purchase.

Charges

In the strict legal sense, a restrictive covenant is regarded as a charge on the property; but the much more usually recognized charge is a mortgage, where the lender holds the property as security for the loan. Normally, borrowing against a property represents the finance required for its purchase in the first place or money raised to improve or convert the property in some way. However, money can be raised against a property to be used for quite different purposes, such as starting a business. To be effective, a mortgage or charge has to be registered with the Land Registry, so normally a freehold property cannot change hands without the parties concerned being aware of all outstanding charges.

Access

Only in fairly extreme circumstances can access restrict the use of your freehold. If you buy a property on a Scottish island, you may well find that you cannot get to it for three months of the year because of storms. If you buy a cottage on some areas of British shoreline, you may find that you are cut off from it twice a day by the tides. At the other end of the scale, communal drives into a housing estate may prevent your access if your neighbours allow their friends to park untidily. An example of a serious access problem was highlighted recently on a Radio 4 programme, in which an unfortunate woman was no longer able to reach her isolated house by car because farm vehicles had churned up the bridleway which led to her house, to such an extent that no vehicle could get through the mud.

All these possible restrictions to *absolute* freehold ownership need to be borne in mind at the time of any freehold purchase. Obviously, some of these items should be picked up by your solicitor but not necessarily all, and it is very important that you take nothing on face value. Ideally, a freehold property should be something which is absolutely yours and, subject only to abiding by the laws of the land, a place in which you can do anything you want.

Leasehold (1) – a general look

A leasehold comes in many guises. At one end of the spectrum are short term leases or licences to occupy, where weekly, monthly or annual rent is paid for a bedsit, flat or house. There is a great demand for this sort of property but in the private sector it is very difficult to find. Because of all the difficulties of evicting tenants, there is a general reluctance to lease private property although, in recent years, efforts have been made to improve legislation in order to make the protection of both landlord and tenant as equitable as possible. It is sometimes possible to rent on a short term basis from a housing association, rather than a private landlord and then, of course, there is the local authority council housing, which we have discussed in detail on page 20.

At the other end of the leasing scale there is long leasehold property, which is subject merely to a small annual ground rent – the main cost being the price one has to pay to acquire the lease. Long leaseholds are granted on both houses and flats and, essentially, these properties are bought and sold in virtually the same way as if they were freehold. Indeed, in many cases their value varies little from an equivalent freehold value. There is essentially no difference between owning a long leasehold property as opposed to a freehold provided, of course, there are a good many years left to run on the lease.

From both a legal and practical point of view, there are significant differences in both your rights and obligations as a short term tenant, as opposed to a long term leaseholder, although in each case you can be described as a tenant. There are no precise legal definitions by which you can identify a long lease, largely because there is a considerable amount of confused middle-ground. This is created by the fact that obviously long leases do come to an end eventually. If, for example, there are only four years to run on an old 99 year lease, this clearly qualifies as a short term lease. The situation is further confused because a statutory form of protection has been built up over the years which gives some tenants the right to stay in possession beyond the term of their original lease, and this applies not only to long term leases, but more recently to shorter term tenancies as well. So . . . if a tenant has a short lease but also has the statutory right to stay where he is, then his tenure of the property is equivalent to being a long leaseholder for practical purposes, even though he does not have the formality of a long period of unexpired lease. As a general rule of thumb, however, a long lease generally means a lease with 21 years, or more, unexpired.

The vast majority of house purchases and sales involve the conveyance of a freehold, whereas flats are always leasehold. Fashions change – this century virtually all housing development has involved the splitting up of large areas of land into small freehold plots. Therefore, modern houses in the private sector – whether built by an individual or by a developer – tend to be freehold. However, in the last century this was not the case. The large estates did become invoived in the development of their land, but the controlling families adopted the general policy of wanting to preserve and increase their freehold land, rather than diminish it. They therefore granted long term ground leases – particularly in cities – and this is particularly evidenced in Central London where practically all property over 100 years old is long leasehold. By way of example, if you decided to buy a house in Mayfair (these days you would need about £1 million) almost certainly you would be a long leaseholder, enjoying the residue of an original lease, granted many years ago and still running at a modest ground rent. These original leases were granted for a range of periods – 99 years is perhaps the most usual but 125 and in some cases even 999 years are quite common.

To demonstrate that any size of building, in any circumstances, can be a leasehold, it is interesting to note that the United States does not own the freehold of the American Embassy in London. When it was built, apparently, the Americans tried to buy the freehold of the site. The owners, The Grosvenor Estate, were prepared to go ahead, provided that America agreed to return all the land confiscated from the British during the War of Independence! As you can imagine, this was certainly not acceptable and even today the American Embassy is still subject to a long leasehold.

People often talk of *buying a flat* which suggest that they are acquiring the freehold. Basically this is just not possible – all flats are leasehold because a flat is a part of a building, and normally a horizontal part. This applies whether the property is a purpose-built block of flats or a house which has been subsequently divided up into flats. Either way you cannot identify and transfer the freehold of part of a building unless it is a vertical part – i.e. top to bottom – in which case, it is no longer a flat, it is a semi-detached or terraced house.

The exception proves the rule – some years ago the authors were involved in the purchase of The Grand Hotel, Southampton Row, in London. Part of the hotel was built over a crypt of an adjacent church and the freehold of that part of the hotel was described as *a 'flying' freehold* – in other words, a freehold property detached from mother earth, so to speak. This has to be very exceptional, however, and it is not a situation you are likely to come across.

THIS IS A CLOSE ENCOUNTER OF THE "FLYING FREEHOLD" KIND.

So, we have identified the difference between the long and short term leasehold. Now it is important to look at both in more detail.

Leasehold (2) – long leases

Long leases are not purely the preserve of former centuries. They are still being created today, mostly for the disposal of flats as a result of a new development or the conversion of an existing building, but also for some house sales.

How is a long leasehold created?

- A freehold land owner may lease a building plot for, say 99 years, to someone who wants to build a house. The house builder can subsequently sell the property but he will only be selling a long lease – the land owner having retained the freehold of the land.
- The freehold land owner may lease a large site to a developer for building a number of houses or flats. Again, when the developer comes to sell, he can only be selling long leases.
- A freehold land owner may sell a freehold site to a developer and the developer may decide to retain the freehold himself and simply sell long leases of the property he builds.
- A freeholder may himself act as a developer but only sell completed houses or flats on a long leasehold basis.
- A freeholder, or someone enjoying a long leasehold on an existing large house, could convert it into flats and these flats can then be sold on new long leases.

As we have already discussed, it is not possible to buy the freehold of a flat. The only way round it would be to buy the entire building in which your flat is housed. In new developments, it is more usual, these days, for the freehold to be held by a specific management company and in these circumstances, you would own a percentage of the freehold. It works like this – if, say, a house is split into four flats, each of which is sold by way of a long lease, then each tenant would be entitled to own 25% of the shares of the company. This usually works very well. As well as solving the problem of title, the company usually acts as a form of housing association, enabling joint decisions to be made as to shared gardens, parking facilities etc, etc, and generally ensuring that the overall standard of the building is maintained. The fact is, though, you still will not own the freehold of your own flat.

Borrowing money to purchase a long leasehold

You can borrow money to buy or improve a leasehold property, provided that the lease has long enough to run. It is quite possible to obtain a normal mortgage which usually runs over a 20-25 year period, provided the lease has at least 55 years unexpired. An unexpired period of less than 55 years will not preclude a mortgage but the percentage of value available as a loan, or the length of the mortgage repayment period, may be restricted. The attitude of the average bank or building society to lending against the unexpired term of a long lease, will normally reflect a prudent view of your own attitude to the lease's value. In other words, forget borrowing money for a moment – what you have to do is to satisfy yourself that the lease is worth the money being asked and if you are able to do this then, chances are, you will find the money to finance it.

There is a different feel to a leasehold because, ultimately, the bricks and mortar will revert back to the freehold owner, at which time the leasehold interest becomes valueless. It is not yours for ever, it has a fixed term of life, and while the lease you have been granted or have purchased may well exceed your own life expectancy, it is still very important that you ensure your investment is justified.

Not all long leasehold property automatically reverts to the freeholder at the end of the term. The Housing Act of 1980 and the 1967 Leasehold Reform Act do give certain tenants the right to buy the freehold, or extend the lease for up to 50 years, or to remain in occupancy at the end of the lease as statutory tenants. There is a very complex set of rules to determine entitlement. Below is a brief resumé, but we would stress that if you feel you may have continuing rights in a leasehold property, you should consult a solicitor.

Circumstances in which you may be entitled to rights:

◆ The Acts mentioned above only apply to houses, not flats. However, semi-detached houses and terraced houses are included.

◆ The lease must normally have been granted originally for a term of not less than 21 years.

◆ The rent being paid must fall within the definition of a low rent. This means that it must be less than two-thirds of the rateable value of the house as at 23rd March, 1965, or when it first had a rateable value, or when the lease began – which ever is the later date.

◆ The tenant must be an individual – i.e. not a company or a business – and has to have occupied the house, as his main residence, for the last three years or for at least three years out of the last ten years.

◆ The relevant rateable value has to be within certain defined limits.

The tenant of a flat does not go unprotected but is subject to a separate rule book. If you have a flat on a long lease and at a low rent, there is a degree of protection under the 1954 Landlord and Tenant Act. The length of the lease, the amount of rent and rateable value of the flat are all relevant in establishing what protection is available under this act, but the general position is this:

◆ At the end of the lease, unless the landlord or tenant gives notice, the tenancy will simply continue on the same terms.

◆ If the landlord gives notice, he can only repossess the property if he can demonstrate the tenant is in breach of the lease or is unfit to continue the tenancy, or if the landlord requires the property for his own family or himself, or is in a position to offer suitable alternative accommodation.

◆ The landlord can give notice to terminate the original tenancy but has to offer a new statutory tenancy, if required.

Further protection to tenants of privately owned blocks of flats is now also available under the 1987 Landlord and Tenant Act. This latest Act provides:

◆ The right of first refusal if the block, or part of the block is intended to be sold – the landlord must, in effect, offer the tenants a chance to buy or to nominate a purchaser.

◆ If the landlord is in breach of his management obligations under the lease, the Court may appoint managers to act in place of the landlord, or where this might not be appropriate the tenants may compulsorily acquire their landlord's interest.

◆ If the lease is unsatisfactory in its terms relating to maintenance or insurance, any party to the lease can apply to the County Court to have the lease varied.

◆ In order to exercise these rights, a tenant must know the name and UK address of his landlord.

It is a complex subject and, bearing in mind the enormous premiums for which long leasehold property changes hands, it is important to obtain really good advice.

AS LEASE HOLDERS YOU ARE RESPONSIBLE FOR THE UPKEEP OF THE ROOF.

Leasehold (3) – short leases

A short lease is not intended to provide any real sense of ownership of a property. The tenant pays rent on a weekly/monthly/quarterly basis, which, broadly speaking, represents a fair price for the accommodation being leased. The rent paid can represent purely the fee for leasing an unfurnished house, flat or a room, or it can include furniture, services and rates. The term of the lease can be anything from a few weeks to a few years. In other words nothing is standard – the rules of short term leasing are infinitely variable. However, there are various terms used to describe various types of lease, which in turn provide various rights to both tenant and landlord.

These are they:

Regulated tenancy

The main object of a regulated tenancy is to give protection to the tenant. The Rent Act of 1977 and the Housing Act of 1980 redefined the basis on which tenants, renting from private landlords, achieved some form of security of tenure. By *private landlords*, we are referring to individuals or property companies as opposed to local authorities or housing associations. Up until August 1974, it was generally recognized that unfurnished accommodation tended to give security of tenure, whereas a landlord renting out a furnished flat could more easily regain possession. Under the 1977 Act, the furnished letting definition has been replaced. Now, the landlord must be resident in the same house or flat, in order to avoid creating a regulated tenancy, and it is this new rule which has created such a shortage of accommodation in the private sector. Generally speaking the letting of a house, a flat or even a single room which has a rateable value within the upper limits laid down in the Act, will create a regulated tenancy if let by a private, non-resident landlord. This is the stumbling block so far as landlords are concerned. Regulated tenancies may not be very appealing to the landlord but they are of benefit to the tenant for the following reasons:

◆ If the tenant dies, then the tenancy may pass to any member of the family who has been living in the accommodation.

◆ The tenancy may be passed by court order to the other spouse in the case of separation or divorce.

◆ The landlord cannot obtain possession without a court order.

◆ The local authority rent officer can be asked by the landlord or tenant to fix and register a fair rent.

It is a complicated business, so to further help you define a regulated tenancy, these

THE LANDLORD GIVES US BREAKFAST TO STOP US HAVING A REGULATED TENANCY

are the occasions when a regulated tenancy cannot be created:

- ◆ Where a low rent is payable (see section on long leases).
- ◆ Where the property is held under a long lease or a service tenancy.
- ◆ Where it is a holiday letting.
- ◆ When the tenant is merely granted licence to occupy (see next section on this subject).
- ◆ Where the rent includes an element of board and attendance.

Protected tenancy

During the term of the original agreement of a regulated tenancy, it is known as a *Protected Tenancy*. This protection can only be passed on in the event of the tenant's death and usually passes to the surviving spouse. It can be passed to any member of the tenant's family who is living with the tenant, but they must have lived with the tenant for at least six months prior to death.

Statutory tenancy

This is the term used to describe a regulated tenancy which has expired. When a regulated tenancy expires, if the original tenant is still in possession, he remains protected and the tenancy continues as a statutory tenancy. In these circumstances he cannot assign or sell the lease to anyone else but he does have continuing personal security of tenure, and if he dies whilst he is still a statutory tenant, then the lease will still pass to his spouse or other family member. In the case where a spouse or family member succeeds to the tenancy, on the death of the original tenant, the new tenancy created is *always* a statutory tenancy, not a protected tenancy. On the death of the original tenant, the transfer to the first successor is automatic. When that first successor dies, the statutory tenancy is again automatically transferable once. This second transfer is subject to the same set of rules – a member of the family living on the premises during the preceding six months. However, when the second successor dies, the tenancy is terminated.

Shorthold tenancy

This form of tenancy has been introduced to provide the tenant with the protection of the fair rent provisions in the 1980 Housing Act, while not inflicting upon the landlord the onerous security of tenure enjoyed under a regulated tenancy. This type of tenancy is quite clearly a political initiative aimed at encouraging the private property owner to rent rather than sell and thus increase the stock of accommodation available on the letting market. A shorthold tenancy must be granted for a fixed term of between one and five years. It is important to mention that such a tenancy cannot be offered in substitution for an existing regulated tenancy, because clearly it would reduce the tenant's security of tenure. The landlord can slide round this, however, by offering alternative accommodation to a tenant in the form of a shorthold agreement. A point worth mentioning – in Greater London registration of a fair rent is mandatory.

Assured tenancy

Another initiative of the 1980 Housing Act, and subsequently the 1986 Housing and Planning Act, is the creation of assured tenancies. Institutions such as pension funds, building societies and development companies may build new residential accommodation, or convert and improve existing buildings for rental under this new form of lease. The rent payable cannot be altered by any authority. At the start of the lease, it is negotiated and agreed between landlord and tenant and the lease can be for whatever length and on whatever terms they decide to agree. At the end of the lease, the tenant has the right to renew for a further term – either at a rent agreed with the landlord or, failing agreement, at an open market rent. The landlord can only refuse to renew if there have been persistent breaches on behalf of the tenant; unreasonable failure to offer a new lease could give rise to a claim for compensation by the tenant.

Licence to occupy

All of the benefits and obligations so far discussed under the sections on leasing result only from the formal landlord and tenant relationship created by a lease. However it is important to recognize that property can be occupied, with the owner's consent, with money passing in consideration for its use and with a proper legal document executed to establish the position – *without creating a legal tenancy*. This is known as *occupation under licence*.

Having a licence to occupy a premises does not provide the occupant with any protection under the fair rent legislation or any security of tenure beyond the specific terms of the licence – or any right to buy. This means that the landlord is not trapped into a relationship which goes any further than the terms of the agreement into which he has entered.

Let us look at some examples of a licence to occupy. It is sometimes granted when you are purchasing a property. While the rituals of conveyancing plod on, the vendor may grant the purchaser a licence to occupy if, for example, the purchaser has already sold his house and would otherwise be homeless. A resident in a home for the elderly has a licence to occupy, as does a lodger. It also applies to staying in a hotel – you are a licensee not a tenant.

These examples are obvious and straightforward and are useful because they serve to highlight the readily recognizable differences between lease and licence. In order to understand whether a lease or a licence has been created, it is very important to look behind the wording of any agreement to occupy premises, and to be quite sure of the intention of the parties involved. Clearly, it has to be in the interests of a landlord to make a lease look like a licence, whereas it has to be in the occupier's interest to try and establish that what looks like a licence agreement is in fact a lease.

The main requirement of a legal tenancy is to grant the tenant the exclusive possession of the premises and this in turn helps to demonstrate the difference between a lease and a licence. Clearly, if you are staying in a hotel, you do not have exclusive possession but equally, as a potential purchaser, you do not have exclusive possession until such time as the sale is completed. It is this factor which represents the main difference between lease and licence. The second main characteristic of a lease is that it must be for a definite period. There are other points to consider as well:

- Having nothing in writing is not a protection for either tenant or landlord. A licence does not have to be in writing but neither does a lease for up to a three year term. For a period longer than three years, a lease should be granted by way of deed, but if an agreement has been accurately recorded in writing, while the landlord may consider it only a licence, it could in fact be a lease, despite the fact that no formal deed has been entered into.

- An employee, living on his employer's premises, is quite definitely only a licensee and this is an important point to bear in mind, for clearly loss of job indicates loss of home.

- A word of comfort for anyone suffering from an overzealous mother-in-law. Friends or family, provided with living accommodation out of the goodness of your heart, are only licensees. When they have outstayed their welcome, you are within your rights to tell them to go and they have no legal redress.

- The most crucial criterion of all in establishing the difference between a licence and a lease is the intention of the parties concerned. This, of course, is very difficult for a court to establish without background evidence so it is important whether you are a tenant or a landlord, that this element is very clearly defined.

Without doubt, one of the effects of the licence to occupy has been to provide landlords with a vehicle for avoiding the Rent Act. In itself, this is no bad thing, for it has made available a considerable amount of accommodation which otherwise landlords would have been reluctant to offer for occupation.

LICENCE dated

Parties : **(1)**

198

("the Licensor")

(2)

("the Licensee")

IT IS HEREBY AGREED that in consideration of the Licensee paying to the Licensor the Licence Fee (as herein stipulated) at the times herein stated the Licensee shall be permitted to use Unit on the floor of the building known as 70, Rosebery Avenue in the London Borough of Islington (hereinafter called "the Building") or such other unit as the Licensor shall allocate to the Licensee in accordance with clause 21 (hereinafter called "the Unit") between the hours of 6.00 a.m. to 9.00 p.m. subject to the following terms and conditions:-

1. This Licence shall be for the period of one month from the date hereof and be continued thereafter from month to month until determined by one month's notice in writing given by one party to the other at their respective addresses appearing above.

2. The Licensee shall pay by way of banker's order to the Licensor in respect of the use of the Unit the monthly Licence fee of £ payable in advance on the first day of each month the first payment to be made on the date hereof, such fee including a fair proportion of the costs incurred by the Licensor in providing services to the Unit.

3. The Licensor may on 1st March 1st June 1st September and 1st December increase the Licence Fee on giving to the Licensee not less than one month's previous written notice of such increase.

4. The Licensee shall on the signing of this Licence pay to the Licensor the sum of £ as a deposit to be held by the Licensor during the continuance of the Licence which sum shall be returnable on the termination of the Licence after any deduction for damage to the Unit or the Building or arrears of Licence Fee or any other sums payable under the terms hereof or any other valid claim of the Licensor against the Licensee.

5. The Licensee shall pay all general rates which shall be assessed on the Unit together with gas electricity and any other charges arising from his particular use of the Unit.

6. The Licensee shall use the Unit solely for the purposes of

7. The Licensee shall be personally present in the Unit at least three full working days in each week and shall accept full responsibility for any of his visitors business associates or employees in respect of the use of the Unit and the general facilities of the Building.

8. The Licensee shall at all times keep the Unit adjoining areas and common facilities in a clean and tidy condition and free from any fire or health hazard and shall as often as occasion shall require cause all waste and refuse at the Unit to be removed and neatly deposited in the refuse collection area from time to time designated by the Licensor.

9. The Licensee shall not cause any nuisance or annoyance to the Licensor or other licensees or occupiers of the Building.

10. The Licensee shall be permitted to use the entrance of the Building and the lift at the Building to gain access to the Unit and shall at all times keep the staircase and corridors of the Building clear and free for access.

11. The Licensee shall be permitted to make reasonable use of the lift and staircase for the transfer of goods but shall not block the said lift and staircase and shall not cause nuisance or annoyance with other Licensees in the use of the lift and staircase.

12. The Licensee shall not make any alterations or additions to the Unit and shall not overload the floor of or the services supplied to the Unit nor introduce any heavy article or equipment into the Unit without the prior written consent of the Licensor.

13. The Licensee shall not use the Unit in such a way whereby any insurance effected in respect of the Unit or the Building might be vitiated or prejudiced.

14. The Licensee shall be responsible for insuring and maintaining the window glass at the Unit.

15. The Licensee shall at his own expense conform to all statutory and other regulations pertaining to his particular use of the Unit and in particular but without prejudice to the generality of the foregoing maintain suitable and serviceable fire extinguishers at the Unit.

16. The Licensee shall not bring noxious substances on to the Unit without the prior consent of the Licensor nor shall he cause damage to the drains of the Building by the use of corrosive polluting or other harmful substances.

17. The Licensee shall observe and perform all the conditions rules and regulations prescribed from time to time by the Licensor for the management and control of the Building.

18. The Licensee shall indemnify and keep the Licensor indemnified from and against all actions proceedings costs claims and demands by third parties in respect of any damage or liability caused by or arising from the use or occupation by the Licensee or the Licensee's servants agents or invitees on the Unit.

Students, particularly, benefit – by and large they are not interested in security of tenure and a licence to occupy suits them very well. Problems only arise where either party is under any form of illusion as to the nature of the agreement into which they have entered. It is a minefield and certainly if you are considering granting a licence to occupy, or believe that although dubbed a licensee, you may well be a tenant, then you should seek the advice of a solicitor for clarification.

Second homes

A second home, in theory, sounds a wonderful idea. A city dweller dreams of a country cottage, while those of us who live in the country plan the day when we can afford a pad in town. Yet are the realities as attractive as the dream? In many instances, they are not. It is difficult, if not well nigh impossible, to hand out specific advice on the subject, for circumstances – financial and personal – vary so much. However, we could suggest you adopt two golden rules when thinking about a second home.

◆ Do not acquire a second home unless it is for a quite specific reason.
◆ Do not borrow a large sum of money to buy your second home.

Let us look at these golden rules in more detail.

Reasons for acquiring a second home

Maybe you see your second home as being the place in which you will ultimately retire. In these circumstances, buying a second home is a good idea. When you do come to retire, not only the property, but also the district will be familiar and already full of fond memories. You can sell your first home free from Capital Gains Tax and there will be no CGT payable on any increase in value of your second home from the moment it becomes your main residence. Maybe you have children at boarding school – a country cottage, purchased near the school, could save literally thousands of pounds of hotel bills over the period of schooling, and provide your children with a bolt-hole to take their friends as they grow older. Perhaps your spouse faces five days a week of heavy commuting and you are frightened of the accident risk which seems an inevitable result of pounding up and down the motorway, year in, year out. A home from home in town could alleviate this.

What we are saying is that a second home must have a practical function. Frankly, we do not consider a holiday cottage necessa-

rily provides sufficient grounds for a second home, as a general rule. Think about it for a moment. If you have small children, perhaps the idea of a country cottage in, shall we say, Devon, does have very definite appeal. They can bucket and spade to their hearts' delight, and you do not have to worry about their making a mess in the hotel dining room. Certainly, up until a child is eight or nine, self-catering works very well. However, by about ten, they will start asking why you cannot have holidays abroad, like their friends do. By sixteen they will not be having holidays with you at all. Do you still want to be committed to going to Devon, year after year? Certainly, while you have a holiday cottage, it is very difficult to justify going anywhere else, so why not simply rent the same cottage a few years running – think of all the money and hassle you will save. Certainly your second home *can* be a place you go to for holidays but we would strongly suggest that this should not be its only function.

Financing your second home

Both building societies and banks will lend money for a second home provided that the property is going to be used at least occasionally by the owners and that any letting is purely on a holiday basis. You should be able to borrow up to 80% of the purchase price, though most lenders will not advance much over £200,000. This means that, in theory at any rate, there is nothing to stop you borrowing money to buy a second home, but we strongly recommend you not to borrow more than perhaps a small sum – for conversion or repair work. The running costs of a second home are likely to be high – they are so much more accident prone than a home which is constantly lived in. Roofs leak and no-one notices, pipes freeze, expensive heating is left on by mistake and if you are letting the property there is always the risk of damage caused by the tenants. Bearing in mind that in recent years bricks and mortar seem to have led a charmed life, so far as value is concerned, you may be tempted to feel that you are justified in borrowing money to buy a second home because of the investment it

represents. Firstly, you will be lucky if your running costs are covered by any rent you will receive from letting the property. Secondly, you will be fortunate indeed if the rate of inflation on your property exceeds the interest you are likely to have to pay on a substantial mortgage. This may seem a jaundiced view, and maybe you have your eye on a property which you can not only let out at a substantial rent for most of the year but will greatly increase in value and more than justify your investment.

If you are intending that your second home should qualify as a business – i.e. you are looking at commercial letting, then the profit you make from your letting is earned income. This has the distinct advantage that you can therefore offset for tax purposes the cost of any interest paid on the loan, plus legitimate running expenses. In order to receive tax relief, the property in question must be in the UK and be available to let throughout the year, and actually let for at least twenty-six weeks of the year.

Letting your second home

This is always a difficult subject, for one is frequently torn in two directions. Letting to friends, family and friends of friends is by far the most comforting way of achieving a small income from your second home – it is also the most difficult. Friends do not expect to pay the full going rate, family do not expect to pay at all and if you are not careful, you will find that it is actually costing you money, rather than providing you with any income. Letting the property commercially has its draw-backs but, by and large, holiday lets are not subject to much abuse. The odd stain on the carpet, the odd smashed plate, is normally the extent of the damage. Letting through an agency is a good idea if your second home is some distance away, but a word of warning – some agents are very good at taking their commission but they are not so good at taking any action if things go wrong. Find a good agent by personal recommendation.

To summarize – a second home is a rich man's pastime, unless it has a quite specific job to do.

Buying overseas

A colleague of ours who has considerable experience in investment property gives his wife a firm instruction before they embark on any holiday, 'Let me look, but never, never let me sign anything.' Our chum suffers from something we have all experienced from time to time. You have a holiday in a place which appeals to you and before you know where you are, you are fantasizing about owning your own little villa/flat/cottage/farmhouse – whatever. Increasingly today, particularly in Europe, realizing these fantasies is all too easy. In Spain, particularly, the pressure to buy a holiday home is considerable, and lulled into a sense of well-being by the sun, sea and endless wine, it is all too easy to make a decision which you will come to regret. Certainly take our friend's advice – never sign anything until you have come home from your holiday. Then, in the cold light of day, set your proposed purchase against the reality of your current commitments and consider carefully.

Much of what we asked you to consider about second homes also applies to buying overseas – only more so. Do you really want the commitment of going to the same place for your holiday every year – how are you going to look after the property long distance – does the property have long term appeal for your family? Still enthusiastic? All right then, let us look at some of the practicalities.

Firstly, before buying any property overseas you must find yourself a good English-speaking lawyer, who is *not* also acting for the vendor. Ideally, you should find someone through personal recommendation – perhaps your own accountant or solicitor may be able to advise you. If not, go to a local bank and see if they can recommend a lawyer. Under no circumstances be fooled into thinking you do not need one. In many countries in Europe, it is not normal practice to involve a lawyer in the purchase of a house. That may be so, but *you* need one and it is worth paying the fees to satisfy yourself that you really do have title and that you are not being ripped off in any way.

Generally in Europe, you need to allow between 10–15% of the purchase price to cover fees and costs, which is perhaps a little higher than in England. However, this will include your own lawyer.

In most European countries, you will get more for your money in terms of property than you will in the UK, but you do need to bear in mind that this also means that prices do not escalate to the same extent, so the increase in value of your overseas property will be far more modest. You will find that there is no exchange control problem with the Bank of England in sending money out of the country to purchase a property. However, before committing yourself to a purchase, do check the position on bringing money back should you decide to sell. Some countries will not allow you to take currency out again. Some will restrict the currency taken out to the amount originally invested – thus making it difficult to realize any profit. Greece is currently a prime example of these sorts of restrictions. If you buy a villa in Greece, that is fine. If you come to sell it, you cannot take the drachmas out of the country. The only way to get your money back is to sell the villa to another foreigner outside the country, which obviously greatly restricts your market.

This is one of the most important questions you do need to ask yourself – what happens if I want to sell? Particularly, if you are buying into a new development of villas or flats you will find foreign agents falling over themselves to make a sale. This is because the developer has put them on a

high commission to shift the properties quickly. However if, for whatever reason, you decide after a few years to dispose of your property, you will find the same agents far less diligent – in fact probably fairly unenthusiastic about the concept of trying to shift a single villa. Take trouble, therefore, to look at the area and see how quickly property is moving, for as far as possible it is very important to ensure that you can get out if you wish.

Taxation

As with any second home, if you come to sell it, then the profit you have made on the property may be subject to Capital Gains Tax. It may also be subject to tax in the country where your home is situated. For example, some property overseas will be subject to inheritance tax in that country, although people get round this by buying the property through a family-controlled non-resident company. Certainly you should discuss this problem with your lawyer.

You also need to be very careful about how much time you spend abroad. If you are living abroad for more than half a year, your entire taxation position will be subject to change. Maybe, in some instances, it is better to be taxed out of this country, if you can, but what you have to be careful about is not to fall between two stools and find yourself being subject to two sets of taxation. You do need to check out this position very carefully indeed.

Finance

Generally, banks and building societies in this country are prepared to lend money to finance the purchase of a property abroad. Normally they charge a slightly higher rate of interest than they would do for a UK mortgage and the terms tend to be slightly more onerous – there will be less money available and they will require repayment over a shorter term. However, supporting the purchase of property abroad is recognized as a growing requirement to the extent that a number of banks and building societies actually have mortgage departments dealing quite specifically with this aspect of the property market.

You may feel our words of warning are over-zealous but we believe you cannot be too cautious about the purchase of a property abroad. Over the years there have been many, many horror stories of developers selling non-existent flats and villas and even today it still goes on. A current scandal involves the Spanish Government threatening to bulldoze sixty villas, mostly belonging to Britons, because the Spanish have decided to turn the site into a nature reserve. The developer of the site had acted in good faith. He had obtained all the necessary local permissions to proceed with the development and to those people buying their dream homes in the sun it must have seemed that they were making a safe and sensible investment. Now it seems their houses will be destroyed and compensation is likely to be a tenth of the price they originally paid for their villas.

Undoubtedly there are a lot of sharks in the business and also a deal of resentment on the part of the countries concerned about having their land bought by foreigners. If, as they see it, you are stupid enough to be taken for a ride, it is considered fair sport. No one is going to go out of their way to point out the dangers of the game, so you just have to make sure you are one move ahead.

Time-share property, both at home and abroad, excites considerable interest. On the face of it, time-share provides the opportunity of owning a holiday property for that period of time when it is relevant to you, without any of the hassle of maintenance, sub-letting etc, etc.

What is time-share? Normally a property company develops a site and creates a number of small houses or, more usually, flats or apartments. Then, taking each apartment, the developer sells space in it, of a duration of one, two or three weeks normally, for a set period of each year. In other words you, the punter, end up by owning, shall we say, an apartment in Majorca for the first two weeks of July each year. In theory it is a brilliant concept. If you have found a holiday resort which suits you perfectly, rather than run to the expense each year of paying a hotel bill or renting a villa, you pay a lump sum which guarantees your holiday in the same place each year, over a set number of years. The time-share arrangement is similar to a leasehold and the holiday period you are buying is likely to be twenty to twenty-five years or even longer. There is a service charge in addition to be paid, in order that the building can be maintained, the furnishings and fittings renewed and replaced where necessary and, if appropriate, the gardens tended. Yet despite the service charge, buying time-share is obviously infinitely cheaper than buying a holiday home and alleviates all the stress and work associated with a second home.

So what is the snag? There are a number. While there are plenty of very well-established, bona-fide time-share developers, the time-share concept does attract the riff-raff because it does appear to be a way to make a fast buck. A greedy developer works out what it will cost him to build a block of apartments, takes each apartment, divides it by fifty-two weeks in the year and sees the potential for an immense profit. He does not look beyond this point and does not consider his obligations of maintenance and renewal. In

addition, his sums will be calculated on the basis of his selling time-share on all the apartments. Perhaps he is only able to sell those with, say, a sea view, in which case, what happens if he runs out of money? There have been many stories in the press to support the view that you do have to be very, very careful with whom you invest your money in time-share or you could lose the lot.

The problem with time-share, however, is not as simple as worrying about tying yourself up with a rogue. It is true that if you choose a large, well-established property company, and preferably buy into an existing site – where you can discuss with established tenants how things are working – then you can be relatively confident that you will get what you have paid for. There are other considerations though, which perhaps can be best described by way of personal experience.

For the last seven years, we have spent the first two weeks of the children's summer holidays in Crete. We stay in the same hotel, in the same numbered apartments, which are separate from the hotel building and right on the edge of the sea. Because the Greeks are not noted for their administrative efficiency, every year we have a fight to secure these two apartments. Even though we book them from one year to the next, we are never really confident that we have got them until we are actually unpacking the suitcases. We asked ourselves, for the purpose of this book, the hypothetical question – if these two apartments became the subject of a time-share, would we take them? The answer is no and the reasons are these:

⬦ While our children have been growing up, it has been an ideal holiday place for us, but our youngest child is now thirteen, and it will not be too many years before she wants to take her holidays independently from us. Crete,

in the last two weeks of July, is both exceptionally hot and exceptionally crowded. Given a choice, we would far rather go in May or June – only the school holidays force us to take July.

⬦ Again, our particular apartments have suited us because we have a range of ages and interests to cater for. Without teenage children to entertain and left to our own devices, we would far rather hire a jeep and wander around the less developed places on the island, staying at the odd taverna.

⬦ The Crete we loved seven years ago has changed enormously with the influx of tourists. Sadly, in another seven years, we may not even want to go there at all.

⬦ If this and other of our books sell well, we might want to look beyond the Greek islands for our holidays of the future – West Indies, here we come! If they don't sell well, we may not be able to go away at all.

This case history demonstrates what you, yourself have to consider about your own and your family's position. Are you really going to want to go on doing the same thing year after year? Supposing your fortunes take a nose-dive and your time-share commitment is abroad – you could find yourself in a position where you simply cannot stump up the air fare to take advantage of the very thing you have paid for. In a way, time-share is falling between two stools – it neither gives you the flexibility of a normal holiday booking, nor the investment potential of owning your own holiday home. Time-share is sufficiently new that there is not a great deal of data to be found on its long-term effects. Early indications are, however, that your time-share interest is not an easy thing of which to dispose. Certainly you are unlikely to make a profit of any substantial nature. At a recent auction, all of the time-share properties changed hands at less than 40% of their original cost. Some agencies are running

time-share swap schemes so that you can, for example, swap your two weeks in July in Majorca, for a week in Miami in May. It is, however, a lot of hassle, takes a lot of organizing and one is tempted to ask whether it would not be simpler to book a straightforward holiday if you want a change of scene.

We have some friends who are a childless, professional couple and have been visiting the same Devon seaside town for the last twenty years at approximately the same time of year. The hotel at which they always stay has just built some time-share apartments and they have bought one. They are thrilled – for them it is the perfect answer for there is no way they can see their life-style changing in the next twenty years. They live in London, they have no intention of moving house, and their whole life is very settled and ordered. For them, time-share is right – for most of us, we suspect, it is not.

Investment property

The meteoric rise in property values in recent years has tempted many people to consider the advantages of investing their money in property. If anything, this view has been strengthened recently by the difficulties of Stock Market investment, and since it is apparent to everyone that the value of property only goes one way – up – it is tempting to become involved.

If you are considering investing in property, the most important thing to recognize is that it is virtually impossible to achieve any measure of success on an income basis. Whatever you have to invest – whether it is £20,000 or £200,000 – the rent you receive, less your management expenses, will not represent a reasonable return on your capital investment. This applies particularly in the case of residential property, but tends to be equally the case with shops, offices and other commercial or industrial property. From an income point of view, therefore, it needs to be recognized that you would be better keeping your money in the bank.

There are two golden rules relating to your personal position which we believe are absolutely fundamental to success so far as investment in property is concerned.

◆ You must have the cash available. In our view, not less than £100,000 – though these days, £200,000 is more likely to be an appropriate minimum. In other words, *do not borrow money in order to make an investment in property.* Even in today's buoyant property market inflation is unlikely to exceed the interest you will be paying.

◆ You need to be a high income earner – or at any rate, you need to be receiving an income which is satisfactory to your needs. In other words, the fact that your investment in property is not going to provide you with an income – or, in fact, may even provide you with negative income – must not worry you.

So why is property considered to be a good investment? It is solely because of its potential growth in value. Growth happens, as a result of one, or a combination of, the following factors:

- General market conditions – supply and demand, inflation, the state of the economy.
- Changes in local environment or services – a new motorway, a new industrial plant – so the area starts moving up in terms of housing standards and type of residence.
- Change of use – changing the use of your property from, say, a warehouse to residential use, a house to an office or a shop to a house.
- A simple refurbishment job – changing the character of the house to give it a more up-market image.
- Redevelopment – a £100,000 building site, plus eight houses costing £60,000 each to build, could produce eight houses worth, say, £130,000 each.
- For the most common of all investors – the owner/occupier – favourable tax treatment, combined with ready availability of mortgages, enables the home owner to greatly enhance his capital position.

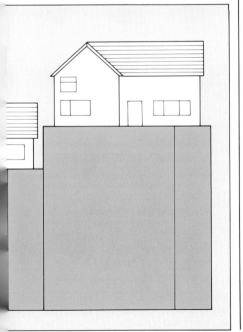

Without doubt, the most worthwhile investment in property is your own home. You may find your ideal house and sit tight over a number of years, perhaps only in old age trading down to realize capital. Alternatively, you may move houses a number of times, trading up on each occasion. Either way, it is likely to be the best investment you will ever make.

If, however, you are looking at investment outside, or in addition to your own home, recognize that an investment in property can never be a passive thing. If you invest money on the Stock Exchange, it is simply a question of making a telephone call and then sitting around and reading a paper. Not so with property – you need to be involved in the management or in some element of the development, whether you are constructing a new building or refurbishing, whether you are renting or simply intending to convert and sell one. If you are a builder yourself, or an architect, then clearly an investment in property is also providing you with a job and in this respect justifies itself. If you do not have these skills, you still need to be involved in other ways. It is not a situation where you can sit back and let the experts get on with it. You need to develop a good feel for your local market. You must have the ability to recognize development and conversion potential. You need to spend a lot of time thinking, talking and investigating. The days are long gone when one could make an easy killing in property. These days everyone is switched on to the fact that in this over-crowded island of ours property is at a premium. You are not going to pick up any unbelievable bargains – they simply do not exist any more.

Investment tips

To make any sense of an investment in property we would suggest you need the following:
- £200,000.
- a thorough knowledge of the area in which you intend to operate.
- a good relationship with one or two estate agents, for you must buy property before it is advertised.
- courage.

Historic buildings

It is a privilege to live in an old building. Forget the ghosts and ghoulies for a moment – old property does have an atmosphere, a special feeling of security and permanence. It also offers status, and if you take your responsibilities seriously, it is enormously satisfying to feel that you have made your contribution to an historic building. Against this, of course, are the inconveniences. An old building is likely to be expensive on maintenance, difficult to heat and clean and fairly low on mod. cons.

Case history

We have a friend called George who lives in North Yorkshire. He has a wonderful old, stone pile – a small stately home really. He is in his forties, clearly very attractive to women but unable to find anyone to marry him – quite literally, he changes his girlfriend each spring. The reason? He has yet to find a woman who can stand living with him through a Yorkshire winter, in his beautiful, but essentially unheatable mansion!

Buildings of historical interest generally fall into one of three categories:

1 Ancient monuments
By definition an ancient monument is not a place in which you will live or work. It is likely to be a ruin, with the odd wall still standing, but restoration is not really viable and the owner is not expected to attempt to maintain it.

2 Listed buildings
Under the Town and Country Planning Act of 1971, the Secretary of State for the Environment was given power to *list* buildings of special architectural or historical interest.

3 The rest
There are a number of very old buildings which are neither ancient monuments nor have they been listed. They may be situated within a conservation area or they may have a listing pending.

What is listing?

Listing can apply to almost any type of building, whatever its shape or size. Familiar buildings of great national importance such as the Houses of Parliament, Blenheim Palace, Battersea Power Station are all listed. Similarly, in towns and villages around the country, you will find a listing on perhaps a row of shops, the town hall, a tythe barn, the village stocks or even a telephone box.

Property is listed in order to protect it, on behalf of the nation, from demolition or from unauthorised alteration or extension. Control of listed buildings is exercised through the local planning authorities, by English Heritage (Historic Buildings and Monuments Commission) in England and equivalent Government departments in Scotland and Wales.

For practical purposes there are three grades of listing within which properties may fall.

Grade 1 – public buildings which are of outstanding national importance or rarity – such as Blenheim Palace, as mentioned above.

Grade 2* – the cream of the more every-day historic property in terms of importance and historic interest.

Grade 2 – the vast majority of listed buildings fall into this third category.

The pros and cons of listing

A listed building may not be demolished or altered without listed building consent from the local planning authority. Work carried out without the authority's permission, or in breach of the conditions applied, may well have to be reinstated. If you fail to obtain consent or act in breach of restrictions imposed, you could be involved in heavy fines or even imprisonment. In contrast to normal planning applications, there is no possibility of being granted retrospective permission, to regularise a default. You simply must not carry out any work without obtaining permission first. Talking to various planning authorities about this point, they advised us that the most common breach is the fitting of replacement windows. In a modern house it would not occur to you to seek planning permission to rip out rotting window frames and replace them with more up to date units. This is something you cannot do to an historic building.

The practical effect of this very tight planning attitude does impose very real restrictions and these restrictions apply internally as well as externally. It would be extremely unwise, therefore, to move into a listed building in the belief that you will be able to undertake extensive alterations to suit your family's requirements. It is also worth mentioning that any alteration work you are allowed to do is likely to be extremely expensive, as bricks will have to be matched, old roof tiles found etc, etc.

The other point you need to recognize is that taking on a listed building is a liability. Because the listing procedure has been adopted in order to ensure the protection of historic buildings, under the terms of listing, failure on the part of the owner to properly maintain the property will give the local authority power to carry out any necessary work or in extreme cases, even to proceed with compulsory acquisition, in order to protect the building.

Owning a listed building is not entirely a catalogue of disadvantages. In a practical sense, for example, grants may be available to help you carry out necessary work. In addition, if you apply for permission to carry out work on the property and are refused permission (or granted permission with very restricted conditions), you may be able to force the local authority to purchase the property. An additional small bonus – repairs and alterations to a listed building, which require and have obtained listing building consent, are free from VAT. If the work does not require consent then, sadly, VAT is payable.

Unlisted historic buildings

If an historic or architecturally important building is not listed, but is threatened by extensive alteration or demolition, a Building Preservation Notice can be served on the owner and/or occupier. This has the effect of halting any proposed work for six months, while a listing is considered.

Historic buildings do come up for sale fairly regularly and many will appear in the window of your local estate agent. However, if it is an historic building in which you specifically want to live, then we would recommend that you subscribe to:

The Period Property Register,
Chobham Park House,
Chobham,
Surrey, GU24 8JD.

Telephone: Chobham (09905) 7983/6128.

The Period Property Register is a monthly publication which advertises historic property for sale, divided into sections such as medieval, Tudor, seventeenth century, Georgian etc, etc. At the back of the magazine period property agents are listed in each area of the country, which should prove helpful.

Conservation areas

The Civic Amenities Act of 1967 and subsequent legislation imposed for the first time a duty upon local planning authorities to identify and designate areas of special architectural or historic interest. These are areas where it is clearly desirable to preserve and enhance the general character and appearance of the locality. Most conservation areas are in towns and cities and can consist of a group of buildings, a street, a number of streets or even a whole recognizable section of a town. In rural surroundings, the whole of a small village might be designated a conservation area.

Within the designated area, there may be individual listed buildings, which have planning protection already identified. However, the object of designating a conservation area is to spread the concept of preservation beyond individual buildings, so as to maintain the whole cohesive appearance and character of a neighbourhood.

In a conservation area, the local planning authority do have more clout when it comes to their ability to refuse applications for alteration or demolition. They are also likely to impose more conditions when planning permission is granted – such as type of bricks used etc, etc. However, there is far more flexibility for alterations and renovations of *unlisted* property in a conservation area, than there is for a listed building, wherever it is situated. It should not be overlooked that to protect the overall appearance of the surroundings, planning will be very fussy about all visual aspects – extensions, new roofs, replacement windows, treatment of stone facing etc, etc and they will also be greatly concerned with the overall *character* of the conservation area.

An example:

Take a small market town in any county in the country. In the old part of the town there are likely to be several listed buildings, sitting comfortably alongside others of considerably less merit. The whole area – which is perhaps the market square – could well be designated a conservation area. In these circumstances, it is obvious that Planning would refuse to allow you to rip down several houses in order to build a petrol station. However, you might be misled into believing that they would have no objection to your selling off the ground floor of your house to a firm of solicitors to use as offices. You would be wrong. Chances are, Planning would turn down such an application for change of use, because it is a conservation area, and in this instance what they would be trying to conserve is the residential nature of the heart of your town.

Case history

We have a friend who is a very experienced property man and has undertaken hundreds of conversions and redevelopments over the years. He was telling us recently of a fundamental mistake he made which cost him, unnecessarily, several hundred pounds. Our chum, Peter, was redeveloping a row of shops in a conservation area, for which he had obtained detailed planning permission. One of the conditions of that permission was that he built in front of the shops a brick wall, and it was specified that the brick wall should be erected from bricks which exactly matched the bricks used in the buildings – in terms of age, texture and colour. Permission also stated that the bricks should be inspected before the wall was erected. Peter was lucky – from a demolished house down the road he found the perfect bricks and enthusiastically set about building the wall. A few weeks later a planning inspector visited the site to see how work was progressing and was horrified to see the wall already erected. Angrily, he told Peter the bricks were not right, the wall was to be demolished immediately and that in line with the

On balance, most of the restrictions likely to be applied to a conservation area are quite easy to live with *provided you play by the rules.*

You may consider Peter's experience a bureaucratic nonsense but the fact is that he did not play the game by the rules. Because he was so experienced in planning and building materials at least he only incurred the cost of additional labour but he could well have ended up with a load of unusable bricks as well.

When buying a property, do ensure that you know if it is in a conservation area. Unlike listed buildings, you do not have to worry to the same extent about your responsibilities but you do have to consider the future requirements of your home. In a few years' time, you might require a second bathroom, a playroom for your growing family or a granny flat. Before committing yourself to purchase, it would be sensible to investigate the likely attitude of the local planning officer.

GOLDEN RULE FOR CONSERVATION AREAS – do remember that planning authorities are not simply concerned with bricks and mortar when it comes to their attitude to a conservation area. They are also concerned with the overall character and image of the place, which can prove very restrictive if you have any major alterations in mind.

conditions of planning consent, the replacement bricks would have to be checked first. Peter did not argue. He had his men take down the wall and store the bricks. Several weeks later he rang the planning inspector and told him he had found some replacement bricks. The planning inspector was shown the same bricks which had formerly been the wall and passed them immediately, saying what an ideal match they were. The wall was then rebuilt.

THE WALL'S FINE EXCEPT FOR THE BRICKS I'VE MARKED WHICH WILL HAVE TO BE REPLACED.

PLANNING OFFICER.

Although national parks, nature reserves and areas of outstanding natural beauty are, by definition, open spaces, you could just be lucky enough to have a home within one of these areas. The National Parks and Access to the Countryside Act of 1948 created a National Parks Commission. More recently, this has been renamed the Countryside Commission and it now operates largely under the terms of the Countryside Act of 1968. The Commission is the body responsible for the protection and improvement of the natural beauty of the countryside and its aim is also to encourage the countryside's use and enjoyment. As with English Heritage, the Commission acts through the local planning authorities, and in this way national parks have been created, nature reserves have been defined and areas of outstanding natural beauty have

been designated. Agriculture, some industrial and commercial activities, tourism and various countryside and water-based pursuits all take place, to some degree, within these areas. There is also an element of private and publicly owned residential accommodation. For example, the Lake District is a national park and within it, businesses thrive and residential accommodation is plentiful. By contrast, on nature reserves in particular, residential accommodation is very scarce and more often than not reserved for keepers and their families.

Planning

The local authorities' planning control of housing within these special countryside surroundings is clearly strict, and within the jurisdiction of the national parks, little housing development is permitted – even local infilling in most cases will be unacceptable. External finishes of your home – i.e. its visual impact on the environment, will need to be maintained and any alteration or development will not only be vetted as to how it will look, but also will be examined for the risk of pollution and the possibility of extra strain on local services. Clearly the areas vary enormously. Again, citing the example of the Lake District, new houses are built, extensions allowed and businesses operated. There has even been new development allowed along lakeside banks in certain circumstances, although this is the subject of mounting criticism. By contrast, the area around the Helford River in Cornwall is far less developed and planning intends that it should be kept that way. This demonstrates that attitudes of different planning authorities are likely to vary considerably.

As with historic buildings, while planning permission is difficult to obtain, when your application is successful you are likely to be eligible for local, or even central, government grants and subsidies (see Grants on pages 154–6).

It may be you are considering buying a house in close proximity to a national park or nature reserve – indeed such an amenity could play a major role in your decision to move. Be cautious – acres of nature reserve on your very doorstep may be lovely to look at, but can you actually make use of them? While we applaud the conservation of our countryside, in some instances it does seem that conservation goes too far. For example, near our home there is a large forest which recently has been designated a nature reserve. The direct result of this on local habitants is that dogs can only be taken for walks on a lead, horse riding is restricted to certain paths and horses are not allowed to be ridden faster than a trot. Sensible, possibly, but the immediate effect on the local community has been to take away a natural amenity which they, their fathers and grandfathers before them, had been free to enjoy. These restrictions come as no hardship to the occasional tourist at weekends but the local community is greatly the poorer. So . . . the lesson to learn from our experience would be not to take such an amenity for granted. Check out precisely what you may or may not do within this designated area.

Most national parks and nature reserves occur in truly rural areas. If you are not used to country living do consider the implications very carefully before committing yourself. Access to schools, local bus services, shopping – all these aspects need to be thought through, and in our view the best time to buy a rural home is in January or February. If the place appeals to you then you will just adore it for the rest of the year!

The National Trust

The National Trust was founded at the turn of the century. It is funded by public subscription, donation and its own operating revenues. The Trust also receives Government grants but only in respect of quite specific properties.

The object of the National Trust is to buy and manage, for the nation, fine buildings, outstanding pieces of land and important estates. The Trust acquires many properties by gift, as a gesture of goodwill. Sometimes it takes on a property in lieu of Inheritance Tax, and sometimes simply because the owners cannot afford the upkeep. Increasingly, though, the Trust is becoming more commercial and it does now require some form of endowment with any property acquired, so that it is not purely a drain on Trust funds. This means the National Trust can, and does, say *no* to properties where it feels that merit is outweighed by the financial implications. The National Trust is the third largest land owner in Great Britain, the first being the Ministry of Defence and the second the Forestry Commission.

There is a tendency when thinking of the National Trust to think in terms of rolling acres, mansions and mile upon mile of unspoilt coastline. Of course all this exists but on those rolling acres, in addition to the stately homes, there are working farms, houses of all shapes and sizes, holiday cottages and a number of commercial concerns. The one thing that all these properties have in common – apart from the fact that they are owned by the National Trust – is that they need people to live in them, manage them and look after them. The National Trust is a big organization: as well as its head office in London, there are sixteen individual regional offices. The Trust is run by experts – experts on historic buildings, experts on planning matters, experts on large scale land management, experts on agricultural land . . . *but it still needs people* to run its farms and live in its houses. The last thing the Trust wants is that its properties should be a series of museums.

If you are interested in living in a National Trust property, the first point to mention is that they are overwhelmed by demand, particularly in the south of England. You cannot buy a property from the National Trust but you can become a tenant, sometimes a very long term tenant, which is clearly the next best thing to buying. The opportunites which are available vary wildly from region to region and from year to year. While the Trust is inundated with requests from people to rent houses or farms in the home counties, farm houses in rural Wales are falling into disrepair for lack of demand.

By way of example, quite recently, the Trust purchased the Sheringham Estate in Norfolk. It was purchased in order to maintain and protect a large area of superb Norfolk landscape. With the land came the historic house, but the Trust could not afford to buy the furniture, the paintings and all the contents which make any house a

home – albeit in this case, a lavish one. The result is that the house is still empty. The Trust has been trying for over a year now to find a tenant prepared to take on the house *and* all its commitments.

In the past it has been possible to acquire National Trust property for a peppercorn rent, in return for guaranteeing to undertake a degree of maintenance, repair and, in some cases, restoration. In these cases a lease was granted for often as long as 99 years. However, experience has taught the Trust that in many instances tenants do not fulfil their obligations. The Trust is then forced into the situation of either having to undertake the repairs itself or see the building fall into a state of disrepair. As part of its new drive towards greater commercialism, the Trust is moving towards granting shorter leases of say, 15–20 years and spending the money itself on the necessary refurbishment so that the property is let at an open market rent. This situation certainly applies in the more popular areas. Indications are that in the more isolated parts of the country the National Trust is more concerned with acquiring the right tenant than making a big commercial success out of the relationship.

Many of the Trust's properties are in simply superb locations and many of the buildings are historic or unusual. If you would like to commit your life to a National Trust property, you should contact the regional office nearest to you and talk to one of their land agents. The National Trust Head Office is:

The National Trust,
36 Queen Anne's Gate,
London,
W1H 9AS.

Telephone: 01-222 9251

Ideally, what you should be looking for is a property which needs money spent on it, for maintenance and refurbishment, and also needs someone to look after it. If it is in an area of low demand, so much the better. In these circumstances you might be able to obtain a lease for say 45 years, at a modest rent, in return for a covenant to restore and maintain the building. It also might be possible to acquire an option to renew beyond the 45 years. What you do have to come to terms with is that a National Trust property will *never* be yours – you will be living there as a trustee. Nonetheless it will feel like yours and it is likely to be very special indeed.

Finally, while you might be told by your regional land agent that the waiting list for National Trust property makes your request hopeless, do bear in mind that the Trust, like any other big landlord, has its share of problems. The Trust owns a fair number of semi-derelict properties to which the NT purse simply cannot stretch. So . . . if you come across that sort of cottage, house or farm and you fall in love with it, why not try and negotiate for it? Offer to pay a nominal ground rent for a long lease in return for a commitment to spend a substantial sum on restoration. You just might touch lucky.

Green belt land and Rural Development Areas

Green belt land

The green belts were established to protect the countryside by preventing urban sprawl. In other words, they are tracts of land between towns, which stop one running into another. In all, approximately 4.5 million acres of land are covered by the green belt, of which 1.2 million acres are in the London Metropolitan green belt area.

Most local authorities have jealously guarded their green belt areas against the demand for development. In recent years there have been moves by the Government to relax building restrictions on agricultural land, but so far as the green belt areas are concerned, they have remained largely untouched. Within green belts, therefore, new housing development is virtually impossible. An odd infill house might be

allowed, but a new house in say, the garden of an existing home, would be very unlikely to be accepted by the planners, unless the garden was extremely substantial. An extension to an existing house would be likely to be approved, however, provided of course all the other normal planning criteria were met.

This really sums up the difference between green belt land and conservation areas. Planners are not so concerned with how the area looks, provided it is not developed further. We have an example of this on our doorstep, living as we do in a little village north of Oxford. Between North Oxford and the dormitory town of Kidlington there is an area of green belt. To be frank it is hideous scrubland and has absolutely nothing to commend it. Its sole purpose is to separate North Oxford from Kidlington and there is no way anyone will obtain permission to build on it – although there are grounds for saying almost anything would be an improvement.

So, if you have, or intend to buy, a house in a green belt area you can be confident that the surroundings will continue to be protected. The part green belt plays in many people's lives is not so much that they live in the area as they overlook it and here again, if your house enjoys the amenity of overlooking a green belt area, you can be confident that your position is protected.

Public demand for the preservation of the green belt has proved to be an important political factor and it was necessary recently for the Government to do some rapid backtracking after tentatively recommending that green belt control should be relaxed. The resultant uproar of criticism left them in no doubt that such a move would do them untold damage at the next election.

However, there is one major loophole in green belt protection and this relates to some agricultural land. After the Second World War, at a time when farmers were being given every encouragement to solve the problems of food shortages, it was generally accepted that the countryside and rural environment had been created by farmers and therefore it was their domain to administer and protect as they saw fit. In consequence it was felt unnecessary for there to be any major planning controls imposed on agriculture. This attitude lingers even today in that if a farmer wants to build a fairly substantial industrial structure – which he chooses to call a barn – provided he is going to use it for agricultural purposes, he can do so without any form of planning consent. At the same time Government policy now actually encourages the re-use of existing rural buildings which have become redundant, whether or not they are in a green belt area. So . . . the farmer can build his 'barn' with no requirement for planning consent, use it for, say, a couple of years and then decide it is redundant – at which time he can dispose of it for industrial use.

Rural Development Areas

While on the one hand green belts are providing protection from urban sprawl, it is recognized that the changing face of agriculture in Great Britain needs to be taken into account. Advanced farming methods and European Common Market policy have combined to create over-capacity in many farming areas, and encouragement has been given to new forms of employment opportunities in rural areas. The Development Commission has adopted priority areas known as *Rural Development Areas*, within which there are a whole range of assisted schemes – subsidized property, finance, training, advice – the whole object being to provide encouragement to new industries and commerce. The emphasis is upon bringing back to life rural communities and it does open up exciting prospects for home ownership, and certainly increased demand will enhance property values in these areas.

If you would like to find out more about Rural Development Areas, start with your local authority or contact CoSIRA (The Council for Small Industries in Rural Areas) whose address is:

141 Castle Street,
Salisbury,
Wiltshire,
SP1 3TP.
Telephone: 0722 336255

Homes equipped for the disabled

By *disabled*, in the context, we are referring specifically to people with a physical impairment which limits their ability to walk and makes them largely dependent upon a wheelchair for mobility. It may be that you suddenly find yourself in the role of carer because someone in your family has had a severe accident or is suffering from some permanent disability – or it could be you, yourself, who are disabled and recognize that over the course of the next few years you may become even less mobile.

Obviously, in these circumstances, the first decision has to be whether you should move or not. Certainly ten or fifteen years ago, being disabled meant that you had to live either in a hospital, a nursing home, or at best a bungalow. All that has changed, for two main reasons:

◆ A combination of design, skill and imagination has resulted in a whole range of sophisticated equipment now being available which enables a house – any house – to be converted into a suitable dwelling for a severely disabled person.

◆ It is now recognized, beyond any doubt, that the best place for a disabled person to live is in the community, leading as normal a life as possible. This is not only best for the individual, it also takes the strain off the already beleaguered National Health Service.

So, if you wish to stay in your own home you can be sure of a great deal of assistance to enable you to do so.

Looking first at the practical aspects of money, whether you are disabled yourself or are in the role of carer, you need to contact your local authority to find out what form of grants and/or equipment are available to you. Help for the disabled is based on a means test. If you are eligible for social security benefits and do not have any hefty savings, you can be sure that most, if not all, the equipment you need will be provided by the State. If, on the other hand, you are working, have a mortgage-free home and considerable savings, then you are liable to have to meet the expense yourself. Either way, whatever your circumstances, we would strongly recommend that where possible you should adapt your existing home in preference to moving. Moving is not only expensive – it is emotionally and physically wearing. A newly disabled person has enough change to cope with – to return to familiar, well-loved surroundings has to be a bonus.

The starting point for assessing the requirements of a disabled person living at home, is to obtain an occupational therapist's report. If you or your dependent relative have been having hospital treatment, it is likely that this report will happen automatically as a routine part of the medi-

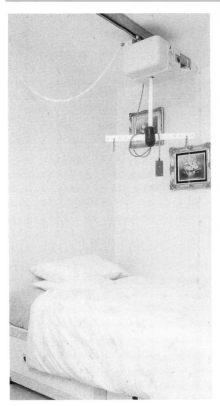

variety of hoists and handles, and these days there is a deal of electronic wizardry in the form of alarms and panic buttons which also may be useful. None of this equipment is cheap but when set against the enormous amount of comfort and independence it can create, is well worthwhile. Stair lifts, for example, start at £1,300, and even a comparatively big lift which can take a wheelchair, or several people standing, can be installed for about £6,500. Not cheap admittedly, but they open up a whole new world to the disabled person. It is even possible to install a completely self-contained, free-standing unit – specially designed for the disabled – containing toilet, shower and washbasin. It takes up just one square metre of floor space.

Golden Rules

Whatever facilities you feel you need *do not start on any of the work if you are going to apply for a council grant.* They are far less likely to award you a grant if you have begun the work. This means you should wait for *written permission* before starting – a verbal agreement is not enough. Also, even if you think you do not qualify for a grant, do go along to your local authority and check. For example, if you are caring for a disabled relative, *it is the disabled person's income and financial circumstances which will be the qualifying factor for assistance* – not yours.

Whether you are intending to move house or staying put, here are some useful addresses of organizations who can help you in the planning of your home:

Access Committee of England
and
Centre on Environment for the
Handicapped,
35 Great Smith Street,
London SW1P 3BJ.

Telephone: 01-222 7980

RADAR (The Royal Association of
Disability & Rehabilitation),
25 Mortimer Street,
London W1N 8AB.

Telephone: 01-637 5400

cal process, prior to discharge from the hospital. However if such a report is not forthcoming, this is something you should organize through the Social Services, for it is vital to have professional guidance as to precisely what practical help will be of greatest benefit to the disability in question. Armed with this report you can then set to work.

The degree of work you have to do so much depends on the circumstances – the extent of the disability, the size of your house and indeed the size of your purse. If a disabled relative is coming to live with you, it may be that you feel the need to build on an entire granny flat, or the problem could be solved simply by the addition of a downstairs bathroom. The kind of adaptations you are likely to make are widening door openings, installing a stair-lift, or if you have the room, an ordinary lift, ramps for the wheelchair, low level kitchen units and shelves, a specially adapted bathroom, a

Homes equipped for the elderly

At this moment, in the United Kingdom, there are ten million elderly people, and over the coming years this figure is going to increase considerably. More of the population are living longer yet facilities for the elderly are even currently not keeping up with demand.

How may the problems of the elderly affect you and your property?

◆ You may be looking after parents or elderly relatives in your own home.

◆ You may be getting elderly yourself.

Looking after parents or elderly relatives

If you are faced with the prospect of looking after an elderly relative, we would suggest that the first thing you should do is to contact Age Concern. Their head office address is as follows:

Age Concern,
Bernard Sunley House,
60 Pitcairn Road,
Mitcham,
Surrey CR4 3LL.

Telephone: 01-640 5431

Age Concern have a great deal of information available on housing for the elderly. They also have a reading list and we would very strongly recommend that you seek their professional advice before taking any steps to alter your home *in any way*. So much, of course, depends upon the type of house in which you live, the health of the elderly relative, your financial resources and perhaps most important of all, your relationship with the elderly person. Fifty years ago, it was considered normal – indeed the family's absolute responsibility – to take in elderly relatives who could no longer fend for themselves. Today, with smaller houses, a more mobile population, and an increasingly pressurised lifestyle, more and more elderly people are having to look to alternative methods of coping with old age, other than relying on relatives. This book is about property and therefore it is not relevant to start moralizing on the pros and cons of taking on responsibility for elderly relatives. However, a word of advice – regardless of how charming and easy-going your elderly relatives may be, they live their lives at a completely different pace from your own. Therefore, if at all possible, try and redesign your house so that your elderly relative has his or her own place – ideally, a completely self-contained granny flat, but if not, at least a couple of rooms which are exclusively for granny. Do remember that the points of stress in family living always centre around the kitchen and bathroom and if granny can be given a kitchenette and a small bathroom of her own, you will greatly reduce the aggravation factor.

As to funding a granny flat, you should find your bank or building society very susceptible to giving you an additional mortgage loan. This can either be permanent or it could be temporary borrowing while granny's house is sold. There are grants available for elderly people on a low income, with little or no savings. Your local authority will be able to advise you whether you are likely to be eligible.

MORNING GRAN.

Growing old

Perhaps the major decision you will have to make as you grow old is whether you should stay put in your existing house or move to something smaller and, in your view, more appropriate. This is a very personal decision. Without doubt there is a tendency to rush into selling the family home once the children have fled the nest and then regretting it later. It is worth looking at alternatives – much can be done to an existing home to make it more labour-saving. Heating can be converted from coal to gas or electricity, a bathroom can be built downstairs, a large garden sold off or let to next door. If you have a big house it could be converted into flats, leaving the ground floor flat and garden for yourself and reletting or selling the rest. Age Concern, mentioned in this section above, have a great deal of helpful advice on housing in retirement and we would strongly recommend that you send for their leaflets before making any firm decision. Grants are available, and it is imperative that you do not start any work before you have established whether you are eligible for a grant, as you will not be awarded the money retrospectively. Contact your local authority for advice.

Finance

If you decide to stay in your existing home, are not eligible for a grant but are short of money, you might consider raising income from a Home Income Plan or Mortgage Annuity Scheme. How this works is that you raise a mortgage on your house and the sum involved is invested to give you an income for life. Certainly if you have a mortgage free house this is a good way of boosting your income. A number of institutions offer home income plans and currently the Abbey National is probably the best. Seek the advice of your bank manager or solicitor before going ahead.

The alternative is a Home Reversion Scheme. This differs from the Home Income Plan in that you actually sell your house to a financial institution, in order to purchase an annuity. You can continue to live in your house for life, are responsible for maintenance and repairs, and on your death, the financial institution simply takes possession of the house. Frankly we do not recommend this – at any rate currently, when property is escalating in value so much. The house you sell today at £60,000, could be worth £160,000 by the time you die, but neither you nor your surviving relatives will benefit from that increase in value.

Moving

If you are going to put yourself through the upheaval of moving into a new home which you feel will be more appropriate for your old age, then do get it right. Avoid if you can, falling into the trap and ending up in a 'retirement ghetto' in Bournemouth, Hastings or Spain. Elderly people should be as much a part of the community as any other. These unnatural communities in which the vast majority of people are elderly, tend to become very stultifying – certainly to the active in mind or body. Bear in mind that your children will have children, and that one of the greatest joys of old age will be your grandchildren, so do try and buy a property large enough to accomodate them. Recognize that you may not always be well. Whilst you have no intention of moving in with your family, having them near enough that they can visit you when you are sick and fetch your shopping when you have a nasty cold, will not only make life easier for you, it will also make life a lot easier for them. Certainly moving into a smaller property can be very rewarding financially, for it is likely to release spare cash. The alternative is sheltered accommodation, but this does come expensive and so much depends on the status and quality of the management. Do be careful before committing yourself. Some sheltered accommodation units offer wonderful facilities – a central restaurant and bar, a warden, room service if you are not well, laundry facilities etc, etc, while others offer very little more than a panic button in case you fall, which is something you can acquire through your GP these days, without the need for special housing.

Sheltered accommodation – old people's homes/nursing homes

In North Oxford currently, a large modern building is being constructed on a prime site for the purpose of providing sheltered accommodation for elderly people. In pursuit of information for this book, we contacted the property developers and asked them for some information as to prices, availability etc, etc. Their answer was fairly staggering. There was absolutely no point in sending us any details, they told us, for not only were the flats all sold (although the first floor is not built yet), but there is also a waiting list for when the first batch of buyers moves on, or dare we say, upwards! This same firm of property developers say they have plans to put in hand a further 900 units across the country in the next two or three years. The purpose of relating this incident is to demonstrate what an apparently vast growth potential there is in this area of the property market and because of this, inevitably, it will attract cowboys.

If you are seriously looking at a way of investing your money in a property conversion, it has to be said that providing flats for the elderly, in the form of sheltered accommodation, has to be one of the surest ways to make money simply because the market is wide open at present. However, it is not a project upon which you should enter lightly for the following reasons:

◆ You need plenty of cash. As we suggested in the last section of this book, in order to invest successfully in property, you need your own capital or a partner's and ideally you need in excess of a quarter of a million pounds. This, of course, is unlikely to be sufficient capital to undertake such a project, but it is vital on this sort of venture to minimise your borrowing.

◆ Providing sheltered accommodation is not as simple or as straightforward as providing flats for students or professional people. It is a very specialist area and to help you provide the right kind of accommodation, you need the full support of all possible interested parties. This means you should discuss the project with the DHSS, with your local authority, with Age Concern and with doctors and nurses specializing in

elderly care. You should also visit as many existing sheltered accommodation units as possible – not only to see what has been achieved on other projects but also to talk to the current owner/occupiers, with a view to seeking their advice as to where they think the accommodation could be improved.

◆ At the moment there is no legislation to specifically control the minimum standard requirements of sheltered accommodation, and so you need to think very long and hard as to what precisely you are going to offer. Some sheltered accommodation offers nothing more than a warden, while others include a restaurant, bar, communal lounge and a variety of services. Clearly the more you can offer, the more you can charge, *provided those services can be maintained*. This is no quick, in and out property deal. You have to consider a long term management structure to run the various facilities, and you have a very real and continuing responsibility towards the occupiers.

The alternative to sheltered accommodation is a nursing home or old people's home. The difference between these two is as the names suggest. A nursing home actually provides nursing facilities, whereas an old people's home simply provides specialist accommodation – a permanent hotel for the elderly, if you like. In discussing these facilities, we are tending to move away from the subject of the property market into a more specialist area. Suffice to say here, therefore, that in order to undertake such a project, you need to be qualified in nursing and elderly care, or at least employ people who are, and we are talking about running a business, not simply converting property. What applies to sheltered accommodation also applies to nursing homes and old people's homes. Do not be tempted to dabble or look on the venture as a way of making a quick buck. Thorough research, careful analysis of the requirements of your neighbourhood and a great deal of advice is what you need before you even seriously consider such a project.

Bed and Breakfast

Without doubt, offering bed and breakfast facilities within your home has to be an ideal way of combining family life with a money-making scheme to augment the family budget. However, an essential requirement for such a project is a real and abiding love of meeting people. Do make sure this applies to you.

Rules and regulations

So far as the planning aspects of bed and breakfast are concerned, most planning departments are happy for you to offer B & B facilities, provided that it does not affect more than half your sleeping accommodation. In other words, if you have four bedrooms in all, you can let two. However, do not become over-excited and assume that it is possible to convert your loft or your cellar to make extra space. While planning departments are happy to be reasonably co-operative about B & B letting, the golden rule is that you must have a certificate from the Fire Authority, who will need to inspect your premises before you go into business – and attics and cellars are frowned upon.

Supplying food to the public

By inference, if you are running a bed and breakfast operation, you will be supplying food – definitely breakfast, and possibly also an evening meal. Before going too far in your thinking, it is important that you go to your local HMSO and obtain a copy of *Your Guide to the Food Hygiene (General) Regulations 1970*. If you have no HMSO near you, this leaflet can be obtained from the Health Education Council, 78 New Oxford Street, London, WC1 1AH.

Strictly speaking, before you embark on any form of catering you should first inform the Environmental Health Department of your Local Authority, and as a result of this, an Environmental Health Officer will come and inspect your kitchen and premises. However, if your catering is at a minimal level this is probably not necessary, provided that you stick rigidly to the rules as laid out in the regulations.

IT'S FIRE REGULATIONS "ALL TOAST MUST BE QUITE COLD BEFORE SERVING

Clearly, the most important aspect is hygiene and cleanliness in the kitchen, and here are brief details of what is required. The walls and ceilings must be clean and well maintained, with no crumbling plaster and the walls should be tiled around the working surfaces. The floors must have an easy to clean surface and the room must be well lit. The kitchen must not lead into a bathroom, toilet or bedroom. No rubbish may be kept in the kitchen and no animal may be allowed to enter. There must be a wash basin for washing hands, completely separate from the sink, and it goes without saying that all equipment must be clean and in good working order. You will need two refrigerators – one for cooked and one for uncooked meat. You will also need several chopping boards so that raw meat is chopped separately from cooked meat, and both separately from vegetables and fruit. Working surfaces must be easy to clean, preferably in stainless steel, with no cracks or joins which can attract dirt and germs. You will also need a fully equipped first-aid kit in the kitchen, and should wear protective clothing, such as an overall. It is all relatively commonsense, but very important to observe. One case of food poisoning could have you closed down overnight – do not take any risks.

Advertising

The most immediate and effective way to advertise your bed and breakfast facilities is to put up a bed and breakfast sign. If you live in a crowded neighbourhood it is best to check this out with your neighbours first. If they disapprove they could cause the planning authority to ask you to remove it. Next, we would recommend that you contact your regional Tourist Board and arrange to register with them. If you have a Tourist Information Centre in your area, you will find them very helpful. Normally they will come and inspect your accommodation and give you advice as to the sort of prices you should be charging.

As well as registering with the Tourist Board, you might also consider undertaking selective advertising. Do not simply advertise in a general newspaper, as this is a waste of money. If you are in an area of the country specializing in a particular sport – sailing, fishing, mountain climbing or whatever – then advertise in specialist magazines. If you are in a town with a big industrial estate up the road, make sure notices go up on all the companies' notice boards.

Advice on conversion

Within the confines of this book it is very difficult to give specific advice on converting your home to accommodate bed and breakfast guests – for the simple reason that everyone's home is so different. However, what we would suggest is that you keep your guests as separate from the family as possible. If you have small children and noisy dogs these can upset your guests, or if your guests are blessed with these appendages, they can upset you! So, try and divide up the house in such a way that the family occupy one area and the guests another. Where possible include bathrooms en suite with guests' rooms, even if each is a small unit of shower, loo and washbasin. Particularly if you are accommodating businessmen visiting the area, having to wait their turn to get into the bathroom in the morning will drive them mad.

Providing your house is big enough and your attitude to people is outgoing, then you could find offering bed and breakfast facilities a very rewarding and profitable experience.

Commercial use (1) – finding the right premises

Although as the introduction suggests, this book concentrates on all aspects of the home, it does not seem appropriate to write a book entitled *The Property Handbook* without offering some advice on commercial property.

If you are looking for a property in which to house your business, then you almost certainly will be looking at a leasehold – either a new lease on a modern, purpose-built property or an existing lease on an established commercial property. As a general rule, we would not recommend buying the freehold of a business premises for two reasons – firstly, it will tie up a great deal of capital which could be otherwise employed in your business, and secondly, businesses can change so dramatically in terms of size and shape, and the premises that seems right today may not be at all suitable in two years' time. The only exception to this, of course, is if you are planning to 'live over the shop'. If your business lends itself to this situation – i.e. you are intending running a restaurant, a retail outlet or perhaps a pub, then it does make a lot of sense to secure the premises by freehold acquisition, thus providing yourself and family with security and splitting the cost of the premises between your home and business.

Whatever type of business you are involved in, and whatever property you acquire, there are still a number of important factors which apply regardless of circumstances:

Location

In deciding upon the location for your business, there are a number of people you should consider – your customers, your suppliers, your workforce and you. Are you within easy reach of your customers? Clearly if you are a retail outlet this is vital, but even if you are a manufacturer supplying direct to the trade, you need to consider where your major customers will be and how your goods will reach them.

The same criterion applies to your suppliers. Will your suppliers be able to deliver goods to you regularly enough? If not then you are going to have to carry higher than acceptable stock levels, which in turn will tie up vital cash.

Consider then your workforce – will you be able to recruit the right type of staff? Business premises right out in the wilds might seem very attractive but what about shopping facilities, public transport, cafés and pubs for lunch hours? If you cannot offer these facilities then you will need to set aside rooms for a canteen, a recreation room and possibly provide transport to and from work. Certain areas of the country have a workforce already skilled in a particular industry. Could this be relevant to your business?

Finally, consider yourself. Do you really want to drive fifty miles to work each day? No, of course not. Make sure your home and your business are as near one another as possible.

Identifying your requirement

Before even looking at what is available on the property market, you first need to decide what you actually require. Certainly, in most instances, it is sensible to allow a little extra space for expansion, but square footage costs money in rent, rates and heating, and you certainly should not be thinking in terms of acquiring a premises vastly larger than your requirements. Analyse what you need in a detailed way – how many square feet of offices, storage, workshop and showroom? How many square feet of employees' facilities? How much room for deliveries, storage and packing? Only then go out into the market place and see what is available.

Subsidized premises and locations

Do consider whether you can obtain any Government assistance in the form of a grant or subsidy. Some areas of the country have been designated as development areas and in these areas regional development grants are available to encourage industrial expansion. As well as grants, there are a number of quite specific projects available, geared towards encouraging job creation and business expansion. Even outside development areas there is help available. Most local authorities have nursery units – small industrial units aimed at providing premises for the new business, where the rents are low and the leases are not too restrictive. For details of nursery units, contact your local authority, and for help and guidance on all subsidized premises and locations, as well as speaking to the local authority, you should also contact the Department of Trade and Industry, 1–19 Victoria Street, London, SW1H 0ET.

Golden rules for taking on a commercial lease

◆ In taking on a new lease, do remember that your prospective landlord will ask for more than he expects to get. Do negotiate – he will tell you that he can offer you only a standard lease but this is rubbish.

◆ Do check very carefully the user clause in any lease and make sure that it will cover not only your existing business but any area into which you might wish to move in the future.

◆ Check out the planning permission and your landlord's title. Do not take anything on face value.

◆ If you are taking over an existing lease, do be wary of dilapidation. Has the existing tenant looked after the property or will you have to face an enormous repair bill when the lease comes to an end?

◆ If you are taking over an existing lease you may be asked to pay a premium by the current leaseholder to reflect that the current rent payable is less than the market rent. A premium may also be sought if you are continuing to operate the same trade as the previous tenant and therefore there is an element of goodwill attached to the premises. Alternatively, it could be that a premium is charged for the value of the existing tenant's fixtures and fittings. Either way, do not pay a premium for something you do not want. If the fixtures and fittings are useless to you, there is no point in paying for them. If the business you intend running is unlikely to benefit from the goodwill of the previous trade, then similarly, why pay for it?

◆ Before buying a freehold for commercial use, acquire a copy of *Planning Permission: A Guide for Industry*, which is available from the HMSO.

◆ Do not ever buy a residential property in the vague hope that planning permission will be granted for business activities – this is unlikely.

◆ If you are looking for an existing industrial freehold in a development area it is worthwhile contacting The Department of Industry, Millbank Tower, Millbank, London, SW1P 4QU, telephone 01-211 6486, who will be able to give you a list of suitable locations, ready for expansion and development.

Commercial use (2) – working from home

Working from home is a very attractive proposition, particularly if you are starting up a new business and want to keep overheads low. However, while one is saved the wear and tear of commuting to work, working from home is not without its share of stress. Self-discipline is the biggest problem and for this reason a room of your own is essential. Whether it means converting the attic or the cellar, or building a hut at the bottom of a garden, a businesslike area which belongs exclusively to you and your work will make the difference between success and failure.

Permission

Strictly speaking, if you plan to run a business from your home, almost certainly you will need approval or permission – either from someone or from some authority. Whether in fact you actively seek that approval is something you will have to judge. Many businesses run successfully from the dining room table for years without causing any inconvenience or concern to anyone. However, if your business becomes obvious to outsiders, or is in any way a nuisance to your neighbours, or if something goes wrong – a fire or an accident – then lack of permission can rebound and can result in fines or even closure.

There are two kinds of restrictions which may affect your ability to run your business from home. The first is a series of contractual relationships into which you may have already entered without even being aware of them. If you own your house, it is possible that at the time you purchased it, you accepted a covenant limiting its use to domestic purposes. Alternatively, you may live in a leasehold property, in which case you need to establish whether the lease (or any tenant's agreement which may exist) prohibits the use of the premises for trading purposes. If you have a mortgage, you are likely to find that there is a restrictive clause concerning the use and occupation of the house. Of course, it may be possible to renegotiate any one of these agreements, but if you are at all uncertain where you stand, ask your solicitor to clarify the position.

The second kind of restriction is that imposed by your Local Authority in the form of Planning, Highways, Health and Safety. Assuming you live in a predominantly residential area, it is obvious that you cannot put petrol pumps in your front garden, nor can you convert your whole house into a nightclub, nor start an engineering works in your garage. However, it is also a fact that many less dramatic activities still need consent from the authorities, and here again there are two facets to that consent:

◆ **Planning permission**
If you want to make a significant alteration to your house in order to accommodate your business, you will need planning permission and/or building regulations approval. This includes building an extension, putting rooms in the loft, or erecting a garage – in fact anything except extremely simple alterations requires you to make an application for planning permission.

◆ **Change of use**
The second consideration is with regard to change of use. The authorities state that consent has to be sought for any *material change of use*. Interpreting material change is difficult, although the fact is that almost any business activity could involve such a change. For example, if you are a farmer and put out a notice saying 'Farmyard Manure for Sale – £2.50 per Bag', then that is material change of use if you have no authority to run a retail outlet from your premises. This aspect of change of use is very restricting – what you have to decide is to what extent you have to comply to the rules.

General advice

If you are not proposing to make any physical alterations to your property, if you are not going to have customers calling, if you are not going to employ any staff on the premises, if you are not wanting a noticeboard outside your house proclaiming who you are – then it could well be that no permission of any sort is needed. Certainly, by tradition, there are a number of occupations which are normally acceptable in a domestic environment – writers, artists, home teachers, designers, to name a few. It is a point worth noting, though, that the common denominator between these people is that they have a virtually non-existent nuisance level.

This, then, is the crux of the matter. Whatever type of business you intend running from home, it must be, for want of a better word, *neighbourly*. Try putting yourself in your neighbour's position and see whether your activity will affect them in any way. This is not for purely altruistic reasons – if your neighbour complains to the local authorities, then they are bound by law to follow up that complaint, and if you have not sought prior permission, you could well find yourself on a slippery slope.

Certainly, if you do proceed with change of use, it must be said that you are likely to become involved in additional costs in order to satisfy specific legislation. For instance, your office layout might be quite adequate for you, but the fire officer may insist on an independent means of escape, in case of emergency. Also, formal approval for a change of use by the planning department will certainly trigger off a revaluation of your house for rating purposes. As a result part of your house will then attract commercial rating, which is higher than domestic rating. In addition, when you sell your house, if part of it has been allocated for commercial use, you will suffer Capital Gains Tax on a portion of any profit realized, because part of your house has ceased to be your own residence.

Insurance

Whether you are seeking planning permission or not, it is essential to check your insurance cover very carefully. Almost certainly your existing household policy will exclude business activities, but you must be covered for these. Insurance companies will dispute claims when full information has not been disclosed. If, for example, your kiln was responsible for burning down your house, and you had no cover for the commercial activity of making ceramic mugs, then your claim would not be met and you could end up living in a tent – seriously.

Seeking planning advice

If you believe that because of the nature of your business you should seek permission to operate from your home, then do not rush straight into submitting an application. First go to see your local planning officer and have a talk 'off the record'. Actively seek the planning officer's advice and listen carefully to what he or she has to say. Do not make any firm proposals. Simply ask – 'If I did this, how would you react?' From such a conversation you will be able to establish whether running your business from home is a viable plan – at least from the planning point of view.

HAND MADE LEATHER GOODS

MY WIFE'S TANNING HER OWN HIDES NOW.

Land and the law

It does not really matter how much or how little land you own or occupy, the joys and sorrows are much the same – it is just a question of scale. You may be the proud owner of a typical three bedroomed house, on a site of approximately one sixth of an acre, or you may live in a stately home surrounded by thousands of your own rolling acres. Either way, what you have in common are walls, fences, boundaries, neighbours, rights of way and access. The larger land owners or occupiers also may be involved in rivers, streams, coastline and forestry.

Ownership or occupation of land generates a feeling of enormous satisfaction and comfort, but it also carries with it obligations and responsibilities. Think about it – second only to arguments over religious persuasion, land and its boundaries has to be the main cause of aggression between men and between nations throughout the centuries. Millions of men and women have died trying to protect their land or acquire someone else's and even today, border disputes and illegal occupation of foreign countries still dominate the news headlines.

With an ever increasing world population and the continual drain on natural resources, land is likely to become even more coveted with each new generation. Thankfully, today, increasingly we turn to the power of the law rather than the power of the sword, to arbitrate on matters of

dispute over land rights. In Britain the legal aspects of ownership and use of land stems from centuries of common law and practice, plus a weight of more recent legislation. All the different variations in relationship – as between you and your landlord, you and your employees, you and your neighbours, you and the general public, you and officialdom – are now the subject of detailed law, but some of it is ancient, complicated and unpredictable. No reference book can be totally comprehensive, no conveyancing lawyer would ever admit to knowing all the answers.

In recent years there has been much talk about *do-it-yourself conveyancing*. Normally, it is only recommended in a case where you are buying a second hand freehold house,

with registered title. However, the effect DIY conveyancing has tended to have is to insinuate to the prospective home owner that the transfer of a property, with all its implications, from one person to another, is a simple matter. It is not. In addition, while so much emphasis tends to be placed on the condition of the house itself, it is often the land where the hidden problems lie – an old right of way long forgotten, arbitrary wayleaves overlooked, a wrongly drawn boundary – it is easy for these details to be ignored or the true implications of them not understood. Our message is this – if you are buying land or intending to occupy it over a number of years, whatever its size or value, always seek professional legal advice.

Finally, do remember that sloppy research when it comes to buying a property could cost you dear and what you do not know about a house and its land is your fault, not the vendors. If, after making your purchase, you discover that a motorway or major trunk road is going to come within quarter of a mile of your garden, that is your fault. If, because you always viewed the house on a Sunday, you did not realize that the house was on the main flight path to a major Air Force base, that is your fault, too. The vendor is under no obligation to catalogue the faults of his property – it is up to you to discover them. Faults in a house are relatively easy to find. If you are stupid enough not to employ a surveyor before you buy a house then you have only yourself to blame. However, providing you have the house properly surveyed, at least you are going into the purchase with your eyes open, knowing where the faults lie. Thorough searches should establish your position in relation to the land, but do not rest there. Conduct your own private research and examination of the neighbourhood and leave no stone unturned. The law of the land is not simply to protect you – particularly from your own ignorance. Whether your new home comes on a small building plot or with a thousand acres, do understand the legal implications of owning your parcel of land, before committing yourself to any purchase.

Walls, fences and boundaries

Boundary disputes are as common in urban environments as they are in rural surroundings. The only difference is that the high value of property in, say, London will justify an argument over inches, whereas in the country, disputes tend to be about the odd few yards. The most likely form of dispute will be about the exact location of the boundary and here are some reasons why a dispute may arise:

◆ The necessity to establish a building line for a new development.

◆ Establishing whether planning consent is required for, say, putting a window in a wall as it is only a few feet from the boundary.

◆ Who owns the boundary marker, whether it be a wall, fence or hedge and who is responsible for repair and maintenance?

◆ Does the boundary marker represent the true boundary?

To resolve these sorts of disputes, first seek documentary evidence. The last conveyance of the property may clarify the position and it is to this you should refer initially. However, things are not necessarily straight forward. You may have a clause in your conveyance which reads more or less as follows:

The purchaser shall erect and maintain at his own expense a brick wall 6ft in height, between points A and B, marked on the attached plan.

That seems straightforward. It suggests immediately that it resolves who owns the wall and who, therefore, is responsible for maintaining it. However, the dispute may be about whether the wall was built in the right place. In addition, you may find it extremely difficult to actually pinpoint A and B on the ground, because the site plan may be too small a scale from which to be able to measure accurately the precise location of the boundary. If this is the case, ideally you want to establish with your neighbour, for the future, some more readily identifiable markers – such as, for example, that the

boundary runs from a line between the side wall of the garage and the garden shed.

On a site plan drawn up when property changes hands – or indeed for any other purpose – the ownership of boundary walls, fences or hedges is indicated by T marks on the *inside* of the boundary. It is an important point to remember, however, that ownership does not necessarily impose an obligation to repair and maintain a boundary wall or fence. If your neighbour owns the wall that divides his property from yours, he is perfectly at liberty to let it fall down, unless he has accepted some express covenant to maintain it. Such a covenant would be noted on the appropriate Land Register, but unfortunately T marks were not noted on Land Registry plans before 1962. This being the case, in most instances, if there is a genuine dispute on location or ownership of boundaries, it can be assumed that plans filed with the Registry before 1962 would only indicate general boundaries.

If you are unable to find any specific evidence in the title deeds, the other way of establishing who owns what is to rely on long standing custom and practice, which in reality very often sets the rules. Here are some general boundary rules:

◆ If a boundary fence is built on your property, or so you believe, then the boundary line will be the other side of the fence. Generally, the fence posts will be on your side and the close boarding will be on your neighbour's side.

◆ Walls, by contrast, can often be joint walls, with shared maintenance and

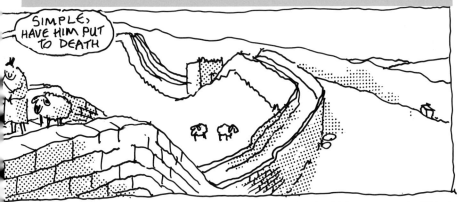

responsibility, in which case the boundary line runs down the middle of the wall.

A boundary hedge is often established by digging a ditch and piling up the earth on your land and planting the hedge on the earth mound created. The normal presumption therefore is that both hedge and ditch are in the land of the creator and it is the area beyond the hedge, furthest away from the ditch, which is the neighbour's land. However, on large scale ordnance survey maps, they tend to show boundaries as being the centre of the hedges and because of this, in the case of a dispute, if there is no firm evidence to the contrary, the ordnance survey line may well be adopted.

Landed bounded by a non-tidal river is deemed to have its boundary at the centre of the river bed. Any gradual erosion of a bank, or the building up on the bank of new deposit, will gradually alter the boundary which will continue to be the centre of the river. The exception to this is if the river has changed course dramatically and permanently by, say, major flooding or as result of human intervention. In this case, the original boundary will stand, even if the course of the river has changed. Occasionally, land is conveyed quite specifically from the river bank only, thus excluding ownership of any part of the river bed.

Land bounded by a tidal river or the seashore is deemed to have its boundary at the high water mark. This is the average high tide level between Spring and Neap tides.

Land bounded by a highway is normally treated in the same way as non-tidal rivers – i.e. the boundary is the centre of the road. The exception to this is where the Highways Authority has actually purchased the bordering land for the road.

Golden Rule

If you take a sensible approach to your purchase of land, you never should have a boundary dispute. Before you commit yourself to a purchase, sort out boundary queries with your neighbours, and once you have agreed who owns what and who is responsible for what, then an exchange of letters will have the matter resolved for all time. If the documentary evidence is unclear, then you and your neighbours should set your own rules and again confirm them in writing, for it is a fact that you cannot rely on the average conveyance documentation being specific on detail. Sorting out the grey areas of possible dispute will not only ensure that you have no aggravation with neighbours but if you should come to sell the property at some time in the future, at least some of the potential legal problems will have been resolved. Boundary differences are not attractive to live with, and a continuing feud with your neighbour can easily threaten the pleasure you would otherwise take in your home.

Public rights of way

The Great British Public at large have a tendency to think it is their right to wander about the countryside as though they owned it. Over recent years this attitude has been accentuated by a number of pressure groups determined to see that rights of way are maintained, and in some instances this has created open warfare between land owners and the public.

It is important to recognize that even on common land – let alone on privately owned land – there is no common law right of access for the public to simply wander about. The public do have a right to use public bridleways and footpaths, and in some instances they may be allowed access to private areas of land by the owners, although certain terms and conditions may apply.

Unfortunately the public's right to use long established paths and bridleways is a considerable irritant to the farming community and, one has to say, with some justification. The footpath, which neatly divides a twenty acre field, makes ploughing, sowing and reaping difficult and puts valuable stock at risk. This applies if the footpath is being used properly but even if most adults do not stray from the path, their children and dogs do, with the result that crops are flattened, stock is harmed and sometimes even killed. The lambing season, of course, is a particular hazard but so is the discarded plastic bag, the gate not properly closed, the cigarette butt not fully extinguished. Small wonder that rights of way upset the farmer, particularly when it is other people's mindless recreation which is threatening his very livelihood.

Certainly there are a number of footpaths which serve genuinely useful and important functions. We have one which goes past our house and which leads directly to our little church. The church is in the middle of a field and there is no other means of reaching it except via the footpath. In many instances footpaths mark the shortest distance between a village and, say, a nearby hamlet which nowadays has been superseded by a perfectly good road. However the rights to the footpaths remain for dog walkers, with all their inherent problems.

The whole situation can so often develop into a permanent running sore – the more aggressive the farmer's reaction to the public, the more protective the local populace seem to become towards the maintenance of their rights.

Re-routing footpaths

Footpaths can be re-routed, even over somebody else's land. Obviously, if someone else is going to be affected, you have to obtain their approval in addition to the approval of the Local Authority and a degree of co-operation from local footpath users. It is no good your taking a cavalier attitude towards an established right of way by simply refusing to recognize it. While it is technically possible to have a right of way extinguished in certain circumstances, it is not easy. One of the best grounds for a right of way removal is complete lack of use, but even this is not straightforward. The moment a proposal to extinguish a public right of way becomes common knowledge – which it will have to do because of the necessary advertising and disclosure formalities – inevitably it will attract the pressure groups into a degree of militancy. While no one may ever use your right of way, that does not mean that the public should have their rights withdrawn. As a general rule it is better to try and re-route rather than extinguish a right of way.

Public footpaths are not always ancient rights of way. Local authorities have power, under the 1980 Highways Act, to create new footpaths. One of the instances where this is most likely to occur is in the creation of a new footpath to make a connection between old established footpaths, with a view to giving continuous walks across an area of the country. While this procedure is normally only undertaken with the consent and approval of the affected land owners – and taking full account of the farming, forestry or sporting implications – local authorities do have the ultimate power to insist

We have some friends called Martin and Sue. Up until eighteen months ago they lived in a delightful Cotswold village in a truly magnificent house with a spectacular swimming pool. For years they had suffered with the problem of a right of way through the village (which also represented a considerable short cut from one side to the other) cutting straight across their beautifully manicured garden, literally within feet of the swimming pool. Strategically placed vegetation helped up to a point but the fact was the garden and swimming pool area afforded no privacy whatsoever. When Martin was promoted to yet a bigger job, they decided to move. The estate agent, whilst enthusiastic about the house and grounds, made a heavy point of the enormous inconvenience and

intrusion such a well used right of way caused. He stressed it would reflect on the price and indeed it did.

Imagine, therefore, Martin and Sue's consternation when the new owners moved in and simply applied to the local council to have the right of way moved, so that it ran round the far end of the garden, well away from the swimming pool area. The new owners did a good job with local public relations – everyone in the village could see how much sense it made for them to request the alteration and their application went through like a dose of salts!

that a right of way be provided, albeit that the owner can appeal against any arbitrary decision in this respect.

Common land

As with rights of way, there is widespread misunderstanding as to public rights over common land. Traditionally common land was provided for local people to graze their stock, gather firewood, dig peat etc, etc, and these rights date back to feudal times when the land was held by the lord of the manor and the people who enjoyed this

common land were his tenants. Such land is now generally owned either by the National Trust, the Church or, in some instances, still by a large private estate, and all common land is registered with the County Councils. However, this does not mean that anyone can still claim common rights, unless those rights have also been officially registered, which is unlikely. Sorry, but that is the way it is and it is also important to stress that as with private land, there is no right of access to common land, other than over designated public footpaths.

Roads and driveways

A *public* highway can be either:
◆ A footpath for pedestrian use only
◆ A bridleway for pedestrians and horses
◆ A road for pedestrians, horses and vehicles

Whatever the category of highway, they are all open to the public for the purpose of travel/movement, without restriction. However, this does not entitle the public to trade, camp or picnic on highways. A public road may have been created by specific statute or by established custom over a long period. In some instances, a highway may provide a right of restricted access or access to a limited section of people. A typical example of this could be a lane leading to a village hall or on to a private estate – in which case it would not be a public highway as such.

If the public start to use a lane/driveway/ road as if it were a public highway, it will be deemed to have been dedicated by the owner for public use, if it can be demonstrated that:
◆ It has been so used for at least twenty years.
◆ That there has been no interruption in it use.
◆ It has been used by the general public as if it was their right so to do – in other words, there has been no restriction placed upon its use.

Restricting public use

When a property changes hands, the new owner may be faced with the fact that the general public have been using his driveway as a public road for as long as anyone can remember. If he is not prepared for this situation to continue, then he will have to demonstrate that the previous owner had merely given permission for access – in other words he will have to prove it is not an established right. To strengthen his case, the new owner should seek to demonstrate that there have always been notices displayed indicating it to be a private driveway, or that there is some form of restriction – such as the gates always being closed at nightfall or whatever.

The highway authorities own most public roads which have been created under statute, but this is not always the case. A road which has become a public highway by long term use and custom, may well be privately owned.

There is no necessary or consistent link between ownership of the land on which a road is built and the obligation to maintain that road. A road may have been properly dedicated to public use but not *adopted* by the highway authority – in other words the highway authority have no obligation to maintain it. If you are looking to buying a property with access over an unadopted road, you need to establish the following points:

- Why has the road not been adopted – is it below the standard required by the local authority?
- What is the cost of bringing the road up to standard?
- What proportion of that cost would be attributable to the house you are buying?
- Can you deduct the cost of road maintenance from the asking price of the house?
- Is it likely that the road will ever be adopted and if so, when?
- If the road is not going to be adopted, what are going to be the routine maintenance costs which you are likely to have to bear?

If your property is serviced by a public road, this does not mean necessarily that you may not have maintenance commitments. The road may be maintained by the highway authority, but still check on the ownership position where the road joins your property, for you may well find that you own the land up to the centre of the road. If this is the case, you need to be aware of the maintenance implications of drains, verges, ditches, embankments, hedges and so forth alongside the road. With local authority spending under considerable pressure currently, you could find yourself in the position of having to foot the bill for everything except the maintenance of the actual road surface.

Road surfaces

Local authorities only have to maintain a road surface to the minimum standard require for normal traffic. If your main access road is not really suitable for heavy traffic but you constantly abuse it with your farm transport, then the highway authority may not be prepared to pay the full cost of maintenance. This applies whether it is you who is abusing the road surface or someone else – say, the local brewery lorries using it as a regular short cut. You may well ask whose responsibility it will be to bear the cost if the highway authority refuse to pay for it all. The answer is, the owner. However, if you are the owner but are not responsible for the broken surfaces, you should be able to reclaim the costs from those who are responsible.

Shared access

It could be that you share a drive with an adjoining house or, in order to reach your house, you have to drive through the outskirts of someone else's property. Either way, it is a hotbed of potential conflict. Do very carefully check out the position with regard to maintenance, parking, litter, noise etc, etc, before committing yourself to the purchase of a property with shared access. For example, finding out after the event that your next door neighbour's teenage children roam home on their motorbikes right under your bedroom window, at 3am nightly could have you wishing you had never bought the wretched house. Make enquiries and establish an absolutely crystal clear agreement between yourselves and your neighbours, in writing, before committing yourself to the property.

The real problem of shared access is that its smooth operation depends upon mutual goodwill between the parties concerned. If you fall out with your neighbours, for any reason, a shared drive can become a nightmare. Do be careful.

Wayleaves

A wayleave is a right of way and it is something you do not want on your property – not if you can help it. In theory the term is used to describe the rights granted by a land owner, or a long term occupier, for some form of pipe or cable to pass over his land. However, this description is perhaps somewhat euphemistic, for some public bodies can exercise these rights compulsorily – a wayleave without a by your leave, so to speak.

Services requiring wayleaves

◆ The services supplied by cable – i.e. electricity, telephone and other communications such as TV and radio. These can take the form of either overhead lines on pylons or poles, or underground cables.

◆ Services supplied by pipeline – i.e. gas, oil, water, sewage and drainage. These are likely to be almost entirely underground pipe lines, though very occasionally they are on the surface.

Effects of wayleaves

Without a doubt the grant of a wayleave must reduce the value of the land and property over which the service runs. Let us look at the disadvantages:

◆ Visual amenity – a 'crop' of pylons does little to enhance the attractiveness of the countryside, and to a lesser extent, poles, valves, stop-cocks and manholes are hardly things of beauty.

◆ TV interference.

◆ Restrictions on subsequent building and excavation work.

◆ Loss of development potential.

◆ Requirement for future access for inspection and maintenance work.

In addition to these long term and largely permanent factors, the application for a wayleave and the process of installation cause considerable short term cost and trauma to the land owner as follows:

◆ His time and trouble.

◆ Professional costs.

◆ Disturbance – of livestock, sporting pursuits etc, etc.

◆ Loss of use.

◆ Actual damage to roads, hedges, ditches etc.

◆ Damage to the land owner's nervous system.

Compensation

A land owner granting a wayleave, therefore, will and must expect to receive compensation in the form of:

◆ An initial payment based on X pounds per hundred metres, plus Y pounds per pylon/manhole cover or whatever.

◆ And/or a continuing annual fee, based on the same principles.

This entitlement to compensation exists, whether the wayleave is granted by negotiation or taken under compulsory powers. It should recognize, not only actual physical loss – such as the lost of a crop – but also loss of amenity – i.e. the interruption of a view. This is all very well but one is forced to ask whether, in some instances, however large the sum, compensation can ever in fact compensate. At this moment, sitting here in our study, writing this book and looking across the fields outside our window, we feel that no sum of money on earth could compensate our loss, should someone choose to erect an electricity cable across the land.

All is not gloom and doom, however. Over the years, the rights of land owners in rural areas have been protected by the NFU and the Country Gentlemen's Asso-

ciation. These organizations have established codes of practice and compensation levels with the major supply industries, on behalf of their members.

Opposing a wayleave

The key to successfully opposing a wayleave application is to mount a campaign *at a very early stage.* All such schemes have to receive final approval at some level and you are most likely to succeed in stopping the application if you can intervene *before* approval is given. Major new grids connecting different parts of the country have to have approval from the relevant central government departments, as well as the county planning authorities. By contrast, a proposal to extend existing overhead power lines by 200 metres would only need local planning approval. Frankly once approval is granted, all the land owner can do is to negotiate fair compensation terms and agree the least intrusive line across the property. However, before approval is granted you may be able to persuade the planners to consider an alternative route.

Ensuring that you do not fall foul of a wayleave – either on your own or on adjoining property – has to be a major consideration when buying a home. At the time of purchasing your property, make sure you know what is underground and what, if any, restrictions have been placed upon the property as a result. Check out with the local authority whether there are any plans for extending services over your land. This should come out in the normal course of searches on a property, but if you feel you are in a potentially vulnerable area, double and treble check to make sure there is no problem.

There is another form of wayleave which is not generally described as such but which is very common in conveyances as between developer and first buyer. This is the right of the developer to run drainage, water, gas and other services in or under your property. You need to know precisely what this covers, although if you want the house, there is usually little you can do about it in practical terms.

Rivers, streams and coastlines

Water, in any form, adds considerably to the value of a property. If your land runs down to the coast, to a lake or to a river, this is perhaps obvious, but even a stream running through the garden will command a considerable premium on the price of a house. Water at the bottom of your garden can provide sport and leisure activities. It can also be a hazard – particularly to small children. If you are lucky enough to have this facility, do also look on it as a responsibility – life jackets should be as much a part of the equipment of your house as pots and pans – and so should waterproofs and endless drying facilities!

Your rights

Your rights with regard to any water which may border or form a part of your property are complicated. They are known as *riparian rights* and in our experience, the average conveyancing solicitor knows very little about them.

◆ **Ownership**
When you buy a property with a riverside frontage on a non-tidal river then almost certainly you will own the bed of the river between your river bank and the centre of the river. In certain instances, it may be that your conveyance specifically indicates that your property ends at your river bank, but this on the whole is unusual. On a tidal river, or on a seashore, your ownership will extend to the average high water mark. It is worth mentioning that no one actually owns the water itself.

◆ **What are riparian rights?**
The owner or occupier of land with frontage onto water enjoys riparian rights which are as follows:
(i) The right to have a flow of water unimpaired, in quantity or quality, by improper acts of owners or users upstream.
(ii) The right to take and use water for *your own domestic purposes and for your livestock*. This common law right

is somewhat restricted by the Water Resources Act of 1963, which introduced the need for a licence to take water. However, it needs to be stressed that a licence is *not* required for purely domestic use or for agricultural use by the owner/occupier – though this would not include spray irrigation. Other than for fire fighting purposes, most other abstraction of water will require a licence.
(iii) The right to take fish – it is ownership of the riverbed which determines the entitlement to fish. Owners with tidal frontage do not have fishing rights, because in virtually all cases tidal rivers and foreshores can be assumed to be Crown property. On non-tidal rivers, however, fishing of your 'half' of the river is normally yours by right, although still subject to a licence from the river authority.
(iv) Mooring rights – you have the automatic right to moor your boat or boats, provided that they do not interfere with normal navigation. However, so far as the use of the boat on the river is concerned, this may well still be the subject of a licence from the relevant river authority.

Public rights

The general public have the right to fish in tidal waters and, with certain limited exceptions, from the foreshore. Tidal rivers and the foreshore, being on the whole Crown property, are available to the public, but this still does not give them the right of access over private land in order to get there.
◆ There is no fishing by right in any non-tidal water, although in some rivers, fishing by the general public has taken place by custom over a long period. However, it is still not a right.
◆ It is most unlikely that you will be able to stop the public from boating up and down the river or coastline in front of your house, for as we have already stated, you do not own the water. Some rivers, lakes and canals have speed restrictions which is helpful and

This particular section of the book is very close to our hearts because our garden borders the River Cherwell and we are very enthusiastic boating people. Our particular stretch of river is in fact an old millstream and not the main channel of the river, and our problem is a constant fight to maintain our water level in order to ensure we can continue to enjoy our boating. Upstream of us, the river joins the main Oxford Canal. British Waterways Board were quick to point out that they have priority over the water, to ensure navigation of the canal in times of drought. The fisheries department of the Thames Water Authority were also equally quick to stress that they, too, have priority over the water in the main stream of the river, to protect their fishermen. So far we have managed to hang on to enough water for ourselves, but this is largely due to a spate of wet summers. Certainly our experience would suggest that maintaining one's riparian rights is not plain sailing!

almost all inland waterways have the requirement for a boating licence. Mooring even momentarily on your land, however, is illegal and you may find 'no mooring' signs are necessary.

Practical problems

The main practical problems of living beside water are as follows:

- **Erosion** – either to river or coastline, reducing both the quantity and quality of your land.
- **Damp** – it is surprising how dampness coming off the water seeps into the house, however cosy and dry you make it.
- **Flooding** – this, of course, can be a very real problem.

Before buying a home close to water, you should check flooding levels over the last fifty years and try and establish some sort of pattern. If there is a serious danger of your home being flooded out, then this should be reflected in the purchase price.

- **The public** – people are enormously attracted to water and if you have water flowing past your door, you can be sure that you will have your fair share of the general public in it, on it or around it.
- **Mosquitos** – not normally a serious problem in this country but nonetheless a considerable inconvenience towards late summer. This also applies to horse flies.

Animals

In this section we are looking quite specifically at farming stock and domestic animals. Wild animals we will deal with under hunting, shooting and fishing.

Animals and the law

◆ **Straying livestock**

If you keep livestock, it is your responsibility to control them. If they stray onto a neighbour's property, generally speaking you are responsible for any damage or disturbance that is caused as a result. The *only* exception to this is if your neighbour has a specific obligation to erect and maintain the fencing which divides your two properties. In this instance, any damage which is caused is your neighbour's problem and if your stock suffer damage in any way, as a result of your neighbour's inadequate fencing, then he is responsible to you for any loss you may have sustained.

If, through carelessness, your livestock get out onto the road, you will be responsible for any damage caused. However, if the stock have good reason to be on the road (they are being moved from field to field/field to milking parlour/going to market) and cause damage, you are not liable unless it can be proved that you were negligent. You are also not responsible if your cattle stray off unfenced common land, because they are entitled to be there unfenced.

◆ **Grazing agreements**

It may be that you have bought a property in the country and have more land than you actually need. In the circumstances, it seems sensible that you should consider letting off your surplus land to a neighbouring farmer. If this is your intention, we would suggest you rent grazing rights, rather than allow the land to be used for arable purposes. There are two reasons for suggesting this:

a) Grazing land is more attractive than arable land. Do you particularly want to look out of your window at a ploughed field?

b) A crop is likely to involve a farmer in a longer lease than you may wish to grant.

The question of length is very important when it comes to grazing rights. If you wish to rent out your land, without giving the tenant any right to renew or any other security of tenure, then you must do it for less than a year – 364 days is perfectly all right. Certainly if you were considering letting out your land for the first time, it would seem very foolish not to take advantage of this ruling on tenancies of less than a year. You need time to establish a relationship with the farmer, to see he pays on time, to see that his animals are not a nuisance and to consider whether you have any alternative use for the land. In order to absolutely preserve this degree of flexibility when it comes to repossession, the grazing rights should not include the use of any buildings, unless they are purely ancillary to the grazing – i.e. a shelter, for instance.

A grazing agreement for a full year or longer can give the tenant protection and continuity far beyond that which you may have intended.

◆ Nuisance

If you choose to live in the country, near a farm, you have absolutely no grounds for complaint about either the noise or the smell. However, if you live in an urban area, you have very good grounds for complaint if your neighbour keeps six unruly dogs and twelve geese, all of which keep you awake day and night. Unacceptable noise levels, caused by neighbours or their animals, can be reported to the local authority, but before doing this, we would suggest two things:

a)   Firstly, do consider very carefully whether you and your family ever make excessive noise.

b)   Before involving yourself and your neighbours in unpleasant court action, see if the matter cannot be settled amicably by an exchange of letters. If all else fails, then Section 58 of The Control of Pollution Act 1974 gives local authorities power to deal with noise. Normally an officer from the Department of Health will investigate and discuss the matter with you. What he has to prove is whether noise amounting to a statutory nuisance exists. If so, a prosecution may follow.

◆ Control of dogs

If you live in an urban environment then it is almost certainly an offence to allow dogs to foul the footpaths and pavements around your home. In many instances this also applies to public parks.

In rural areas the main problem is of a different kind – that of worrying livestock. It is an offence for a dog to kill or injure livestock, irrespective of whether or not you know your dog is on the loose or indeed even capable of causing trouble. If a farmer finds a dog on his land, with no one apparently looking after it and no means of knowing to whom the animal belongs, he may shoot it if it has been worrying his stock. If a farmer finds a dog about to worry his stock or indeed actually worrying them, he may shoot the animal whether the owner is present or not.

We would go so far as to recommend that if you have a genuine aversion to animals, you should very seriously consider whether it is appropriate for you to live in the country. There is no real escape from animals in rural districts, whether they be livestock, domestic or wild. While you may not love them, you have to at least learn to live with them and recognize their place and their rights in the community.

In principle, the owner of land also owns the sporting rights. In practice, however, this may not be the case since sporting rights can be easily separated from the ownership of the land. This can be done in a number of ways. The owner of the land, who may also be the occupier, may have acquired the land without its shooting rights, or may have chosen to sell or lease out those rights if he does not wish to use them. The owner of the land may not be the occupier and if this is the case then he may pass on the sporting rights to his tenant. Alternatively, he might lease out the land without the sporting rights, retaining these for his own pleasure or, indeed, sell or lease them separately. Yet again, a tenant may take a lease on the land, including sporting rights and sub-let, issue a licence or sell his limited interest in the sporting rights.

Hunting

Whatever type of animal is being hunted, the Master of Hounds must obtain prior consent from land owners/occupiers before hunting over any private land. At the time permission is sought, the basis will be agreed upon which compensation will be paid in the event of any damage being done. There is no obligation upon you to allow hunting over your land if you do not wish it. If permission is not obtained then the hunt will be trespassing and the Master and officials of the hunt will be held responsible. Even if the hounds stray on to unauthorized land and no one follows them, it is still trespass.

Whether or not you allow hunting over your land is a very personal decision, based on your general attitude towards the sport. Certainly, refusal to allow your land to be used for hunting – if traditionally, it is a favourite spot – is bound to cause a lot of local illfeeling. To the uninitiated, it is assumed that hunting is an upper-class sport, the sole property of the privileged. This is not the case. The butcher, the baker and the candlestick maker are as likely to enjoy a day's hunt as the local gentry.

Shooting

As with hunting, shooting can only take place with the permission of the land owner/occupier. There is no public right to shoot, even over farmland. The one exception to this is that irrespective of who owns the sporting rights, the *occupier* of land is entitled to kill rabbits and hares but only if they are a direct threat to his crops.

In Great Britain, all birds in the wild are protected, subject only to:

◆ Custom – in that it is generally recognized that birds may be killed if they threaten serious damage to stock, fish, crops or feed, if they threaten to spread disease or if they are themselves disabled.

◆ Limited periods of killing of certain species covered by the game laws.

There is a nice old country law relating to the knocking down of a pheasant. If you accidentally run over a pheasant, country custom has it that you should not stop the car, put the bird in your boot and take it home to the pot. You are supposed to leave it for the next motorist who comes along. This country custom, of course, is aimed at discouraging the deliberate mowing down of pheasants!

Fishing

Ownership of fishing rights relates to the ownership of the soil below the river or lake (see earlier section on rivers, streams and coastlines on page 74). The right to fish may be leased or sold by the owner of the river bed, on whatever terms he may determine. However, the relevant water authority is responsible for the issuing of fishing licences, and on most rivers and lakes in Great Britain, it is illegal to take fish without a licence, even if you have the fishing rights. Licences can either be issued to individual owners or to a club for multiple use.

Even if you have the rights to fish and are licensed, you still need to adhere very strictly to the provisions of the 1975 Salmon and Fresh Water Fisheries Act and the local bylaws. These define what you may catch, when you may catch it and how you may catch it.

In all your sporting pursuits, irrespective of the law of the land, do follow the country code. Different areas have different traditions and it is a foolish person who flouts these – particularly if a newcomer to the district. There is nothing wrong with tradition and if you are going to enter into the spirit of the sport, then for your enjoyment and for everybody else's you should play by the rules, whether, strictly speaking, you agree with them or not.

Sewers and drains

Public sewers and sewage works are the responsibility of the various regional water authorities, as a result of the Water Act of 1973. The water authorities may construct a sewer more or less wherever they like – under a street, under or over land, regardless of who owns that land. They are obliged to give *reasonable notice* of their intention to build a sewer, to the owner and to the occupier of any land which will be affected. However, there is not even a prescribed period of notice though practice suggests that twenty-eight days is considered normal. The notice will take the form of a statement as to the dimension of the sewer and the exact site proposed. However it is not a request – it is simply information, for there is no provision for objections from either owners or occupiers to the laying of a sewer. The only saving grace is that there is compensation. The

water authorities are under no obligation to purchase the land but they do recognize the requirement to offer compensation – not only for damage done to the land but also for any inconvenience caused. As far as possible, the water authorities will reinstate the land to its former condition but recognizing that, say, trees may not be replaceable, they will pay compensation for any losses of amenity which cannot be physically replaced. It all sounds rather arbitrary and indeed it is. For this reason it is sensible to discuss any possible drainage plans with the appropriate water authority before purchasing a property.

Public health

The various district councils are responsible for the nation's health, although they have parcelled out some of this responsibility to other bodies. For example, the water authorities are responsible for supplying water and the local authorities are responsible for ensuring that the water is pure, wholesome and adequate. Local authorities are also responsible for the following:

- Wells
- Tanks
- Water butts
- Septic tanks
- Cesspools
- Litter
- Rubbish
- Refuse
- Waste

Local authorities are responsible for ensuring that private water supplies from, say, wells meet the required standard and that cesspools are emptied regularly. If they consider a supply of water unsafe, they have the power to close it down, as indeed they have the power to empty cesspools regularly and charge the occupiers of the premises accordingly. They are also responsible for the removal of rubbish and litter – whether it be paper dropped on pavement or bridleway or abandoned cars, prams, etc. In an effort to avoid the dumping of rubbish, these days local authorities are providing official dumps, to encourage people not to abandon their waste.

Nuisance

Overflowing cesspools, polluted water and rubbish, all fall under the category of nuisance – as does noise, smell, straw and stubble burning and pollution. Your local authority have a number of very useful booklets on the subject of nuisance of varying kinds – how to cope with it and how, in some instances, to gain compensation. Whether your argument is with an individual person or an organisation, local authorities do have powers to deal with statutory nuisances by serving abatement notices. If the abatement notices are ignored then the matter will be taken up in a magistrates' court. To put together a case of nuisance, you must be able to demonstrate that the nuisance is unreasonable and you must also have a legal interest in the land affected – i.e. you must either own it or must have a licence to occupy it.

Nuisance can take the form of actual physical damage, loss of amenity or destruction of the environment. Former knowledge of a nuisance does not preclude you from taking action. For example, supposing you bought a country cottage adjacent to a farm, with an unacceptably enormous dung heap piled up against the side of your fence which smelled out the whole cottage. Assuming you were brave enough to go ahead with the purchase of the cottage, you would be perfectly entitled to complain to the local authority, even though you were well aware of the dung heap's existence before the property became yours.

A natural catastrophe may equally be deemed to be a nuisance. If next door's landscaped garden gets washed away during a storm and causes a landslide which demolishes your greenhouse, that is nuisance. It perhaps should be emphasized that the object of establishing the nuisance factor is either to get it stopped – as in the case of noise or pollution – or to obtain compensation where actual damage has been done.

Estate agents

If you are seeking a property, then it is only logical that you put your name on the books of a number of estate agents. A few points to remember though:

◆ Estate agents – unless instructed otherwise – work for the vendor and are paid on commission, so it is in the estate agent's interest to sell the property to you at the highest possible price.

◆ This also tends to mean that you are foisted off with a great deal of information on entirely unsuitable property.

◆ Recognize that an estate agent is always going to present the house in which you are interested in the best possible light. Information as to likely development potential, state of the roof, lack of damp course or whatever, has to be dragged out of the average estate agent and then, frankly, cannot be relied upon.

We are not suggesting by the above remarks that estate agents go out of their way to mislead the potential buyer. However, we do have to stress that they are on the vendor's side, because the vendor is going to pay the bill and it is important not to lose sight of this fact.

In certain circumstances, this situation can be reversed. If you feel that you can justify actually appointing an agent to find a property for you, then clearly he is acting for you. As a general rule, it is far better to do your own looking but there are occasions where you might be justified in seeking an agent's help:

◆ Perhaps you are looking for a property abroad or are living abroad and looking for a property in this country.

◆ Perhaps you are living in the north of England and moving to the south or vice versa.

◆ Perhaps you are just too busy in your working life to take time off to look for a new property.

In these circumstances, an agent will normally charge a 1% commission on buying price. The brief you give your agents needs to be very specific and confirmed in writing, and in theory, at any rate, they should not involve you at all until they have found a property which is likely to be almost exactly what you want. In these circumstances, once you have seen the property and liked it, the agents will negotiate the price for you.

There are also some specialist agencies providing a home finding service, which includes far more than simply tracking down the right house. They also find the finance, organize removals, interior decoration and will even find new schools for your children. This sort of service though does not come cheap.

For most of us looking for a new prop-

Personal experience of a house hunter

A few months ago we decided to buy a flat in North Oxford. We approached five estate agents and had our names put down on their books. We were very precise as to what we wanted – it had to be a ground floor flat, in one of about twelve streets. The property was to be used as a hideaway, in which we could write, so we were quite specific that we did not want a house – we were looking for a one to two bedroomed flat. Within twenty-four hours of approaching local estate agents, circulars started arriving through the post offering semi-detached houses in Headington (the other side of Oxford), detached houses in Cowley, country cottages in the surrounding villages and very, very occasionally a flat in North Oxford, though almost never on the ground floor. It is hardly surprising, therefore, that when we eventually found the flat we wanted, it was the result of some friends of ours telling us about a flat development a few doors up the road from them. The development in question was offering not one, but two ground floor flats and it is interesting to

erty, an estate agent's window is as likely a place to start as any, and there is reason to believe that the service currently supplied by estate agents is likely to improve. There have been some major reshuffles in recent years in the estate agency business and many institutions have broadened their financial services base by the acquisition of whole groups of estate agents. There are about five such major organizations building up at present and each is working towards offering a service throughout the whole of the UK. Between them, they will shortly control between four and five thousand different estate agency offices, and this will represent a very large part of the overall market. In most industries, losing the individual touch would be something to mourn but in the estate agency business it seems likely that this grouping together will tend to improve the nature of the service.

note that at no time did any of the estate agents we approached suggest these flats were available.

Linked to nationwide computer systems, they should soon be able to pinpoint available property for you in any street in the country – and certainly there is room for improvement.

Estate agent contacts

The large groups of estate agents are increasingly able to offer a very powerful link into the money market and in the insurance world. They have financial experts, either at each branch or within easy reach of each branch. If you happen to buy your new home through one of these major agents, you may well find that they can save you money on your mortgage. Some of these big agency groups are actually linked to a particular banking source, while others go direct to the mortgage market as a whole. Either way they have 'clout' and are likely to be able to put together a mortgage package for you that will suit your particular requirements.

Alternatives to estate agents

In looking for property, of course, your local newspaper takes a lot of beating. In addition there are publications such as *Dalton's Weekly*, *Exchange and Mart*, and, for expensive properties, *Country Life*. Some of the national newspapers run property pages on certain days of the week and if you are looking for a property of special interest – perhaps close to good fishing or a golf course – certain specialist magazines may well be able to help you. There is also nothing wrong with knocking on doors, and this particularly applies if you have pinpointed a particular street or a particular village in which you would like to live – in other words if your requirements are very precise. Make enquiries in the neighbourhood – at the pub, in the nearest shops – to see if anyone knows if a house is likely to come on the market. If so, do not be afraid to present yourself at the front door. The potential vendor will be as pleased as you to avoid the need for an estate agent and the resulting fee, if between you you can find an acceptable selling price.

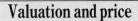

Valuation and price

UTTON

Superb opportunity early Victorian cottage situated in good size plot, 2 receps, kit, cloakroom, 2 double beds, needs renovation.

O/A £65,000

BURY WEST

£198,000

17th century farm house, exposed timber. Ref:M/5114

Picturesque det cottage in sought after location. Fully modernised. Sep diner, fully fitted kit/break rm, 3 beds, Early viewing recommended.

ARBOY
£120,000

£70,000

LEASEHOLD

SOLD

Spacious chalet-style home, cul-de-sac loc. Recently extended and in exc. dec. order. Luxury fitted kitchen/breakfast rm, 3 beds. 80' gdn.

SIVES
£82,500

If you are buying a home, it is likely that your start point for negotiation will be the asking price, which will either take the form of a fixed sum or will request 'offers in the region of £X'. In Scotland, you are likely to make your offer by means of a sealed tender, and in any part of the UK it is possible that you will acquire your home at an auction, but the vast majority of purchasers will be responding to an asking price.

Whether you are buying a house, a flat or a bungalow, there are a number of factors which you need to take into account in order to judge whether the asking price is reasonable:

◆ Make comparisons with similar property in the area, offering the same type of accommodation, (four beds/two reception/two bathrooms, or whatever) and the same quality, finish and state of repair.

◆ Look at the location – is it coming up or going down? This can be easily judged by looking at the other properties in the area.

◆ Planning potential – are you likely to be able to build on, to meet your future requirements – i.e. a granny flat, a garage, a second bathroom or a conservatory?

◆ If you are buying a leasehold property you need to study the security of tenure, the value of the unexpired portion of the lease, the management charges and the likelihood of being able to purchase the freehold.

In addition to these factors which relate solely to the property itself, there may be others which relate wholly to your personal needs and circumstances. For example:

◆ Timing can play a major part in assessing what a house is actually worth to you. A house available immediately could save you renting interim accommodation or perhaps could save a term's school fees. It could also enable you to take advantage of an offer which has been made on your existing house. These factors set against the asking price could justify your paying a little more perhaps than you had intended.

◆ The property may be worth the asking price or close to it, because it specifically meets your requirements – the right-sized garden to accommodate your hobby or a big enough house to run your business from home.

◆ Location – the property may be worth a great deal to you because of where it is – close enough to the local school so that the children can walk there, or perhaps it is very close to your parents' house so that you can keep an eye on them and they in turn can baby-sit.

It is these kinds of factors which may be worth a few extra thousand to you in order to clinch the deal, because in the long term you will be saving money or time, or both, in other ways. Do take time to assess the picture as a whole – weighing extra expenses against possible savings.

If you are buying something less straightforward than a standard home – such as a shop with living accommodation, a farm or a barn for conversion, clearly there are other factors you should take into account.

◆ The commercial viability of the whole project, which is likely to involve an accountant and your bank manager.

◆ How much money is going to be needed over and above the purchase price of the property?

◆ How long will the whole project take? – if your farm or shop will not provide an income for the first two years, you need to take account of this. If your barn will be unlivable in for a year, you need to take account of the fact that you will have to rent somewhere to house the family in the meantime.

The price asked, and subsequently achieved, for the house in which you are interested will be determined by a combination of some or all of the factors mentioned here. However, by far the biggest influence is likely to be the question of comparability and for this reason you must know and understand the local market. There is no point in quibbling about £2–3,000 on, say, a purchase price of £120,000, if you know that a very similar house down the road is selling for £130,000. Just thank your lucky stars and accept the price. Similarly, if the vendor is being unreasonable and asking way over what is clearly the local norm, you have to ask yourself whether you really want the property badly enough for other reasons to justify over-paying.

It is important, when making the comparison of your potential property with others, to bear in mind that the comparison must be made with the *local* market. While it is very well documented that house prices between the North and South of England vary enormously, it is just as true that house prices may vary from street to street, from town to town and from village to village. A pretty village, four miles from a town centre, will command a better price for its houses than a not so pretty village three miles away. Two apparently identical streets, running parallel to one another, may have a variance in asking price because one contains the local dairy. As a result, milk floats droning up and down the street in the early hours of the morning cause a sufficient disturbance to reduce the house prices.

Negotiation procedure

This is the procedure you should adopt for opening negotiation on the purchase of any house or flat, freehold or leasehold:

- Judge whether the price is right for the property, as it is described and as you see it with a layman's eye, i.e. judge its face value prior to a survey.
- Make sure that in principle you can raise the money to make the purchase.
- If the property is what you want and is within your price range, offer between 5–10% less than the asking price – subject to contract. Say you can exchange and complete quickly, give the vendors your solicitor's name, address and telephone number and ask if your surveyor can come round immediately.
- If possible, deal direct with the vendor, not through the estate agent. This is important because you need to judge the genuine reaction to your offer, which will be masked by an estate agent's intervention.

No one is completely honest and straightforward when it comes to selling or buying a house because so much is at stake. If the vendor says that three other people have already offered the asking price, you need to ask yourself why therefore he has not signed one of them up and taken the house off the market. You have to try and judge whether or not there are really any other buyers genuinely interested or whether the vendor is bluffing. This initial reaction to your offer is a crucial stage and the more personal a feel you can get, the better.

Many people put in an offer knowing they are unlikely to be pressing ahead with it. While you are trying to assess the vendor's position, he will be looking to you for signs of your genuine intentions. If he truly believes that you are genuine and are prepared to go ahead with the sale at the price you have offered, then he is far more likely to drop his price. For this reason, stress your requirement for a surveyor to look round the property and make sure your solicitor is active in getting in touch with the vendor's solicitor. This will indicate your serious intent.

Once you have made your offer, haggled and agreed a price, you have to be seen to be actively pursuing the purchase. The vendor will have made a mental commitment to you but there still may be snags ahead – your surveyor may uncover a serious roof problem or your solicitor may come across some nasty clause in the conveyance, in which case negotiations will need to be opened again to reflect the problems. In this instance, you need to be making the point that whoever becomes interested in the property in the future will sooner or later come across the same stumbling blocks and will accordingly reduce their price. In other words, he may as well negotiate with you now than go through the whole charade again with a new buyer in a few months' time.

Newly built or fairly modern houses will have a more definite market value than older property, because it is normally easier to establish comparisons. Similarly, it is less likely that there will be any major problems arising from the survey and therefore the whole process should be easier.

Always try and find out as much as you can about the vendor. How long has the property been on the market and has the vendor found a new place to live? If so, is he under pressure to complete the sale? Have any previous deals fallen through and if so, why? Indeed, why is the vendor selling at all? All these pointers will help you to negotiate the best possible deal.

Option to purchase

In certain circumstances it may be possible for you to negotiate an option to buy a property. For some reasons the property could be in a state of flux – perhaps it is waiting the outcome of a planning application or perhaps there is the possibility of redevelopment in the area, such as a motorway, which could drastically affect the price one way or the other if it goes ahead. In these circumstances, you could pay a sum of, say, a few thousand pounds, to

secure the property for a specific period –
usually of three to six months at an agreed
price. This is not a practice widely adopted
because the circumstances do have to be
very special to make such a situation valid.

However, it could be something to consider
in the event of the property you wish to
purchase being subject to some major
change.

Buying a freehold (1) – a step-by-step guide

In this section we are not dealing with the legal implications of buying freehold. Here we are concerned with the practicalities, and these are perhaps best examined in the form of a step-by-step guide.

Step one

Having viewed the property of your choice you must first ask yourself whether it is worth the price the vendor is seeking. We have dealt with this aspect in more detail in the previous section, but essentially assessing the worth of a house has to be a combination of two factors – comparing the property's value with similar property in the same area and assessing whether your personal circumstances, for whatever reasons, makes the property worth the asking price *to you.*

Step two

Having established that the house is worth the money being asked, you then have to decide whether you can afford to buy it. This is not simply a question of establishing whether you can borrow the money. We will be discussing finance of purchases later in the book but essentially, these days, borrowing money to purchase a property is easy. What you have to decide is whether you are going to be able to service the mortgage repayments.

Step three

Having decided that you are prepared to buy the house at more or less the asking price, put in an offer, preferably direct to the vendor – but via an agent if you have to – offering somewhere between 5–10% less than the asking price. This offer should be made *subject to contract* and *subject to survey*. *Subject to contract* is an absolutely necessary phrase to ensure that your offer letter cannot be interpreted as a contract to buy – you can always back out of your offer before you sign a contract. *Subject to survey* is sensible as there is little point in spending the money on a survey before you know your offer is accepted, but without a survey you cannot be sure that the offer price is justified.

Step four

Following your offer there is likely to be some negotiation on price. As a buyer, do remember that knocking a few hundred pounds off the price may be satisfactory but could put you in the position of losing the property. If you have decided you want the house, can afford to buy it and you are near the point of having your offer accepted, there is no point in haggling down to the last penny.

Step five

Having had your offer accepted, the next stage is to find out everything you can about the property and this you should do quickly – both for your own sake and the vendor's. These are the avenues to explore:

◆ A survey. If you are borrowing money from a building society or bank, they automatically will require a survey. You may accept their surveyor as being able to do a good enough job – on the grounds that the house is relatively new and trouble-free – or you may feel that in addition to the building society survey, you want a private survey as well. Only you can decide the potential risk factors involved and so much depends on the age and state of the property. It is particularly important, with an older property, to check on the condition of the drainage system, because it is all too easy to assume that all is well. To find out, after you move in, that you need a new septic tank and land drains can be a costly and worrying experience.

◆ Physically you need to feel and touch the house again. Clearly it is not fair to constantly visit the house while it still belongs to the vendor but having had your offer accepted, it is not unreasonable to ask to go back to measure up for curtains and carpets (which incidentally the vendor will find comforting as it shows the sincerity of your offer). On your return visit poke about – look under stairs, in cupboards, check ceilings, under carpets. What are you looking for? The problems, of course – damp, obvious roof faults, missing tiles, rotting timbers, gutter trouble, cracks in the walls – but also the opportunities. Often it takes fresh eyes to realize the full potential of a property. Never mind major conversions – look to knocking down a wall here, putting a window in there – it may make an enormous difference to the property.

Step six

It is at this stage you should agree a price for the fixtures and fittings – curtains, carpets and furnishings. Any or all of these may appeal to you, and certainly, if the vendor is willing to sell any of them, the price is likely to be considerably cheaper than starting from scratch with everything new. If your budget is tight, it might well be worthwhile making an offer for curtains and carpets, even if they are not entirely to your liking.

Step seven

Once the deal is done you need to appoint a solicitor. We will deal with this in detail in the legal section of this book. Suffice to say here that your solicitor, as part of preparing a contract, will conduct all the usual searches to ensure that the owner has correct title to the property, that there are no arbitrary covenants and that there is no demolition order or compulsory purchase hanging over the property.

However, this does not mean that you can sit back and rest on your laurels – far from it. Firstly, go and introduce yourself to the neighbours. Neighbours can literally make or blight your life. Clearly you are interested in them in a personality sense, but also you need to sort out with them any problems of potential mutual interest, such as boundaries, shared parking or drive-ways. Any agreements reached should be put in writing.

Ask questions around the local community. Chat up the local publican, the nearest shop and anyone who is willing to talk about your new home. Learn everything you can.

Step eight

If you are wishing to make any extensive alterations to the house it is at this stage – before you are committed to the property – that you should have an informal meeting with your local planning department. If they advise you that there is little likelihood of being granted planning permission then this may radically alter your views as to whether to proceed with the purchase.

Step nine

Having satisfied yourself on all aspects of your property to the point where you really feel confident that you know what you are getting, then you are ready to exchange contracts. Both your solicitor and the vendor's will have drawn up a contract to buy and sell and these are quite literally exchanged and signed by the opposite party. It is at this point that normally you pay 10% of the purchase price as a deposit. The exchange of contracts does commit you to the property. At the time of exchange the completion date will be fixed. Completion normally takes four weeks from date of exchange but there is no reason for this. Exchange and completion can happen on the same day – it all depends on your circumstances.

Buying a freehold (2) – wheeling and dealing

Most property transactions these days involve a degree of synchronization and it is this aspect of buying and selling a house which causes the most anguish. By synchronization we mean, of course, the selling of your existing property and the buying of a new one – all geared to happen not only on the same day but at the same time, so that you literally move out of one house and into another.

I AM THE GHOST OF PROPERTY CHAINS PAST

UNDER OFFER

Chains

A chain strikes terror into the heart of the average person contemplating a move of house, for it means that you are putting your fate in someone else's hands. A property chain is really self-explanatory. Down the line somewhere Mr A is buying a house from Mr B, Mr B is buying a house from Mr C and Mr C is buying your house. You in turn are buying Mr D's house, who is buying one from Mr E. If anywhere along this chain somebody changes his mind, pulls out or cannot raise the money, then all the deals collapse. In recent years there has been considerable publicity on the methods of chain breaking. For example, one of the potential buyers cannot, say, raise the money for the deposit, all the others involved in the chain have clubbed together and provided the deposit, just to unlock the situation.

It is a nightmare and it is not helped by the fact that there are a number of people around who consider it perfectly acceptable to put in an offer for a house which they know they are unlikely to be able to buy, thus putting everyone involved, up and down the chain from them, in a false position.

Avoiding the chain

There are two obvious ways in which you can avoid the chain – either by selling your house before you have found a new one or vice versa. We personally have always taken the view, when moving house, that the most important thing to do is to find the place we want to live. Having found it, we have made an offer and if necessary we have gone ahead with a bridging loan while waiting to sell our existing house. This is not something we would recommend for the faint-hearted. It can be agonizing waiting for an offer to come in on your existing house, while you know the interest clock is ticking away on your loan.

The reverse is also not without its headaches. Accepting an excellent offer for your house with nowhere to go, means that you may well have to suffer the trauma of living in rented accommodation for a while, putting your furniture into store and the animals into kennels, which is both expensive and emotionally unsettling.

In theory, being a cash buyer should mean that the purchase of a property is easier. However, this is certainly not always the case. Just because you have cash to offer, it does not mean the person you are buying from can simply vacate his property at the drop of a hat. He, too, is looking for somewhere else to live and he may be at the bottom of a chain. Your offer to sit down and write out a cheque there and then, while very attractive, may not be either feasible or practical for the vendor.

The case for a bridging loan

There are two types of bridging – a closed bridging loan and an open bridging loan:

A closed bridging loan

A closed bridging loan is more or less an academic exercise so far as you and your banker are concerned and represents little risk to either of you. You may have exchanged or be on the point of exchanging contracts on the sale of your house and the purchase of a new one, but for some reason the completion of the sale of both houses may not be occurring at the same time. This could be a question of choice. On your new property you might have to undertake a great deal of work, so that you might delay completion on the sale of your existing house for a month, to allow the builders to move in to your new house ahead of the family. Alternatively, the delay of completion could be requested by the vendor for similar problems he is experiencing with his new house. Either way, no bank manager is going to refuse to lend you the completion money on your purchase, if you have signed a contract on the sale of your existing house, unless the house you are buying is vastly higher in value than the one you are selling. Even if something ghastly did go wrong with the selling of your house, do remember that you would have the deposit monies which would more than cover the interest on your bridging loan and

give you a little breathing space to find a new buyer.

Open bridging loans

Open bridging loans are another kettle of fish altogether and as we have already mentioned, you need a strong stomach to cope. Here you persuade your bank or building society to lend you the money to make your new purchase, when you have not signed the contract for the sale of your existing home. Understandably, financial institutions are reluctant to offer this sort of bridging loan, for although the property market is buoyant, it is also volatile. Whether you will be granted an open ended bridging loan depends almost entirely on relationships. If you have enjoyed a good working relationship with your bank or building society over a number of years and know the manager personally – if he is aware of your job, your status, your salary – then he may well be prepared to offer you funding. Alternatively, the variation in value between the two properties could make an open bridging loan acceptable to a financial institution. For example, supposing you have reached retirement age and are trading down. If your current house is worth £185,000, you have a very small mortgage, and you are intending to move down to a cottage in Cornwall worth £90,000, then you should have no problem in bridging the purchase of the cottage, even if you have not entered into a contract to sell your existing home. As the heading of this section suggests, the buying of a property does need a degree of native cunning. Otherwise thoroughly nice people tell appalling lies in their desperation to secure the sale of their home. Take nothing on face value. Check and double check and do not be afraid to follow your instincts if you suspect someone is bluffing or misleading you in any way.

Buying a long lease

Long leases apply mostly to flats, town houses and properties owned by such bodies as the National Trust and the Church Commissioners who are not prepared to release freeholds. Most of what we have said about the purchase of a freehold applies equally to long leases, but there are some additional factors for you to consider:

◆ Value – now and in the future
◆ Finance
◆ Running costs
◆ Responsibilities/relationships

Let us look at these factors in detail.

Value

If you are buying a lease of say 999 years, with 910 years to go, then clearly it is equivalent in value terms to purchasing a freehold. Lesser periods are not so straightforward. A new 99-year lease would be equivalent in value to a freehold but not if there are, say, only 45 years to run. What you have to consider in buying a long lease is not so much its value at the moment you buy it, but what it is likely to be worth when you come to sell it. There comes a time when every lease reaches its watershed, from which time onwards, the value starts dropping. In buying your lease, with the example of 45 years left to run, you need to bear in mind that in 45 years' time, the leasehold interest will be worth precisely *nothing*.

It would be most unwise to assume that when buying a long leasehold property you will have any greater safeguard to your security of tenure than that granted to you under the term of the lease. In other words, do not assume that there will be any statutory rights available at the end of the lease which will enable you to stay on as a tenant beyond the end of the lease or provide you with, say, an option to buy the freehold. This does not mean to say that currently you may not have rights, nor indeed that in 45 years' time those rights might actually have improved. This is the point really, it is an unknown quantity – landlord and tenant law can, and does, change and you have no way of knowing what the position will be in the years ahead.

If you have 30 years or less to go on a lease, then you have to face the fact that when you come to sell in a number of years' time, you are not likely to fetch the same sort of sum as you would if you owned the freehold. In justifying how much you should pay for the lease, you must take into account the diminishing value of your purchase.

If you have 10 years or less to go – in other words you are buying the last few years of a long lease – then what you are having to look at is a purely financial calculation. How much will it cost you, per year, to live in the property and how does this relate to paying rent on the open market?

Example – lease with 10 years unexpired –

Open market rental	£3,000 per year
Ground rent	£50 per year
Annual rent saved by purchase of lease	£2,950 per year
Total rent saved over 10 years	£29,500

Based purely on the figures in this example, if you were contemplating taking over this mythical lease, you should be prepared to pay a premium of between £25,000 and £28,000 but not more.

Do bear in mind that the value of the 'fag end' of a long lease is nothing to do with the value of the bricks and mortar. You are purely looking at what it is worth to you to occupy the premises over a number of years.

Finance

Banks and building societies will happily provide mortgage facilities to support the purchase of a long leasehold property, provided that they can see that the value of their security will be maintained throughout the period of any loan. For a normal mortgage this means they will be looking for an unexpired period of lease, of about 30 years *beyond* the end of the mortgage. This period of time is mentioned here as an indication of attitude rather than a rigid ruling. Therefore, if you are having problems raising a long term mortgage on a property with, say, only 40 years to run, do not give up hope – shop around. You should also bear in mind that if there is any doubt about the strength of the security in terms of value, you will either be asked to settle for a shorter term mortgage or you will have to pay over the odds in terms of interest rates.

Running costs

There is usually no problem attached to the purchase of the residue of an old long lease – normally the only running costs you are likely to incur will be a modest ground rent.

However, supposing you are buying a newly converted flat, in, say, a refurbished Victorian house. The refurbishment of the house is likely to be someone's propety deal on which they are wanting to make a profit, and therefore their attitudes to running costs will be extremely commercial. Take care, therefore – there may be manage-ment charges for maintenance of the building, insurance, security, heating and lighting of common areas, gardening, etc, etc. You need to know precisely what you are letting yourself in for, you need to study the small print and ask questions. For example, who bears the cost of upkeep of unlet or unsold flats and who bears the costs which should have been charged to the occupiers of these empty flats? If the development has not been as successful as it should have been in terms of selling off the flats, the developer will be anxious to recoup every penny from you he can – make sure he has no legal right to do so.

Responsibilities/relationships

If you are buying a long lease on a flat, inevitably you are going to be dragged into some form of relationship with your immediate neighbours – across the corridor, upstairs or downstairs. You will also have an ongoing relationship with your landlord and/or his agent and/or a management company. You need to be very clear as to where your responsbilities start and end. For example, if you have bought a ground floor flat, do you have to pay a contribution to the roof repairs or the lift running costs? If you live on the top floor, do you have to contribute to the costs of a flooded basement? You could well find yourself resenting the contribution you have to make towards your co-tenants' existence, or vice versa. It would be sensible to sit down with other tenants and the landlord or agent, and discuss a series of hypothetical situations to see just how the rules and regulations work in practice.

It is for the reasons outlined above that the purchase of a long lease is not, in many respects, as straightforward as the purchase of a freehold and therefore you need to proceed with possibly even more caution than you would with a freehold. Again, make comparisons – check out other lease-hold property in the area which has changed hands recently for this will give you an indication, not only of what you should pay, but also what you can expect to receive as and when you come to sell the property.

I APPOLOGISED FOR THE PARTY AND SHE SAID I WOULD SLEEP FOR THE REMAINDER OF THE 999 YEAR LEASE

Taking a short lease

In practical, rather than in legal terminology, taking a short lease means entering into a relatively short term relationship with a landlord. The types of lease available are infinitely variable and details of these are outlined on pages 30–31. Leases can run for several years, months or even weeks and can apply equally well to houses or flats – furnished or unfurnished. Normally, taking on rented accommodation means simply signing a lease and starting to pay rent, though the landlord will certainly require a month's rent in advance, if not more. If the accommodation is furnished then an inventory will be presented to you for you to sign. First check very carefully that all the contents listed are in fact in the property and that they are in good condition. During the period of your lease it will be your responsibility to see that these fixtures and fittings suffer only *fair wear and tear* and you will be expected to make good any loss or serious damage.

Assignment of a lease

Rather than dealing direct with the landlord, it could be that an existing tenant assigns the lease to you, together with its financial commitments and various obligations. Normally before an assignment is possible a landlord has to approve the new lessee, but this is not often a problem. In the case of an assignment, you may be asked to pay a premium to the existing tenant –

◆ for the benefit of the tenant's furnishings and fittings, or
◆ because the rent payable under the lease is substantially lower than market value.

Taking on a short term rental commitment involves assessing whether you feel you are getting value for money. You need to weigh up the pros and cons of 'wasting' rental money which could otherwise go towards a mortgage against the advantages of having no long term commitment. Perhaps you are a student or newly married and unsettled in your job, perhaps you are living in a particular area of the country only temporarily – the possibilities are endless. However, just because the commitment is short term, it does not mean that the lease should not be taken very seriously, for there are some very important points you should consider:

◆ Who is responsible for all the outgoings of the flat – rates, water, electricity, gas, external maintenance, internal repairs and decorations, insurance, security? How many of these services are going to be charged to you? You need to be aware of them and you need to know how much they are going to cost.

◆ Do check the inventory very carefully and make notes of damaged, stained or faulty items. Point these out to the landlord and then confirm them in writing.

◆ Make a detailed list of all parts of the building which need repair and a careful description of the state of decoration on a room-by-room basis. The object of this is to ensure that you do not find yourself responsible at the end of your lease, for putting things right which were needing attention when you took over, or in the case of the inventory, being responsible for six dining-room chairs when there were only four at the time you took over.

◆ Who is the landlord? Do you deal direct with him or through an agent? Is the agent helpful and concerned with any problems you may have or simply anxious to get the property off his books? If it is the latter – beware – as you are likely to have trouble all through your lease. If your circumstances change, do you see yourself being able to assign the lease? If it is a lease which you feel no one else is likely to want, is it because there is something wrong with it?
Check out the position carefully on pets and small children, as many leases preclude these.
Try and meet your neighbours, in advance of committing yourself. Particularly if you are taking a flat, living cheek by jowl with unpleasant neighbours can be most uncomfortable

When I was eighteen, I moved into a damp basement in Chelsea with two school chums. It was all very exciting – my first time away from home. It was a five-year lease of which there were still two years to run. The flat had always been occupied by four girls and there was still one girl in residence, left over from the former sharings, with whom the three of us got on well. Over the next couple of years the fourth member changed several times, but the three of us remained constant. The flat was the basement of an old Victorian house and above it lived a family called Jenkins. They had children of our sort of age and were a very pleasant couple, who regularly asked us in for sherry and looked after us if we were ill – very much proxy parents.

When we first moved into the flat, the thing that struck us was how ghastly the furniture was – it was literally falling to bits. So we loaded it all into a cupboard, raided our parents' attics and moved in our own furniture. The Jenkinses were well aware of what we had done because we asked them for their permission first.

The two years passed by and the lease came to an end. Imagine our horror when Mr Jenkins came to inspect the furniture before we left, took one look at it and proposed to charge us £200 for its deterioration. It *was* in a terrible state but it was not our fault – it was something that had happened when the furniture had been used by previous tenants. Mr Jenkins, our friend, became an ogre in seconds. He said it was our responsibility to recompense him for the damage and insisted on payment. We reminded him we had never used the furniture but he was simply not interested, and in hindsight, I can see his point of view. He had granted a five-year lease – girls had come and gone during that period and so far as he was concerned, the person left with the lease was the person responsible for any damage sustained during the five-year period. We could not reclaim the costs from any of the former tenants because we did not know where any of them were living – but then neither did Mr Jenkins. What we should have done before putting the furniture in the cupboard was ask him to inspect it and then confirm the dilapidation in writing. In those circumstances he would not have been able to charge us.

IT DOES SAY THREE PIECE SUITE.

INVENTORY

Estate agents

When you come to sell your property, you have two alternatives – either to appoint an agent to sell it for you or to find a buyer yourself.

Trying to sell your property privately in theory sounds very attractive. It avoids the need for you to pay any agents' fees, and particularly if you are selling your house to someone you know, it could avoid a great deal of uncertainty as to the validity of the offer being made. Against this, you have to consider the disadvantage of not reaching a wider market – the imponderable factor – have you agreed the best possible price?

Most people, when they come to sell a property, appoint an estate agent and we would recommend you to do so. A good agent should more than earn his fee, but this is the point – what you have to ensure is that you appoint the *right* agent. This is what you should do:

1   Study comparable property in your area by scouring the local papers and looking in the windows of local agents. The object of this exercise is to obtain a feel of what *you* think your house/flat is worth.

2   Approach five or six local agents, including all the large agencies. Tell them you are thinking of selling, invite them to come round and inspect the property and ask for their advice as to price/timing/marketing.

3   Ask each visiting agent the following questions:

◆   How much is the property worth?
◆   What will the agent charge?
◆   What will the agent do for his fees?
◆   What will you have to pay over and above the fee in terms of brochure and advertising spend?
◆   What is the extent of his firm's coverage – do they, for example, have a London office?

General advice on selecting an agent

◆   You have to be convinced that the agent you intend to appoint is going to obtain the right price for you – which in this case is the highest price – quickly.

He must know the area, understand the attractions of your home and above all believe in the asking price. He must be prepared to sell himself and his firm's services to you. If he cannot sell himself successfully, then he probably cannot sell your home successfully to a prospective buyer.

◆   The fee an estate agent will charge should be between 1%–2%, plus VAT, except in London where it is not uncommon for a fee of 2½% to be charged.

◆   Do not try and sell your house by a combination of private advertising and the appointment of an agent. Either sell through an agent or not – you should not try to mix the two.

◆   We would strongly recommend that you do not appoint more than one agent. If you do, you will find they are less interested in obtaining the highest possible price and are more concerned about being first to find a buyer. So, appoint a sole agent but limit the appointment to, say, two months and if he has not been successful with a sale by then, you may want to reconsider and appoint a fresh agent. In addition, a

sole agency fee is likely to be slightly cheaper than if you appoint several agents.

◆ Do not appoint the cheapest agent, appoint the best. Look at the letterhead. You are looking for FRICS – Fellow of the Royal Institute of Chartered Surveyors. You are looking for an agent who can convince you that he knows the market, understands your property, has the biggest spread of offices, contacts and marketing skill. He must be able to present the property in the right way and have a reliable team of staff. Do bear in mind that if you are either working or living some distance from the property you are trying to sell, the agent will hold a set of keys and show people round in your absence. A useful service in the hands of the right agent.

We will be dealing with price and valuation in the next section of this book, but while talking quite specifically about estate agents, it is important to make a point on price. An estate agent is not a property guru and his assessment of what price you can obtain for your property may well not be right. This particularly applies when your property does not conform to a standard set of criteria. When an estate agent quotes you a price, he is quoting what he believes is the right price to ask in order to sell your property quickly and with minimum of fuss. This is fair enough, but it may not be the highest price you can obtain for the property. As you well know, an extra £5,000 on the price could make all the difference to being able to afford carpets in your new house, whereas to an estate agent, 1½% of £5,000 is barely worth having. We are not suggesting that estate agents are non-professional in their attitude to price. However they are trying to move a great deal of property, fast, and the price they suggest to you will be the one they know they will be able to achieve without too much effort. Bearing this in mind, whatever price they quote you, you should be able to persuade them to ask a little more, and if the price being quoted is substantially lower than what you had in mind, then talk to another agent. While it would be foolish to be unrealistic about the value of your house, it is likely to be the biggest asset you have and you do not want to be intimidated into believing it is worth less than you imagined just because some estate agent is out to make a quick deal.

Estate agents' boards

There is a degree of snob value attached to an estate agent's board. If your property is sufficiently up-market, it is considered *not quite the thing* to have a board outside. Perhaps, if you are selling a stately home this is the case, but for the vast majority of property we would strongly recommend that you allow an estate agent's sign board to be erected. So, it is inconvenient when complete strangers knock on your door and ask to be shown round but they could just be your buyer and you cannot afford to let them get away. You are trying to appeal to the widest possible market. You want as many people as possible desperate for your house, so that you can obtain the best possible price, so why jib at anything that will help you sell quickly and well?

You know your property better than anyone else – both the good points and the bad. Minimize the bad points in practical terms and banish them from your mind. You have got to be positive! So far as the good points are concerned, make sure you have thought them through so that you can quote them both to your agent and your prospective buyers.

Make a list, concentrating on those things that other houses/flats in the area may not have, necessarily –

The double garage	The conservatory
The extra bedroom	Extra insulation
The second	The new kitchen
bathroom	units
Double glazing	Security locks
The view across the	The shrubs you
valley	planted last year . . .
The patio	

What you are trying to justify in your own mind is that, when compared with the other houses in your vicinity, you can make out a case for asking a higher price. As we stressed under the previous section on estate agents, before talking to anyone you must have worked out, in your own mind, a price which you believe is realistic and stick to it. Certainly, you will be prepared to accept that your property is worth more than you thought but you should not easily admit to it being worth less.

Making comparisons with other property is vital but do make sure you are comparing like with like. Your chum's house, forty miles away, may have been built by the same developer and may be identical in every way, but that forty miles could make an enormous difference. Your area may be far more desirable than his. Time, too, plays a vital role. So, you know what your next door neighbour's house sold for seven months ago but seven months is a long time in property, and you have every reason to suppose that since then the price will have risen. Do trust your judgement and as indicated in the last section, estate agents are not always right.

About three years ago we sold our house – a converted Cotswold stone village school. In our own minds, having done our local research, we reckoned the property was worth about £110,000. We called in five estate agents – imagine our horror when the lowest suggested a price of £75,000 and the highest £90,000. Admittedly it was a difficult property to value – there was only a very small garden where the playground had once been and no garage. However, we knew it was a unique property and felt it was just a question of waiting for the right people to come along who would appreciate it for what it was. Eventually, the agent who had suggested £90,000 agreed to put the house on the market for £100,000. Reluctantly we conceded this since it seemed reasonable to meet half way between the agent's expectations that we could get £90,000 and our own hoped-for price of £110,000.

Over the following weekend we agonized over our decision, looked in a few more estate agents' windows and came to the conclusion it was still under-priced. So Monday morning, we rang the agent again and said we wanted him to put it on the market for £115,000. He was absolutely against it and we

recognized that if we were going to insist on this higher price he was going to need some sort of incentive to try hard enough. We therefore offered him the standard commission of 1½% on a price of up to £100,000, plus 10% on anything he managed to sell the house for over that figure. We sold in three weeks for £115,000.

WARNING. There are several lessons to be learnt from our story. Firstly, the only person's judgement whom you should completely trust on price is your own. Secondly, if you are going to force an agent to offer your house at a higher price than he believes achievable, then you have to offer him some additional 'carrot' to make him try hard. Finally, even with that extra 'carrot', those last few thousand pounds on the price will not be obtained unless you have given a sole agency. This sort of deal does challenge agents' professionalism and you might imagine that they would be reluctant to acknowledge that this form of split commission will achieve a higher sale price. Not so, in our experience. It is not the first deal we have done in this manner and we can promise you it really does work.

Negative factors

As we mentioned earlier, do not take too much account of negative factors and do not allow what you know to be wrong with your house to affect the price once you and the agent have set it. So, you know the gutters leak, the central heating is on its last legs, the road outside is very congested twice a day because of the school runs, the new bypass is coming to within half a mile of the house, etc, etc. All right, so these are not very wonderful aspects of your property but do not discount the price because of

them. You may drop your asking price a little because the buyer is a genuine cash buyer who is anxious to exchange contracts immediately, or because you have found your ideal new house and want to move quickly. Fine, these are valid reasons for discounting a little but you should not reduce your price because the buyer has pointed out some fault, of which you are only too aware and which was in your mind when you set the price. A serious buyer is very unlikely to be put off by anything other than a very major problem.

Once your property is ready to go on the market, your agent will draw up the particulars either as a broad sheet or in brochure form. Make sure you approve these particulars before they are printed as often vital details are left out – like the second bathroom. Obtain a copy of all the newspapers in which your property is being advertised and again check for errors and omissions. If there are any, make your agent repeat the advertising free of charge.

So, what happens next?

◆ If four weeks later no one has come to see round your property either you got the price wrong or you picked the wrong agent. It is more than likely to be the latter, so cancel the appointment and instruct your second choice. Only with the new agents should you re-examine the price, to see if it should be amended in any way – but do not be influenced by the unsuccessful agent.

◆ We have recommended that you should put up a sign board to maximize coverage. One counter to this advice, however, is that if you find it difficult to sell your property, a *For Sale* notice up outside your house for many weeks is likely to have a derogatory affect on the kind of offer people will make. It is a difficult decision but on balance we would still recommend the use of the board – coupled with a decent advertising programme in appropriate newspapers, it should bring in the potential buyers.

◆ If, as hopefully happens, you are besieged with viewers – wonderful, but stay cool! Find out as much as you can about your prospective buyers, exactly as if you were interviewing somebody for a job. You simply cannot know enough about them, because if you do have several people after your property, price is only one of the considerations. What you need to ensure is that the offer you accept is from people who are going to be as good as their word. After showing someone round the house who has

...AND THIS IS THE WINE CELLER. WE REALLY SHOULDN'T SELL THE PLACE IT COULD BE WORTH A BOMB.

TICK TICK

expressed definite interest in your property, make careful notes which you can pass on to your agent. Also *learn* from each set of people you show round the house. If the patch of damp under the hall stairs is noticed when you show the first people round, then for heavens sake do something about it before you show round the next lot.

◆ A prospective buyer may well try to negotiate with you direct (indeed, this is what we recommend to you to do if you are buying). However, as the seller, you must not negotiate direct with your potential buyer! Insist that your agent handles it. The potential buyer must deal direct with him, for your agent will be much tougher and more professional than you.

◆ We have told you to find out as much as you can about your prospective buyers. The reverse of this is to tell them absolutely nothing about you and your family and circumstances. Answer all their questions on the property, of course, but for heaven's sake do not

be drawn into admitting you are desperate to sell the property because you are already committed on a new one or that your daughter starts school 200 miles away on Thursday week, or whatever. The less they know about you, the better.

There is so much bluff and counterbluff involved in the business of selling a home. So much personal happiness is at stake, and it is very difficult for you to keep your head when you are desperate for a sale so that you can snap up the house of your dreams. However, showing any vulnerability or over-eagerness, or even the smallest hint of desperation is a terrible mistake. Every worried, anxious frown is probably worth a £1,000 note! Keep firmly in your mind as you show round yet another couple, that you are in no hurry to sell and that if, in the kindness of your heart, you decide to let them have your highly desirable house at the price being asked, they will be very lucky people indeed!

If you are considering selling your house or flat within the next few months, look around to see what needs to be done to smarten up the place *inexpensively*.

Do not

◆ double glaze
◆ install central heating
◆ redecorate throughout
◆ replace windows
◆ damp proof
◆ insulate

Do

◆ mend the odd cupboard door which has a tendency to hang open and display the muddle inside
◆ slap a coat of emulsion on shabby walls
◆ paint the skirting here and there
◆ fill / make good / paint the occasional tired window sill
◆ seal and paint over the damp patches

What you are trying to achieve is a basic, quick cosmetic job. There is absolutely no point in spending much money on improving your property just a few months before you move. You will not be able to recoup the money spent by an equivalent increase in purchase price, nor will you have had the time to enjoy the pleasure and comfort from the new work you have carried out. Do remember that prospective buyers actually like to spot the potential, they like to feel cleverer than you, to whisper behind their hands – 'I wonder why they never knocked these two rooms into one, or turned that window into a French window out into the garden?' No two people's taste is the same so you can never prepare for sale the perfect house. There is even a tendency for the prospective buyer to feel that if the house is too perfect, either it is covering up some major fault or they are being asked to pay over the odds for someone else's personal taste. This does not mean that it is perfectly all right to present your house for sale falling to pieces, but we would honestly suggest that a few well chosen comments like – 'We've always wanted to extend the kitchen here or put a conservatory out there but never had the time/money' – are actually selling points.

Legalities

Having prepared the house/flat for sale and organized the marketing via your agent, it is time to liaise with your solicitor. Ensure that:

◆ He has the deeds and that any information on these is readily available.
◆ He puts in hand immediately the local authority searches. In some areas of the country there is a long delay on searches, which is one of the reasons that property sales can take so long. If you put searches in hand immediately the property goes on the market you could save time at a crucial stage later on. Of course, a search produced by *your* solicitor may not fully satisfy the purchaser's solicitor because not all the questions may have been asked and it will not be completely up-to-date. However, a combination of your basic search plus a personal search by the purchaser should resolve all queries relatively quickly.

Fixtures and fittings

Carpets / curtains / furniture / light fittings /cooker – you may be prepared to sell any or all of these but *do not include them in the purchase price*. They must be itemised separately because otherwise you will find yourself paying the agent's commission on these items. The agent's job is to sell your house and it is on that price alone he should be paid. Look around your house – many of the items will have been bought quite specifically for the surroundings – a colour matched cooker, a dressing table which exactly matches the fitted wardrobe, a circular table which fits precisely into the dining space under the stairs, and above all, the carpets and curtains – carpets laid to fit, curtains made to match. Of course, many of these items you will want to take with you, because they will fit into your new home and in any case they will be of sentimental value. However, equally you may be mov-

ing into a completely different style of house which needs a new look.

Before your first potential buyer arrives, go round the house and list all the items you would be prepared to sell and then work out what it would cost the buyer to start from scratch in purchasing them. Presenting the buyer with the replacement cost will almost certainly have him bidding for some, if not all, of the items.

As a separate exercise, list everything which you are leaving – either because it is a fixture or because it is simply not worth your while taking. Kitchen units might well fall into this category. There is little point in wrecking the kitchen, particularly if the units will not fit into your new house. It is very important to make it clear to the buyer exactly what he is getting for his money.

Expressing the purchase price

Let us suppose you have agreed a sale for £85,000 and in addition have sold curtains and carpets for £5,000. As mentioned above, the first thing is to make it absolutely clear to the agent that his fee relates to the £85,000 and that the £5,000 worth of carpets and curtains are a separate, private sale on which he will receive no commission. This should not be a contentious issue – the agent should readily accept the position.

So far as the purchaser is concerned, he may want the price expressed in a number of ways. For example, if he is tight for cash, he may want as much of the fixtures and fittings applied to his mortgage as possible,

in which case he may want the purchase price shown as £89,500, with fixtures and fittings at £500. Alternatively, he may have no problem putting his hands on the capital but would like to minimize the cost of Stamp Duty, in which case he may want the house price shown at £80,000 and the fixtures and fittings at £10,000. Either way, this does not matter at all to you, provided your agent is clear as to how much commission he will receive.

Moving out

If at all possible, do not vacate your old home *before* you have exchanged contracts. If you do have to move out – perhaps because of the job in a new town – then it is very important to leave the carpets down, the curtains up, the electricity switched on and central heating on low. Even without the furniture, the property can still feel warm and welcoming. When you have moved out, be prepared to spend a day or so making the place look spick and span, even being prepared to paint the odd wall where pictures have left marks and of course sweeping away the dirt and fluff which will have accumulated under furniture over the years.

Selling an empty property is far from ideal. Not only does the property lose its character but, by inference, if you have moved out, you must be in a hurry to conclude a deal and the prospective buyer will feel he can start bargaining with you on the price.

On pages 30–31 we have dealt with tenants' rights with regard to the different sorts of short term leases available. Here we are not looking at the legalities of disposing of a short lease but rather more the practicalities.

Parting company with your short term lease will occur in one of two different circumstances:

◆ Your lease has come to an end, you do not wish to renew and it is simply a question of vacating the property with the minimum amount of expense and fuss.

◆ For some reason your plans have changed and you wish to vacate the property and cease paying rent, before the lease has expired.

Let us look at these two situations in more detail.

The end of a lease

As with the vacating of any property, in any circumstances, there are certain practical considerations – contacting the Electricity Board, British Gas and British Telecom and ask them to send you a final account on the day of your departure. If you are responsible for paying rates, then here again you will need your rates paid up to the last day of the tenancy. These matters can be soon dealt with and it would be sensible to send your landlord proof that all bills have been paid up to the end of the lease period, to avoid queries or quibbles from future tenants.

That apart, vacating a short term leasehold, particularly where the property is fully furnished, should be like walking out of a hotel room. However, where emotions run high and complications arise is with regard to dilapidations. In all rented accommodation – furnished or unfurnished – the landlord must accept 'fair wear and tear'. What exactly is meant by fair wear and tear? A facile example – if you walk over the same piece of carpet, day in day out, over the space of a couple of years, it may start to show signs of wear. This is not your fault.

However, if you have a wild party and someone empties a bottle of red wine over the carpet and the resultant stain cannot be removed, the landlord could reasonably claim that this is not fair wear and tear.

Under the terms of a short lease, you are living on somebody else's premises and in most instances using somebody else's fixtures and fittings. You need to take care of them and if something drastic happens then you need to recognize that they have to be replaced. Burning a hole in a saucepan means you should buy a new saucepan.

However scrupulously fair you are about keeping track of your landlord's possessions, you may be saddled with a landlord who is out to cause trouble when it comes to dilapidations. So far as furniture, fixtures and fittings are concerned, on taking up the lease you will be given an inventory which the landlord will leave with you. As soon as you have moved in, check that inventory (preferably with the landlord or his agent present) and report in writing immediately any missing items or any items which were

damaged at the time you took over the lease. Keep a copy of that letter which you can produce at the end of the lease if the landlord tries to hold you responsible for any missing or damaged items.

Most landlords understandably do not like tenants hanging anything on the walls. If it has been stated under the terms of the lease that you must not bang nails into the walls, you will probably have to pay for the repair of any holes you make.

Your lease is very likely to contain a clause that there should be no children or pets on the premises. You may have contravened this clause by keeping a cat which has gone undetected because the landlord does not live on the premises. When the landlord comes to inspect the flat at the end of the lease, do be careful to disguise the cat's former occupancy – do not be careless just because you are leaving. A litter tray or food bowl will alert the landlord to the fact that you have had a cat on the premises and he then will be looking for every scratch on the carpet, every stain, every piece of torn wallpaper – all of which he will attribute to the cat and all of which will lead to a demand for compensation since you have been in breach of the terms of the lease.

Disposing of a lease before termination

A change of plans may find you with six or nine months to run on your short lease, while, for whatever reason, you wish to vacate the premises immediately. With a short lease, in most circumstances you cannot pass on the tenancy for a profit unless:

◆   The property contains your own fixtures and fittings, which you are able to sell on to the new tenant, or

◆   The market rental has increased considerably since you signed the lease so that the rent you are enjoying is well below what is being paid elsewhere in the area.

Under the terms of the average lease the landlord cannot object to its being assigned to a new tenant, unless he has very strong grounds of objection. The terminology normally used is – 'Only with the landlord's consent, such consent not to be unreasonably withheld'. The problem, of course, is finding someone to take over the lease and take over with it the responsibilities of any dilapidations.

The alternative to an assignment, but again, still with the consent of the landlord, is to sub-let the premises. In other words, you remain the tenant, responsible to the landlord for all the terms and conditions of the lease, but a friend or sub-tenant moves in and pays an equivalent or higher rent direct to you. This can, obviously, lead to problems – your friend might stop paying rent, in which case you would still be responsible, and secondly your chum might wreck the place and here again you would be responsible for the dilapidation. If you sub-let, make sure that you and the sub-tenant sign a proper inventory at the time you hand over, so between the two of you, you each know who is responsible for what.

If you know you have nothing to gain from assigning the lease, you can alternatively consider approaching your landlord to see if the lease can be terminated by mutual consent. Any agreement between two parties can be varied, with both parties' consent, and it could well be that terminating the lease early on a mutual basis suits your landlord as much as it suits you. If he tries to suggest that terminating the lease early is going to cost him money, remind him he can obtain probably a higher rent from a new tenant. If there is any suggestion that you should pay any form of compensation for early release from the tenancy, then revert to the original plan and find someone to whom you can assign the lease.

Whether you are occupying the property under a lease or merely under licence, the landlord is quite within his rights to expect you to continue up to the end of the agreed period – certainly there is no reason for him to be at a loss because you want to withdraw early. Bear in mind that under a licence you cannot assign or underlet – because the agreement is personal to you. Early withdrawal from a licence, will therefore involve you in a haggle with your landlord to let you off the hook.

There are a number of reasons why you might wish to lease or sub-lease a property which you own or rent:

◆ You may have a holiday home which you do not use all the year round.

◆ You may have a city pad which is only used occasionally.

◆ Your parents may have died and you may be reluctant to sell the family home, preferring to let it pro tem.

◆ You may have a large house in which you and your spouse rattle around since the children left home, but which you are very reluctant to leave. Letting off part of it could be the solution.

◆ You could be considering buying a number of premises which you intend to rent out as an investment.

So far as the first four points are concerned, you need to proceed with extreme caution. So far as No. 5 is concerned, do not even consider renting out property if you are looking for a reasonable return on your investment. A combination of factors makes it difficult to make money, in an income sense, out of buying a few small properties and renting them out on a commercial basis. The various legislation, as between landlord and tenant, is certainly smiling more on the landlord these days than, say, ten years ago but it is still arbitrary (see full details of this in our section entitled Ownership and

---

CONTRACT OF SALE

The National Conditions of Sale, Twentieth Edition

Vendor

Purchaser

Registered Land

District Land Registry:

Title Number:

Agreed rate of interest:

	£
Purchase price	£
Deposit	£
Balance payable	
Price fixed for chattels or valuation money (if any)	£
Total	£

Property and interest therein sold

Completion date:

Vendor sells as

AGREED that the Vendor sells and the Purchaser buys as above, subject to the Special Conditions endorsed hereon and to the National Conditions of Sale Twentieth Edition so far as the latter Conditions are not inconsistent with the Special Conditions.

19

• Signed   Date

• This is a form of legal document. Neither the form nor the National Conditions of Sale which the form embodies, were produced or drafted for use, without technical assistance, by persons unfamiliar with the law and practice of conveyancing.

Tenure, pages 24–33). In addition, there is only so much one can charge for rent, against which you have to offset property maintenance and management costs, the risk of unreliable tenants, who don't pay the rent and who wreck the premises, legal fees involved over the years and the strain on the nerves. So . . . for whatever reason it may suit you to grant a lease on the premises you own or lease yourself, do not kid yourself it is going to be a lucrative exercise and certainly do not try and make a business out of it.

Before considering allowing anybody to occupy your property temporarily, short term or long term, you do need solicitor's advice and help – even if the person concerned is a friend or perhaps *especially* if the person concerned is a friend. It is very dangerous to let anyone simply take up occupation without some legal means of getting them out. This means a properly structured lease or licence to occupy.

Before even considering leasing out a property in which you have an interest, there are two major factors to consider.

- If you own a freehold which is subject to a mortgage you will almost certainly need to obtain permission from the lender before letting any part of the property.
- If you are intending to sub-let all or part of a leasehold, you must first have the landlord's consent

Having satisfied yourself on these two points, the next thing to consider is the length of lease you intend granting.

- If you are letting the premises because you do not want it to stand empty but you are not sure what you intend doing with it ultimately, then we would strongly recommend that you go for a licence to occupy. This essentially lets your tenant live on the premises for any period of less than a year, without enjoying any tenant's rights of renewal. A short leasehold could give you the same protection, but over a longer period.
- If you intend letting off part of the house in which you live, the fact that you are a resident landlord does pro-

tect you up to a point from tenants' being able to renew leases or have options to purchase – still you need to tread carefully.

- Alternatively, you may be quite certain that you will never in your lifetime have any use for the property but for some reason you are reluctant to part with it completely. The most likely situation that could cause this is the death of a parent, resulting in your inheriting your own family home. For whatever reason, it may not be convenient for you to live there yourself but perhaps you can envisage that one day your children might like to do so. Perhaps you could do with some capital now, because those children of yours need educating before they can start inheriting houses. This being the case you could perhaps grant a 30-year lease, for which you should receive a substantial premium. Properly constructed, at the end of the lease, the property will revert to your family.
- What applies to actual bricks and mortar of course applies to land as well. You can lease out the land around your home which you do not need, either to be used as farmland or perhaps for someone to build a house upon.
- One of the easiest letting situations is a holiday let. You can rent out your cottage or seaside flat as a holiday rent on an exchange of letters and the only problem likely to arise is occasional damage or excessive wear.

The variation are endless and so are the complications. Because of this, even with something as simple as a holiday let, do check out the position with your solicitor and seek his advice before the granting of any lease

A WORD OF CAUTION – Landlord and tenant law does change. It would be sensible not to start granting leases close to a General Election without studying the manifesto of all parties concerned. This, of course, does not apply to a short lease but it is worth considering if you are thinking of granting a longer term lease.

Granting a lease (2) – the vetting of a prospective tenant

What makes the difference between a good let and a bad let is the tenant. This, of course, is never more true than if the tenant is going to be living on the same premises as yourself, in which case you do have to very vigilant in your vetting procedure. Here are a few hints:

- Take up thorough financial references – a bank, of course, a solicitor, an employer, if your tenant is employed, or an accountant if he runs his own business. Ask, too, for a couple of personal references and if possible one relating to somewhere your tenant might have an account – the local garage perhaps. Where possible take up these references by telephone. Very few people give bad references by letter, for fear of being libellous, but over the telephone they are far more likely to tell you the truth about your prospective tenant.

- Ask your prospective tenants why they want to rent rather than buy and then consider the validity of their explanation. Most financially secure, honest, intelligent people (and let us assume that is what you want in your tenant) would be far more likely to buy than rent. Therefore they have to have a very good reason for renting. Perhaps they are doing a post-grad. course at university or a two-year training course with a local firm. Perhaps they have just returned from abroad and want to look around before settling down. Perhaps they have recently divorced or separated. There can be some logical explanations but do think about them very carefully. Gone are the days where people save up to do things – provided you have a steady income and an unsullied financial record, these days most banks and building societies are falling over backwards to lend you money to buy a house. Paying off a mortgage has to make more sense than renting, therefore a tenant's reason for renting has to be a good one. If it is not, then

probably he is in some sort of financial mess, in which case you should not touch him with the proverbial barge pole.

- One of the largest areas for private letting involves students and, despite their youth, students are often very good tenants – intelligent, hard-working people who have no intention of over-staying their welcome, since the moment their university or college career is over they are off to conquer the big, bad world. Nonetheless grants are spread thin these days and we would suggest that if you are intending to rent to a student, try and obtain a rent guarantee from the parent.

- One of the most satisfactory ways of renting out your property is to couples from the armed forces or employed by a large company. If you have an Army

or RAF base near you or a large international company, you will find that there is a considerable requirement for local accommodation – mostly for married people, with and without children. In these circumstances, you can have a steady trade of lettings, usually of about one to two years in duration. The rent is guaranteed by the Army or the company concerned, and they, too, are responsible for ensuring that at the end of the tenancy period the premises are vacated. This is very useful since it saves the need for advertising, gives you protection and yet you are not in any way committed to taking someone you do not like. You are free to interview prospective tenants in exactly the same way as if you were dealing on the open market and if, subsequently, you

have any problems with a tenant, the 'big brother' organization concerned will always sort them out for you.

◆ Finally, do put a great deal of store by how people look and behave. Untidy, scruffy people usually live in untidy, scruffy homes. People who are late for appointments are usually late for everything which probably includes paying the rent. We are not asking you to be unnecessarily prejudiced but to recognize that it is very easy to let somebody walk into your property and occupy it, but that once they have stopped paying rent and/or started breaking up the place, you will find it very, very difficult to come out of the whole situation without having lost a great deal of time and money in the process.

Forced disposal

Never before has there been so much loan money available to the potential home owner and a slightly cavalier attitude towards lending and borrowing money has developed and, not surprisingly, is creating a number of casualties. In most instances, what happens to people is that they simply cannot keep up monthly payments to the bank or building society. More serious, in some instances, people use the security of their home to borrow money for some purpose other than a straightforward home purchase, and here they may find themselves dealing with less reputable money lenders. Either way, what you must remember if you get yourself into a mess personally is that *it is never too late to save your home* – however far behind you are with repayments, however severe your debts. What you must do is *Fight*.

Let us look at the worst position. If a lender has a *charge* on your house – whether it is the mortgage company or not – and he takes the view that you are not going to sort yourself out, then ultimately he can apply to the County Court for a Possession Order. Once this order is made, the lender can take over your home and sell it in order to get his money back. It is this situation which you have to stop. Firstly, if you are dealing with a reputable building society, bank or money lender, then it is not in their interests to evict you from your home. No building society likes 'blood on their hands'. If you have children particularly, they are very loath to take the ultimate step. This being the case, they will look at almost any reasonable proposal you care to put to them in order to avoid taking such action. Try not to look on them as the enemy. You and your building society are both in a mess and somehow, between you, you have to find a way out of it.

A step-by-step guide to forced disposal

◆ As soon as you are behind with your mortgage repayments, your lender is bound to write to you and ask you to bring your payments up-to-date.

◆ If you do not reply to this letter, or bring the payments up-to-date, your lender will write again – this time threatening legal proceedings.

◆ If you again ignore this, your lender is likely to send details of your mortgage to their solicitors, with the instruction to pursue the matter through the courts.

◆ To avoid court action, it is imperative that you do respond to these letters. Explain your difficulties and ask for time to pay. Offering to pay off the arrears at so much per month while continuing normal payments, without doubt will be acceptable. However, if your financial position is sufficiently severe that this is not possible, then go to see your mortgage company and try and renegotiate the mortgage. If you explain your position, then you may find that the mortgage company will re-calculate your mortgage, giving you longer to pay and with smaller monthly payments. There is absolutely no point in trying to string them along – it is far better to come clean and tell the truth.

◆ If you have ignored the threatening letters, the next stage will be that the court will issue a summons. The summons will order you to appear in court on a certain date and with the summons will come a document entitled 'Particulars of Claim' which will detail the mortgage agreement and the amount of arrears outstanding. If all you need is time to clear your arrears, you can apply for an adjournment. Ideally you should do this through the lender's solicitors or you can apply direct to the court. We would not recommend that you apply for an adjournment to give you time to pay unless you really can pay with more time. If the matter is going to end up in court, there is little point in aggravating everyone at this stage by pretending you can solve the problem if you can't.

◆ If the court hearing goes ahead, then you will have ample opportunity to state your predicament and ask for time to pay. What may happen is that the lender may be granted a suspended Possession Order which is something, if at all possible, you should try to avoid. A suspended Possession Order means that the lender cannot evict you while you are maintaining the payments agreed during the court hearing, but if these payments fall into arrears then a possession warrant can be produced and the bailiffs can go ahead with eviction without the need to refer back to court again. If the case is going the wrong way and the judge feels the amount of money you are offering is too small, ask for an adjournment to give you more time. You cannot keep using the adjournment device to stave off eviction but when your home is at stake it is very unlikely the judge will refuse you additional time to try and find the money.

One of the reasons that you may be in financial trouble is because you have suffered a severe reduction in income. This in turn may qualify you for Supplementary Benefit. Visit the local DHSS and explain your predicament. If you are already receiving Supplementary Benefit most certainly they will be prepared to come to some sort of arrangement with the lender, whereby part of your benefit is paid direct to reduce your debts. In addition, so far as the arrears are concerned, if you can demonstrate that lack of housing is going to put your family seriously at risk, you may be awarded benefit in the form of a lump sum to help clear the arrears. It also would be worthwhile contacting your local Social Services Department if you have children, and asking them to make a payment towards arrears to avoid your children being made homeless. There are also a number of charities who help people faced with homelessness – your local library should be able to supply you with a list of these.

If all else fails, a Possession Order is awarded and you are evicted, the position is that the lender will sell your home and take what is owed from the proceeds, plus fees, and hand to you the balance. A forced sale is never a good idea – local people become aware of it and this causes the price to drop. If a Possession Order is inevitable, ask the court for time to sell your home yourself, while you are still living in it. Sold in the normal way, on the open market, you at least can be sure of getting the best possible price.

Do remember that it is in no one's interest for you to lose your home. So, help everyone to help you by not putting your head in the sand, by telling the truth and by being realistic about your current and future financial position.

Compulsory acquisition of land

There are a number of specific areas to consider under this heading:
Compulsory Purchase Orders
Compulsory acquisition of listed buildings
Purchase notices
Blight
Let us look at each of these in turn.

Compulsory Purchase Orders (CPO)

Compulsory purchase powers are normally in the hands of the local authority. The words *Compulsory Purchase Order* are very emotive and strike terror into the heart of the average home and land owner. However, although a CPO is not something to be envied, there is adequate and reasonable compensation available and also the opportunity to object – both to the order in principle and to the amount of compensation being paid. The only exception to this is in times of war. If the nation is in danger, then the Government has the right to acquire land by compulsory purchase regardless of objections.

The procedure

If the Local Authority wish to obtain part or all of your land, you will receive a CPO through the post, which will state the reason for the acquisition and the time limit set for objections – which can be as little as twenty-one days. In addition to serving an individual notice on each land owner and occupier involved, the Local Authority also has to publish an advertisement of its intention in a local newspaper in two successive weeks, stating where the hearing will take place and the closing date for objections.

Whether you are an owner or an occupier, you are entitled to object to a CPO and in view of the likely short time limit for objections, you should submit an objection immediately and then consider how to handle the matter. It has to be said that the chances of defeating a proposed compulsory acquisition are slight, although sometimes successful. More likely some degree of compromise will be reached, either with regard to the amount of compensation to be paid or with regard to which piece of land is affected.

If either owner or occupier objects to the CPO, then there must be a hearing. However this only relates to objections about the validity of the scheme, not the amount of compensation. If the objection is about money only, then no hearing will take place. An Inspector will be appointed who will probably visit the site and then will listen to the arguments and objections on both sides. He will not make the decision but will write a letter to the Minister responsible, with a recommendation which may or may not be accepted. In due course, owners and occupiers will be advised of the Minister's decision. If the order is to go ahead then the Local Authority will issue a Notice to Treat, after which a purchase price is agreed and the land acquired.

One of the reasons that a local authority may wish to acquire some of your land is for the building of a new road or motorway. In these circumstances there is usually discussion many months or even years before you receive any form of CPO as to the proposed new route for the road. *This is the time for your objections.* While the route is still open to negotiation, those who shout loudest and make the most fuss are likely to have some influence on the situation. Once the route is set and the compulsory purchase procedures have been started, it is virtually impossible to obtain a re-routing.

If your land is treated with a CPO, there are two Acts you should read. One is the Land Compensation Act 1973, the other the Compulsory Purchase Act 1965, both of which are available from HMSO. There are also a number of useful booklets, published by the Department of the Environment covering various aspects of compulsory purchase and compensation. These, too, are available from HMSO.

Compulsory acquisition of listed buildings

If you are the owner of a listed building you will be well aware that even minor repairs and alterations to the property are the subject of planning consent. What you may not be aware of is that the onus is upon you to preserve your listed building. If your Local Authority consider that your property is not being maintained properly, they can serve a Repairs Notice under Section 115 of the Town and Country Planning Act 1971. The Notice will specify what work the authority consider is necessary for the proper preservation of the building and they are likely to give you two months to undertake such work. If you fail, then the authority has the right to make a Compulsory Purchase Order and submit it to the Secretary of State for confirmation.

Purchase notices

The Local Authorities cannot have it all their own way. In certain circumstances where planning permission for a development has been refused, the land may not be able to be used for any other beneficial purpose – in other words the land is neither useful nor saleable. In these circumstances, a Purchase Notice may be served on the local planning authority, which requires them to buy the land from you. A Purchase Notice can be issued by the owner of the land, and the local planning authority has three months in which to make a decision. They can either buy the land, as requested, or reverse their decision regarding planning permission and allow you to go ahead with the development.

Blight

If your land is going to be severely affected by development resulting from compulsory purchase proposals – not necessarily of your land but also of adjoining land – then you can issue your local planning authority with a Blight Notice. The rules on blight are very precise and you need advice as to whether you qualify. If it is accepted that your land has been blighted as a result of a Compulsory Purchase Order, then the Local Authority are required to pay you the difference between the blighted and unblighted value of your property.

Going . . . going . . . gone

A salutory true story – by Alan Fowler

In 1979, with some reluctance, it was decided that we should sell the old water mill in which we had lived for only two years. I thought I knew the two local estate agents who could handle the sale most effectively, so both were invited to inspect the property and advise on value. Each offered almost identical advice on price, albeit quoting a wide spread of between £80,000 and £100,000. One agent said it would attract a great deal of interest at auction, while the other recommended the more usual route. I decided to go to auction.

The glossy auction brochure was produced. The mill was advertised both locally and nationally. 'For Sale' signs were erected. We started showing viewers around – about two or three weeks prior to auction. No guideline price was quoted on the particulars, We had a dozen, perhaps twenty people around. Three couples came back several times. Two made offers of over £80,000 but the agents advised that we should press on to the auction. Interestingly, no one had the property surveyed.

A few days before the auction, I asked the agent at what level we should set the reserve price. 'Join us for lunch before the auction, and we can talk about the reserve then,' was his response.
Pre-lunch drinks –

Agent: 'I am a bit worried by the price of oil – the market is rather nervous. I suggest you put the reserve at £78,000.'

Me: 'How can you say that, when you have told me to turn down offers of over £80,000 in the last few days?'

Agent: 'Well, you think about it over lunch.'

After lunch –

Me: 'We have decided that the reserve should be £83,000.'

Agent: 'Well, I don't think you will sell at that price, but if that's what you want . . . I tell you what . . . you stand at the back, and if I cannot get more than, say, £79,000, I will say to the room. "Am I going to sell this property for £79,000 ladies and gentlemen?" – you give me a nod if you want me to do so.'

The auction was nerve wracking but at last our house came under the hammer –

Agent: 'Ladies and gentlemen, the delightful, secluded old water mill . . . etc, etc. Can someone please make me an offer?'

Silence . . . complete silence – despite the fact that we had identified the two or three very interested viewers amongst the forty or fifty people in the room.

Agent: 'Come along ladies and gentlemen, I'm not here this afternoon to waste your time, and you are not here to waste mine. Can I please have an opening offer for this charming residence?'
'Seventy nine thousand . . . Thank you sir.'
'Eighty?'
'Eighty one thousand?'
'Eighty two thousand.'
'Eighty three thousand pounds . . . Thank you, Sir . . . sold.'
There was no attempt to talk the price up . . . no encouragement for the bidders to go on – that was it.

After the sale –

Me: 'Well, at least I was right about the price.'

Agent: 'Yes, but only just. You realize that there was only one person bidding – the rest was my imagination.'

The reason for relating this story is that you will see that I very nearly sold the old water mill for £5,000 less than the final figure achieved – in fact I would have done if I had followed the auctioneer's advice. Yet the price we finally achieved at auction was no greater than I was offered by the interested parties visiting the house a week or two earlier, and we would have been saved the awful nail-biting trauma at the auction itself. When you consider that the auctioneer in fact sold on a false premise, creating a second bidder where none existed, you could also say that the buyer did not do too well either. For my part, I would never sell at auction again.

Buying at auction

Never is the phrase 'caveat emptor' – buyer beware – more appropriate than when buying at auction. The onus is entirely on you to find out all you need to know before the auction.

◆ You need to be certain as to the condition of the property, which means looking round it in the normal way and having it surveyed. If you are borrowing money, your mortgage company will require a survey in any event but you may feel a private survey is also necessary.

◆ Title/searches/enquiries – most of this information will be within the auction particulars or available for inspection at the vendor's solicitors. Make sure you have studied these details carefully.

◆ You need to have secured your finance arrangements prior to the auction. Immediately the property comes under the hammer, a contract is signed and you will be expected to pay a 10% deposit at the auction room. Normally you will have to complete in twenty-eight days from that date and failure to do so will involve you in paying very high interest rates to the vendor for every day you exceed the deadline.

What is vital is to set yourself an absolute top price beyond which you will not go, however high the bidding and however much you want the property.

Auction room madness is an auctioneer and vendor's dream but it can get people into a lot of trouble. Preferably go to the auction with a friend or partner who can be relied upon to stop you bidding if you start to become over-excited.

If a house is up for auction and it is the house you want, try and do a deal with the vendor prior to auction. One of the reasons the vendor may be selling by auction is because he is in a hurry and you can take advantage of this situation by offering to exchange and complete well ahead of a sale by auction.

Selling at auction

Fees and selling costs are more or less the same as they would be selling through the normal agency route, assuming of course that in any event you would be producing a brochure. Possibly the main advantage of going to auction is not, as may be thought, the chance of a higher price but of achieving a definite sale with a set time scale – i.e. assuming the auction is properly promoted, you know you will be exchanging contracts on such and such a date and completing twenty-eight days later. If, perhaps, you are going to live abroad or are moving to a different part of the country, this could be helpful.

An auction, of course, does not mean that you have no opportunity to sell in any other way. A desperate buyer, who really wants your house, could well be wound up, prior to the auction, and you might decide it is in your interest to accept this offer. If you do make a sale prior to auction, do insist on exactly the same terms as you would have done at auction. Only accept a bid for an immediate exchange of contracts, followed by completion in twenty-eight days. If the buyer will not do this, tell him to wait for the auction.

If your house does not reach its reserve at auction then there is still the opportunity to do a deal after the auction. Presumably there will be a number of interested parties present who may well approach you with offers. While the price may well not be as high as you had hoped, at least a deal can be done.

New building

It is widely recognised that if you want to build a new house (or several new houses forming an estate), you cannot simply find a nice green field with splendid views and start building. You must have local authority planning permission.

The likelihood of obtaining planning permission is dependent upon a whole range of bureaucratioc and practical factors:

◆ To stand a reasonable chance of obtaining planning permission, it is important that your proposed new building is in an area already designated for residential development. Every local authority has a master plan for all the land within its planning control. This plan designates certain areas for quite specific use and it is important that the site for your intended house falls inside an area set aside for residential development. In other words, if your proposal does not conform to the master plan, the chances of your obtaining planning permission are slender – if not negligible. Do establish this point first before spending too much time and money on developing your ideas.

◆ Either as part of the local authority master plan, or closely allied to it, are various specific areas in which new development is very, very tightly restricted. These are the green belt areas, the national parks, the nature reserves, the areas of outstanding natural beauty and the conservation areas. We have discussed these already in the section on page 50: suffice to say here that if you wish to erect a building in any one of these special areas, your chances of success are extremely slender unless the building is for a purpose related quite specifically to the area – i.e., a cottage for a gamekeeper in a national park.

◆ Having looked at the two areas where you are least likely to obtain planning consent, probably the circumstance in which you are most likely to be successful is infilling an existing residential area. The ideal site is an old house with

a large garden, preferably standing on the corner of two roads. Alternatively, a site tucked away behind an existing row of shops or houses – with easy access to a main or side road – again stands a very good chance of receiving approval.

◆ If your proposed new building involves demolition of a listed building, then listed building consent is needed, in addition to planning approval. This also applies to unlisted buildings in conservation areas. The penalties for not obtaining these consents are severe, resulting in unlimited fines and/or imprisonment.

◆ One of the most important factors necessary for a suitable new building site is suitable access. Whereas your plot may have adequate road frontage to allow for access, if the road is already a busy and dangerous one, the highway authority may well object to there being an additional point of access. Do check out your site with the highway authority *before* spending money on a planning application.

Planning application procedures

An application for the erection of a new building will require the accompaniment of detailed plans. In view of this, your application is most likely to be submitted by an architect, who will be well used to the necessary forms and procedure. Once your application has been received by the planning authorities, your application will be advertised locally and a notice posted on the site itself. In addition, most local authorities will advise your neighbours direct that an application is being submitted by you. The object of all this publicity is to ensure that all interested parties have the opportunity to object or make observations. Particularly where a new building is concerned, it is important you recognize that the development is bound to have some impact on your proposed neighbours, This being the case, we would strongly recommend that before you submit any application to the planning authority, you first visit your neighbours and discuss your plans with them. This will give them the feeling that they have some say in what is going on, and keeping them fully informed at an early stage may well stop them objecting later on.

Outline planning applications

To avoid the initial expense of drawing up plans, it is possible to apply for outline planning permission. This means that you are asking the planning authority to approve in principle the concept of a new building being erected on the site in question – subject, of course, to detailed plans meeting their approval at a later date. This is a very useful device if you have not yet purchased the site but want to establish if doing so would be viable. In these circumstances, if you do not actually own the land you will need to submit a Certificate B which indicates that the owners of the land are aware of your application. Similarly, many people disposing of land and not wishing to go to the time and expense of obtaining detailed planning permission, will make application for outline planning permission which is likely to greatly enhance the value of their land.

Tactics

Before making application to your local authority, it is sensible to have an informal chat with the planning officer, to see whether your application is likely to meet with approval. The planning officer will stress that he cannot speak for the committee, and this is true. The planning committee, headed by a chairman, is the decision-making body, although its members do usually heed the planning officer's advice and guidance.

There are various procedures you can adopt for lobbying members of the committee – the most usual is to obtain their home addresses (your local councillor should help you to do this) and write to them direct, on a one-to-one basis, explaining why you feel your application is valid. We would strongly recommend that you do not adopt this rather drastic tactic if your planning application is likely to be successful, as you will be running the risk of placing too much emphasis on what should be a standard application, However if your application is very controversial and causing much local objection, this could be a good move.

The decision

Your local planning authority may react in one of three ways to your application.
- The committee may grant permission without conditions.
- The committee may refuse permission.
- The committee may grant permission, subject to certain conditions. These conditions could relate to the structure of the building or possibly the time allowed for work to be completed.

Normally planning permission is valid for five years, in that development must have started on the site within a five year period, in order for the application to continue to be valid.

Conversions and additions

Planning departments tend to have the reputation for being peopled by ogres. To many of us they are seen as stumbling blocks – the problem which stands between us and doing what we want with our home. *However, it is a fact that most planning applications made by householders are successful.* A realistic application, properly submitted, stands an excellent chance of being accepted, although there are no hard and fast rules which will ensure its success. Each application is judged on its particular merits, as appropriate to the property and environment. This, of course, does lead to some planning authorities having a reputation for being harsh, while others appear more lax. The most fatal mistake you can make is to under-estimate the power of the planning authorities or simply refuse to take them seriously. Cocking a snook at authority occasionally can be hard to resist, but this is not to be recommended when it comes to the planners.

Later in this section on planning, we will be looking in detail at the procedure for submitting an application, Here we are concerned with the 'do's and don'ts' related to any conversion or addition you may wish to make to your home.

Firstly, it needs to be recognized that you have very real problems if you live in a *special* property or in a *special* area. By *special*, we mean that if your house is a listed building, or you live in a national park, a conservation area, or an area of outstanding natural beauty, not only will you need to seek permission in more circumstances than in a normal environment, you are also more likely to have your application rejected as planning controls are more stringent. Here then are some guidelines:

- General ruling – in the case of most property, you can extend your house by up to 15% of its existing gross volume without planning permission. However, if you live in a terraced house or in one of the *special* areas mentioned above, you can only extend by up to 10%. In order to extend without planning permission, the new addition must not be built higher than the existing roof line, nor extend nearer that part of your boundary which borders a public highway.

- Internal alterations – you may make whatever internal alterations you wish to your home, provided that:
  a) You are not changing its use – i.e. turning a house into flats – or
  b) you are not living in a listed building.
  If either of these circumstances apply, you need respectively, planning permission for *change of use*, or *listed building consent*. For the rest of us, without the need for planning permission, we can happily knock down an interior wall to make a room larger, convert an extra bedroom into a bathroom, or the scullery and larder into an open plan kitchen. This also applies to loft and cellar conversions but do bear in mind that if you are going to create a new window you will almost certainly need planning permission.

- External alterations – there is nothing to stop you changing the appearance of your home. Obviously you can paint it, you can also pebble-dash it or stone-clad it without any form of permission. You can also put shutters on your windows and change your window frames without permissionm, unless,

of course, you live in a listed building. If, however, you are changing the shape of your window – i.e. a bay window instead of a sash window, then you probably will need permission. You may also erect a porch without permission, provided that no part of the porch is higher than three metres, nor covers an area of more than two square metres, and is not less than two metres from any boundary between you and the public highway.

◆ Additional buildings – what applies to house extensions also applies to conservatories, stables, sheds, garages, greenhouses and swimming pools. Buildings of this nature, erected purely for the benefit of the occupants of the house, which are not higher than four metres or placed no nearer the public highway than your existing house or cover no more than half the garden, are unlikely to need planning permission – provided they fall within the 10% or 15% ruling, whichever is appropriate.

◆ Separate dwellings – if you are wishing to build a granny flat or a service flat for staff, then you do need permission, whatever the type of structure *if it is going to be a separate dwelling house.* However, provision of an additional room or rooms for someone who is going to live as part of the household, means that the planning laws come

under the same rules as for an extension – i.e. the 10% or 15% ruling. In other words, you need a communicating door. What applies to a building also applies to caravans and houseboats. You may park a caravan in your driveway, or indeed a boat on the driveway or a river if you have one, provided it is used by the occupants of the house for pleasure purposes. The moment you let anyone occupy it as a separate dwelling, then planning permission is needed.

◆ Demolition – unless your house is a listed building, you do not need planning permission to knock down any part of it. This applies to the main building or to any outbuilding on your land. You may also knock down fences and walls and fell trees in your garden, provided that the trees are not protected by a Tree Preservation Order.

◆ Sundry items – *you do not need planning permission to*:
a)   Erect a television aerial, if it is for domestic use.
b)   Erect a fence or wall, provided it is not more than 2 metres high, or 1 metre high if it is on a boundary adjoining a highway.
c)   Plant a hedge of any height.
d)   Alter the basic structure of your garden – i.e. turn grass to concrete to provide extra parking, or the reverse.
e)   Erect a central heating tank, provided that its capacity is no greater than 3,500 litres and it is for domestic use.
– *you do need planning permission to*:
a)   Erect a flag pole or radio mast.
b)   Construct an additional means of access from your home – i.e. a path or driveway, unless that path or driveway is opening out onto an unclassified road.
c)   Run a business from home – see page 62 for full details on this.

These then are the broad outlines of planning rules as they apply to conversion and additions to private houses. For further information, contact your local planning authority who, truly, you will find are extremely helpful.

Change of use

All land and buildings have an established, recognized use, which is accepted by the local planning authority. If you intend to change that use, you must have planning approval, irrespective of whether it is going to involve any alteration or reconstruction of the existing buildings. In other words, the external appearance can change not at all but this still does not preclude you from requiring planning approval. If you fail to seek planning permission for a change of use, you can be forced to abandon whatever new use you have applied to your land or building and revert instead to its original use.

You can apply for change of use whether you are a tenant or an owner, though obviously in the case of a tenant, you do need to seek the owner's approval first. As a tenant, it is important before committing yourself to a property to check out that you may use it as the landlord has indicated to you that you may. This particularly applies to so-called commercial property which was formerly residential – the landlord may not have obtained consent for change of use.

What applies to tenants, equally well applies in the case of owners. As part of your general searches on any property you intend buying, it is important to establish use, particularly where your use may be somewhat controversial – i.e. a shop in a row of houses, a suite of offices in a house, a converted barn or old school, a workshop in a residential area . . . Just because the existing owner is using the premises in a certain way, it does not mean necessarily that he obtained change of use consent before doing so. If after you have purchased the property, the planning authorities were to discover that you were using the property wrongly, the fact that you bought the property in good faith would not excuse you from having to revert to the property's original use. Change of use does not have to apply to a whole property or indeed a whole piece of land. You can seek permission to use a room or a floor of a building or a garage, or two acres out of fifty for a different use from the rest. These are the most usual circumstances which give rise to change of use applications:

Working from home – office/workshop
Residential to office
Residential to workshop
Residential to retail
Warehouse to industrial
Houses to flats
Flats to hotel
Farm to retail
Garage to self-catering flat

If you wish to change the use of your existing property or one you intend buying or renting, it is advisable to first seek informal advice from your local planning authority. What you need to know is their general attitude towards the use you have in mind, and, frankly, if at this informal stage they clearly indicate they are dead against your proposal, there is little point in pursuing it. Neighbours, too, can play an important role. A strong objection from your neighbourhood is likely to be taken very seriously by the planning authorities and in itself is enough to cause your application to be rejected. So, sound out your neighbours – if you are going to have to apply for change of use there is little point in attempting to keep this information from them.

In many instances, it is tempting to take the view that the planning authorities are likely to turn a blind eye to your activities. This is fine, provided you do not suffer at the time you come to sell your property. Let us take two examples of working from home.

◆ If you are running a theatre booking agency from home, this may involve a few visitors but essentially your business is conducted mainly by telephone. Not only will planning not really want to know what you are doing, but your business is easily transferable to your new home and will involve no increase or decrease in value of your existing home.

◆ If you are running a thriving bed and breakfast business, on a sufficiently large scale that it should have had permission from the planners, but you have not sought it, what happens when you come to sell? Clearly, you are likely to receive more money for sell-

ing your home as a business than as a private residence, yet without planning permission, no buyer is going to pay you much of a premium for the considerable business you may have built up over the years.

Stop notices

If you are using your land or buildings in a way which does not have approval from the planning authorities, then they have the right to stop your activities. In some instances they issue an *enforcement notice*. However, from their point of view this is not terribly satisfactory as you are allowed to launch an appeal and until that appeal is heard, you may continue your activities as before. The more favoured method is a *stop notice* which prohibits specific activities from being carried out and will state a date from which activities must cease. A stop notice is issued personally – either to the owner or occupier of the land or property – and there is no procedure for an appeal against it, although compensation may be payable for any loss arising from it – in other words, if ultimately the stop notice is revoked.

Our advice is always to apply for permission for any material change of use – particularly if the new use is going to involve you in an outlay of capital. Ignoring the rules can prove a very expensive exercise.

Procedure and appeal

If you need to apply for planning permission, then these are the steps you should take:

◆ We would strongly advise that before putting in any application, you have a preliminary, off the record, discussion with the planning officer to see whether your application is likely to be accepted. Your application will be passed or rejected by the planning committee, but the committee is influenced by the planning officer's advice. Therefore while the committee might give you permission where the planning officer thinks it is inappropriate or vice versa, this is unlikely, and the planning officer's view is generally vital to your success or failure. Listen carefully to what he says. If he has objections, see if there is an area of compromise and if at all possible, amend and refine your application to reflect his views.

◆ When you are ready to make your application, you should contact the planning department for the necessary application form. At the time they will tell you how many copies of the form are required, depending upon the nature of your application. If you are going to be employing an architect, the architect will make application on your behalf at the time of submitting his drawings. If you are making the application yourself, you will not find it difficult. There are helpful notes provided with the form.

◆ Fees – you will normally have to pay a fee to the local authority at the time of submitting your application, For the average household alteration or extension, this is currently £30. However, if you are applying for change of use, or building and converting a number of dwellings the fee will alter. In certain circumstances you may be exempt from paying a fee – if you are converting a house for a disabled person or if you are re-submitting an application which has been modified.

I'LL TEACH THEM TO IGNORE OUR OBJECTION TO THEIR EXTENSION.

◆ Once the planning authority has received your application and fee, a copy of your application will be placed in the planning register. The planning register is a public reference point and anyone may go and study your application. The planning authority may also notify the highways authority, if appropriate, and inform your neighbours. In some instances, where major work is involved, the planning authority will place advertisements in local papers at their own expense. For most applications, a notice will be displayed on the site.

◆ Decisions should have been reached within six weeks of your application, though in some instances, with a complicated application, it can take as long as three months. If you have heard nothing from the authorities within eight weeks, you should ring them and ask them what has caused the delay.

Neighbours, and indeed any member of the public, can object to or comment on your planning application but they cannot stop it – only the committee makes the decision. However, neighbours with a genuine grudge do carry weight. For this reason before you put in an application, do discuss it with your neighbours. Interested parties have twenty-one days in which to make any comment or lodge an objection. The procedure is that the planning officer puts these objections before the committee. Much depends on the planning officer's views of the objections – he may well advise that they should be ignored, or if he feels the committee should turn down your application, he will use the objections as one reason for so doing. Beware of watch dog committees, who might have grounds to object to your application and if possible, lobby these in advance of your application.

Your application may be accepted subject to certain conditions – this could be with regard to the materials you use or there may be a time limit within which you must complete the work. Some of these conditions can be onerous, but normally a compromise can be found.

If your planning application is successful, you normally have five years within which to start work. Consent will lapse unless you commence within this period – although you can apply for it to be renewed.

If your planning application is refused, the authority has to give you a reason for its decision. It may be possible that you can overcome the objections by altering the siting of your building work or changing the design in some way, in which case, a fresh application is likely to be successful. However, before putting in a fresh application, you should have further discussions with the planning officer, to make sure that the original objections have been overcome in your new approach.

If you are not prepared to accept the committee's objections, you can appeal direct to the Secretary of State for the Environment. This applies if you have been refused planning permission or if you have been granted planning permission but with conditions which you consider too onerous. You do need to give a great deal of thought before appealing to the Secretary of State – planning committee decisions are not easily over-ruled. Before considering an appeal, we would suggest that you obtain a copy of *Planning Appeals – A Guide*, which is free, and available either from your local planning authority or from The Secretary of the Department of the Environment, Tollgate House, Houlton Street, Bristol, BS2 9DJ. You need to appeal within six months of receipt of your local committee's decision and you do need to accept that it is a lengthy and sometimes expensive procedure.

Building without planning permission

What happens if you have gone ahead with some building work without planning permission, when in fact permission was required? The matter may be quite easily resolved. If you explain your mistake to planning, they may be prepared to regularize the situation by inviting you to put in an application for the work you have carried out. Assuming the application is successful then the matter is at an end. If, however, your application is refused, or you are not prepared to put in an application, then planning will serve you with an enforcement notice which requires you to demolish the work you have carried out. You do not need to comply with this enforcement notice, provided you appeal against it. However, once your appeal has been heard, if it is unsuccessful then you do have to go ahead with the demolition to avoid prosecution.

Building regulations

The need for your building work to have building regulations clearance is quite separate from planning permission, The planning committee is not concerned with whether a new piece of building is properly constructed and structurally sound – this is the function of building regulations. Just because you have received planning permission, it does not mean you will obtain building regulations clearance and vice versa – in fact one is in no way dependent upon the other. Buildings which do not require planning permission (as in the 10%/15% extension rule) may still require building regulations approval. In many respects building regulations are more onerous than planning since they cover a much wider area of responsibility. These are the main areas they cover:

- Structural stability
- Preparation of the site
- Moisture content of building
- Ventilation and height of rooms
- All sanitary aspects – WCs, shower, bath, etc.
- Insulation
- Stairways and balustrades
- Chimneys and flues
- Safety in fire
- Refuse disposal

As you will see from this list, practically all building work is likely to be subject to building regulations approval. As a general rule, garden sheds, greenhouses and detached garages are unlikely to require building regulations clearance, simply because they are not dwelling houses and therefore do not require such deep foundations or plumbing services. However almost every other type of building does require you to make a building regulations application.

If you are employing a builder – and most certainly if you are employing an architect – then these professional people should be well versed in the subject of building regulations. However a small, local builder – little more than an odd job man – may not be. You, as perhaps a DIY enthusiast, may be equally ignorant. In these circumstances, do contact your local authority and ask for advice – there is no point in trying to duck the issue. They will not try and make life difficult for you and there is little point in ignoring the requirements of the building regulations.

Any building which has been converted, altered or built from scratch which does not meet building regulations standards, will have to be brought up to those standards, or otherwise may have to be demolished. You will be liable to a fine for what is termed 'a criminal offence' and there is an additional daily fine for every day the building remains erected after an order for demolition. The responsibility for a building which does not conform to building regulations is that of the builder, but you cannot hide behind his skirts on this issue. A halt in the building programme is bound to prove expensive and the partial or complete demolition of your building work will be heartbreaking as well as expensive.

Building regulations procedure

Before work starts, the builder must serve the district surveyor, at your local authority, with a series of written notices. Initially a complete set of plans should be submitted, together with details of the material to be used. Where fairly large structures are involved there will also be the requirement for details of loads and stresses on walls. Initial agreement to this application will take about five weeks. If the district surveyor is not happy with the proposal, then he must give reasons for his objections and again, as with planning, you can appeal to the Secretary of State.

When building work is about to commence, the builder must serve a notice of commencement of work to the district surveyor. Inspections will then take place at various stages throughout the work. For example, the builder should give forty-eight hours' notice before the foundations and drains are covered in. If by the time an inspector comes on site, the foundations and drains have already been covered, then he will probably have an inspection trench dug so the work can be viewed – this is expensive both in time and money. It is important, therefore, to be aware of these stages and to make sure that the builders do not overlook an inspection. A missed inspection could at worst cause work to be partially demolished or at best a badly organized builder may have work halted for vital days until an inspection has taken place.

Building without building regulations approval

As with planning, if you find you have gone ahead and built without building regulations clearance, it is not necessarily the end of the world. Provided the work has been carried out well, using proper materials, then in all probability it will comply with the rules, and the building inspectors will be able to issue their approval retrospectively. Again though, as with planning permission, there is no point in evading the issue. At some stage it is bound to come out that you do not have building regulations approval – particularly if you come to sell the property. What you must avoid is the whole situation rebounding on you, for the price of your so-called short cut could be fines and/or demolition.

For further information on building regulations, there are a number of detailed guides available from book shops in the £12–£14 bracket. Alternatively, published by the HMSO, is a complete set of building regulations which costs approximately £80.

Conveyancing – solicitors

It has become fashionable over recent years to think in terms of undertaking your own conveyancing – indeed, there have been a number of books on the subject propounding the advantages of DIY conveyancing and suggesting that there is little need to employ a solicitor when buying a house. We absolutely disagree with this view. The decision to buy a home has to be one of the most important you will ever make in your life – certainly in a material sense. You will be committing yourself to tens of thousands of pounds – possibly even hundreds of thousands of pounds – and the success or otherwise of your purchase will have an enormous impact on your everyday life. Given these circumstances, is it sensible to begrudge spending an extra few hundred pounds just to ensure that you get it right? Of course not. Think about the mechanics of moving for a moment. Everyone recognizes that moving homes is one of the most traumatic episodes in a person's life. Given that, why add to the strain by trying to handle the legalities as well? Leave it to the experts.

In practical terms, you cannot really undertake your own conveyancing unless the person you are buying from is employing a solicitor – somebody has to know what they are doing! In addition, unless you are purchasing a registered, secondhand, freehold, where title is entirely straightforward, you should not even attempt to do your own conveyancing – this means that unregistered property and land, flats and newly built houses, all require a solicitor.

If you are borrowing money to purchase your house, you may find that your bank or building society will insist on your employing a solicitor. There is a compromise here in that the mortgage company will almost certainly require their own solicitor or legal department to arrange the details of the mortgage transaction and generally become involved in the formalities of the house purchase. If you are employing a solicitor and your mortgage company is as well, there are grounds for saying there is a duplication of effort and so you could ask your mortgage company to allow their sol-

icitor to act for you as well. Here again though, we are not really in favour of this. Take an example – supposing you are buying a house for, say, £100,000, with a £40,000 mortgage. So far as the lender's solicitors are concerned, they are interested primarily in that £40,000, since that is the commitment which they are protecting for their client. Supposing your conveyance includes a few awkward covenants which could have some effect on the future value of your property – the bank or building society is unlikely to be concerned at all. However, if you employ your own solicitor, he is looking at safeguarding the total £100,000 because that is *your* commitment. In theory, entering into a direct professional relationship with your mortgage company's solicitor should overcome this bias, but first, last and always the solicitor in question will tend to be looking at the property from the lender's point of view and we still feel it would be better for you to employ your own entirely independent solicitor.

Having stressed at some length the need to involve your own solicitor in the purchase of your house, we are not suggesting that you simply hand the problem over to him lock, stock and barrel. What is important when employing a solicitor – or indeed any professional person – is to make sure that you understand what is going on so that you can make sure that your solicitor does a good job for you and covers all the ground that needs covering. This, then, is really what this section of the book is all about – ensuring that you understand the legal implications of buying and selling property, so that you can ensure that everybody acts in your best interest and that nothing is left to chance.

Choosing a solicitor

Ideally, as with all professional help, it is best if you can use a solicitor who has been personally recommended to you. Recognize, however, that there is a difference between the various departments in a solicitor's office. Your family may have dealt with the same solicitor over the years, who has drawn up wills and sorted out the odd family problem. However, when you approach him to help you with the purchase of your house, you will find you are referred to his conveyancing partner. It is important to make the point here that just because a firm of solicitors are good at handling one type of business, they may not necessarily be good at handling another.

Case history

To demonstrate this point, we have a friend who leads a fairly exotic life, wheeling and dealing in the City. He employs a very high-powered firm of solicitors, who have brilliantly manoeuvred him in and out of big business deals over a number of years. Recently our chum purchased a flat in London and naturally used his firm of solicitors to handle the purchase for him. It was then he discovered that this brilliant firm employed one ancient, vague and enormously inefficient partner to deal with all their conveyancing, who in his confused incompetence nearly lost the property altogether for our friend!

What needs to be learnt from this story is that you should be looking for a good *conveyancing* solicitor, not just a good firm of solicitors.

As with buying anything else, buying the services of a solicitor should involve your shopping around for the best deal. It is easy to become intimidated by the professions but this is one occasion when you must not do so. Ask your solicitor to quote you, in advance, as to what his fees will be. We deal with fees and costs in more detail on page 140, but it is important to tie down your solicitor to an agreed charge in advance.

If you are dissatisfied with the services of your solicitor – if you feel he has been negligent or has charged you too much – your only real redress is to report him to the Law Society, who will arbitrate between you and the solicitor and force him to make amends, if they consider he has stepped out of line or failed in his duty to you. In theory this sounds very satisfactory. Our experience of trying to force the Law Society to investigate a solicitor's conveyancing charges would indicate that the Society is not enthusiastically active in this field of complaint. You could also complain to the Consumer's Association but, best of all, make sure you obtain the right solicitor and have sufficient knowledge of your own to ensure he does his job properly.

Enquiries before contract

Once your offer is accepted for the purchase of a house or flat, one of the first formalities that either you or your agent will undertake is to give details of the transaction to your solicitor. If you are selling as well as buying, then he will be handling both transactions for you.

Having received his instructions, your solicitor's first main task will be to deal with the enquiries before contract, If you are buying, it will be your solicitor's responsibility to issue a list of enquiries which the seller has to answer. If you are selling, then your solicitor will receive the enquiries. It is standard practice, and it is important here to mention the law with regard to enquiries. *The seller is under no obligation to tell the buyer anything about the property unless he asks.* The only exception to this is if there is any defect in title. This means that if, for example, a motorway is going to be built in a few years' time, a couple of hundred yards from your boundary wall, the seller is under *no* obligation whatsoever to tell you.

Enquiries before contract are usually made by using a standard enquiries form. This form is being constantly revised and updated to make it as relevant as possible to the most recent property law. However, you do need to recognize that it is in a standard format and therefore does not take account of any special circumstances.

Enquiries from the seller's point of view

When your solicitor receives an enquiry form, much of the information he will complete himself. The first twelve questions of the form are known as *general enquiries* and deal with such subjects as boundaries, guarantees, fixtures and fittings, disputes, services and planning. Questions 13 and 14 deal with development land and new properties and so highlight quite specific enquiries. There is then a section known as *additional enquiries* and this contains those enquiries which relate specifically to the property in question. Hopefully, from your point of view, these enquiries will be of a minor nature – sometimes there are no additional enquiries at all, as from the buyer's point of view they cause additional cost and delay. It is over these additional enquiries that your solicitor is likely to need help. Some of the questions may be a little awkward and where possible give 'yes' or 'no' answers – there is no need to elaborate. What is essential is that you tell the truth.

Enquiries from the buyer's point of view

The section on additional enquiries is very important from the buyer's point of view, for it is here you will be able to satisfy any specific queries you may have with regard to your particular property. It is in the additional enquiries section where you might query such things as television and radio reception, if your new home is in a valley surrounded by trees, where you may query the behaviour of neighbours, parking restrictions outside your house and drainage problems such as a septic tank. It is also in this section that you will deal with fixtures and fittings and highlight any aspect of the property which you feel needs safeguarding. A friend of ours recently bought a cottage, with a truly magnificent formal garden. As a great gardener, this aspect of the property was particularly important to him. Although he had been reassured by the vendors that the garden would be left intact, he nonetheless included this undertaking in additional enquiries – asking the question and receiving the answer that no plants or trees would be removed. This was a very sensible precaution in the circumstances.

Leasehold properties

If you are purchasing a leasehold, then there are five specific questions on the back of the enquiry form. These relate to the ownership of the property, any licences granted to the lessor – both past and present – details of how a lessor's consent is obtained in the event of a sale, covenants and the position with regard to the maintenance of the building as a whole.

One of the most important aspects to remember, as a buyer, when it comes to the enquiries is that it is highly likely that your solicitor does not know the property you are buying – certainly not as intimately as you do. It is therefore vital to look at every potential problem relating to the property and if you have any doubt, raise it with your solicitor to be included in additional enquiries – whether your query is with regard to boundaries, footpaths, neighbours, the actual bricks and mortar, the land, the services, whatever. If you have a niggle that is worrying you then bang it down as an enquiry.

Another very important point to make is that you should not exclude from your enquiries any query that you have raised direct with the vendors and which they have answered to your satisfaction. The fact is they could have been lying and while they might lie to your face, they are unlikely to lie in writing on an enquiries form. Take nothing on face value and if you have any doubts on any aspect of your purchase, the right time to raise it is in the enquiries before contract.

Answers to enquiries should be studied with great care and if you are not satisfied, then fresh questions should be asked. Do remember, as a buyer, that it is not the solicitor who needs to be satisfied, it is *you*. You should go on asking questions until you have all the answers you need and if the vendor is not able to supply those answers then you may have to consider withdrawing your offer.

The legal term applied to the purchase of property is the rule of *caveat emptor* which means *let the buyer beware* and emphasizes the point that it is the buyer's responsibility to ask the right questions.

Local searches

Local authority searches are a fundamental part of every purchase. Normally these searches are carried out on your behalf by your solicitor and the problem is that it can prove quite a lengthy procedure,. In many areas, searches will take no longer than two or three weeks but in some – particularly in London boroughs – you could be faced with a delay of up to three months. Clearly, if you are looking for a quick purchase this is a considerable handicap, the only consolation being that the delay applies to everyone.

The object of searches is to establish that nothing restrictive or arbitrary is registered against the property you intend to buy in the register of local land charges. A search will disclose entries in the register with regard to any sort of charges of a public nature, either financial or restrictive, which may have been imposed upon the property, and which may affect the property either immediately or in the future.

Restrictive charges

Perhaps one of the most familiar restrictive charges to a city dweller is the smokeless zone, which means that you are not allowed to burn any fuel in your house which will create smoke. Other such restrictive charges could involve not cutting down trees or being responsible for trimming your hedge, in order to keep the pavement uncluttered. If you are buying a listed building this, too, will show up in searches, since its very listing does restrict your use of the property.

Searches will also tell you about the future plans of your property. If there is a compulsory purchase order – perhaps made by the council because they want to widen the road – then this would be revealed. Perhaps the area is considered unfit for human habitation and therefore is going to be purchased by the council and torn down. Again, this would be registered. (Clearly, in the case of compulsory purchase it would be very unwise to proceed with the purchase.) Even before compulsory purchase orders are formalized, all plans, such as road widening schemes and pipeline laying,

should be recorded in the Land Registry, but it is important to recognize that searches are not foolproof. Every day new information is added to them, so that when your searches are twenty-four hours old, they are already out of date. This means that while your solicitor is following through the very practical and necessary standard searches, you should also be doing your own research, which means listening to local gossip, asking questions, keeping your ear to the ground and thoroughly investigating any worrying rumours.

Conducting personal searches

If you are either doing your own conveyancing or wish to speed up the searches, you, or if appropriate, your solicitor, can make personal inspection of the register as an alternative to the submission of written searches. In this case you need to:

◆ Make sure you approach the right council.
◆ Make an appointment in advance, with the council.
◆ Seek some advice as to what you are looking for since lack of experience could have you missing vital information.

Do bear in mind that if you are requiring a mortgage to purchase your home, you may well find that the building society or bank is not prepared to accept a personal search and will insist on the formality of the written response to a normal search. In these circumstances, there is really nothing you can do to speed up the situation.

If you or your solicitor conduct an official search and the local authority fail to notify you of something important, then they are liable and will have to pay you compensation if you suffer any loss as a result, whereas if you conduct a personal search, and fail to notice something important, you have nobody but yourself to blame.

Shortly before we signed the contract on our home, we were told by a local friend that there were plans to turn the cement works, some two miles from our house, into the biggest cement works in Europe. No such plans showed up in the local authority searches, yet our friend was adamant that we should not be buying the house, so close to the works. We therefore conducted our own investigation and found that the reverse was true – there had been plans to develop the cement works but local objection had been so great that in fact work was ceasing on the site and it was going to become a distribution depot only. In our case, therefore, the rumour had no foundation but we would have been very unwise to have ignored it.

AN INDUSTRIALIST HAD THE FOLLIES BUILT ON HIS ESTATE WHEN HE BECAME HOMESICK FOR THE NORTH.

Title

Title is the legal word for ownership. Before you can sell a property, you have to prove that you actually own it. Before you can buy a property, you have to know that the seller owns what he is selling and so is in a position to pass it on to you. Either way, what you are looking for is evidence of title. One of the problems with establishing title is that although the 1925 Land Registration Act was responsible for creating the Land Registry, not all property in England, Wales and Scotland is registered – indeed the registration of land in Scotland only came into being in 1980. In all, about 85% of property in England and Wales is now registered but there are still areas where registration is not compulsory.

Registered property

When you own a registered freehold property, you are issued with a land certificate by the Land Registry in your district. The land certificate, which shows all of the details on the register in respect of the property, is your evidence of title. This certificate is in the form of a three part booklet –

Section A consists of a brief description of the property and of any rights enjoyed by it – i.e. rights of way or party walls etc.

Section B is a record of the owners and any changes in ownership.

Section C records any covenants which affect the property, and any mortgages or rights granted over it.

If you are purchasing a property which has registered title, then the seller's solicitor will send to your solicitor copies of the entry on the register, together with a plan of the property and any relevant documents noted on the register. Your solicitor will also be given authority to examine the register and what he will be looking for is any changes to the register since the date the copies were issued.

All charges on a property to support a loan have to be registered in order to be enforced. Very likely the vendor will have a mortgage, in which case this will be registered, but if he is, say, a compulsive gambler who has been forced to pledge his house to meet his gambling debts, this financial charge would appear too on the Land Registry. Clearly, it is vital that as a buyer you are aware of all charges relating to the property. This way, your solicitor can make sure that the loans are discharged before completion.

Unregistered property

If the property you are buying is unregistered, then proving title is somewhat more complicated. Your ownership of unregistered freehold is evidenced by the title deeds, which consist of the conveyance of the property to you plus the deeds, or extracts from them, of transactions involving the property over at least the previous fifteen years.

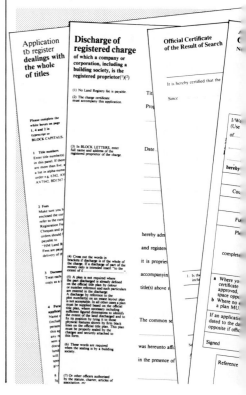

The vendor's solicitors will send the buyer's solicitors details of the title deeds, going back over a period of at least fifteen years. It will then be the job of the buyer's solicitors to check the deeds in detail, to make sure that on each transaction title was properly transferred. He will be looking, not only at the property itself, but at boundaries, rights of way, mortgages etc, to see that no details have been altered or neglected with each transfer of the property. In order to do this effectively, he will need to refer to the Land Charges Register which is based in Plymouth. It is at the Land Charges Registry that details of unregistered property are held, recorded under the name of the owner, rather than the name of the property. This being the case, inevitably your solicitor will be involved in considerably more work than with registered property.

Leasehold property

Where a leasehold house or flat is concerned, then your solicitor will have to examine the lease in detail and so far as the property itself is concerned, he will need to establish that the landlord has the right to lease the property to you. This will either involve establishing his title if you are leasing your flat directly from the freehold owner, or investigating the head lease if you are sub-leasing the property from another leaseholder.

Contracts and completion

Virtually all transactions in everyday life – buying/selling/supply of services – can be carried out with nothing in writing. A verbal contract is perfectly valid so long as at least one of the parties to it can provide some sort of evidence as to the terms. You do not need a written contract to buy a cooker, hire a car, have the lawnmower mended – although in some instances, it might be sensible to have one! However, the exception to the rule is the purchase and sale of property which does have to be evidenced in writing.

In principle, there is nothing to stop your buying a house, just as you might buy a cooker. You can knock on the door of a cottage which is for sale and ask the selling price. If the vendor is asking £48,000, you can say it is too high, but that you will give him, say, £46,000. If the vendor agrees, there and then you can sit down, write out a cheque and hand it over. All you need to do then is both sign a brief letter evidencing the deal, and that would be an end to it.

However, sensibly, you simply cannot buy a house in this way – although this is not to say that deals have not been done like it in the past. The trouble is these days, too much is at stake and there are so many outside influences which can vastly affect the value and future of the property you are buying. For this reason, neither buyer nor seller should take any short-cuts. The buyer needs to know all about the property, as does his bank or building society, and the seller needs to know that the buyer really can perform along the lines he has indicated. From this standpoint, therefore, custom and practice have developed to form the current routine, whereby once the buyer's and seller's solicitors have established what it is that their respective clients are buying and selling, a contract is agreed which sets out the deal, with all the necessary provisos.

Mechanics of exchange

Ninety per cent of contracts for the purchase of a house or a flat are in a standard form, incorporating either the national conditions of sale or the Law Society's conditions. Two identical contracts will be produced and signed respectively by buyer and seller. This happens when the buyer is sufficiently happy that he knows enough about the property, has found the money and can agree a completion date, and when the seller is satisfied that the buyer can complete and that he, the seller, can move out before that completion date. Once all parties are satisfied, contracts can be exchanged and this then commits the buyer to buy and the seller to sell. At the point of exchanging contracts, normally, the buyer hands over a 10% deposit, and normally completion occurs twenty-eight days after exchange – at which point ownership passes from seller to buyer.

Buyer's checklist before exchange

◆ Make sure you and your solicitor are satisfied with the enquiries you have made.

◆ Make sure your searches and evidence of title are satisfactory, subject only to last minute confirmation.

◆ Make sure that you have a mortgage offer in writing, if you require one. Do not exchange on a verbal offer.

◆ Make sure that your surveyor's report is satisfactory and there are no major structural problems with the property you intend buying.

◆ Make sure that you have the property insured from the moment you exchange contracts. It becomes your responsibility at this stage – not at completion.

◆ Make sure you are able to fund the 10% deposit required at the time of exchange.

◆ Before committing yourself to the exchange of contracts, do make sure that you wish to proceed with the purchase. You stand to lose a lot of money and cause everyone a great deal of trouble and heartache if you fail to complete.

Mechanics of completion

On the date of completion, your obligation as buyer is to hand over the money, and as seller to hand over title to the property, and the keys. As the buyer, your mortgage loan will have been sent direct to your solicitors. If you are buying and selling on the same day and have a mortgage on the house you are selling, this will be discharged by your solicitor from the proceeds of the sale and the balance will be put towards the purchase of your new property. Obviously you have to make available to your solicitor any funds which are not coming from your mortgage company, and in this respect your solicitor will ask you to send your cheque to him at least three days before completion, so that the cheque can be cleared through the bank. You are not required to be present at completion. Time of completion will be agreed between the solicitors, from which will follow the time at which you can occupy your new home. The deeds will be sent direct to you unless you have a mortgage, in which case they will be retained by the lender.

Failure to complete

Failure to complete leaves the injured party (buyer or seller) entitled to claim damages for breach of contract. If the seller fails to complete the sale and hand over the property, the buyer is entitled to recover the deposit and then sue for any damages suffered. However, usually when there is failure to complete, it is on the part of the buyer, rather than the seller. The most likely cause is that he finds he cannot produce the money. If completion is delayed for just a few days beyond the contracted date, then all that will be lost will be a few days' interest on the balance of the money due. However, if failure to complete extends beyond a few days, the seller should issue a completion notice. This gives the buyer a little over two weeks' notice that completion is required. Failure to complete the deal within that time will entitle the seller to retain the deposit and pursue his claim for any damages over and above the interest which the buyer will have been expected to pay. As you can see, failure to complete is an expensive business which serves to emphasize that exchange of contracts is not something into which you enter lightly.

YOU CAN'T SUDDENLY CHANGE YOUR MIND ON COMPLETION DAY.

Costs, fees and duties

Let us look at both selling and buying
individually, since the costs involved do
vary considerably between the two.

Selling

Estate Agent

An estate agent should charge you between
1–2% of the selling price of your house and
in some instances will ask for a contribution
towards advertising and promotion. The
promotion costs on a reasonably inexpensive house are likely to be very slight, since
they probably will only involve local advertising. However, if you are selling an
extremely valuable property, in order to
obtain the widest possible coverage you
may well have a full colour brochure prepared and advertise in prestige newspapers
and magazines. The precise percentage an
estate agent will charge you will depend
both on the agent and on your circumstances. For example, if you are selling a
weekend cottage and therefore are not
permanently in residence, then your agent
is going to have to show round every
potential buyer, rather than leaving you to
do it. This is bound to put up the costs.
Agency fees in London tend to be higher
than the national norm – 2½% is quite
common. Fees generally are likely to be
less if you appoint a sole agent, as opposed
to instructing several agents.

Solicitor

Your solicitor is likely to charge between
½–1% of the selling price. His fees will vary
slightly according to how much trouble he
has had with the buyer's solicitors.

Here are some typical examples of the
likely costs involved in selling your home:

Selling Price	£50,000	£100,000	£200,000
Estate Agent	750	1500	3500
Brochure/ advertising	-	250	400
Solicitor	350	750	1250

Note: VAT needs to be added

Buying

Estate agent

There is normally no estate agent's fee
involved in buying a house, unless you have
especially commissioned an agent to find a
property for you.

Surveyor

A structural survey is likely to vary in cost
between £150 and £300 on the average
home. The minimum fee is likely to be £100
and in order to estimate what you are likely
to have to pay, you should think in terms of
£100 plus £1 per £1,000 of value as a rough
guide. If you are buying your home with a
mortgage, then it is likely that you will need
a valuation for mortgage purposes. This will
cost about half the fee charged for a structural survey.

Solicitor

Although buying is a more responsible job
than selling, the same amount of work is
actually involved for both sets of solicitors
when a property changes hands. For this
reason, therefore, you can expect much the
same sort of fee whether you are buying or
selling – i.e. between ½–1%. If you are
buying a registered property this is easier
and therefore cheaper to handle. This
means you can expect the solicitor's total
cost, including Land Registry fees, to be
about the same for a registered property as
an unregistered property where no Land
Registry fees are involved.

Solicitor acting for the building society/bank

There is a fairly standard set of fees recommended for solicitors acting for building
societies and banks. If they are acting
purely for the mortgage company – in other
words not for you as well – then their

charge will relate not to the value of the property as a whole but to the amount of the mortgage. If the mortgage company solicitors act for you as well as the bank or building society you could pay a little less in total than if you had two sets of solicitor's fees.

Stamp duty

You will pay 1% on the purchase price if it exceeds £30,000. There is no stamp duty on property changing hands at below £30,000.

Here are some typical examples of the likely costs involved when buying a property:

	£29,500	£50,000	£100,000	£200,000
Purchase price	£29,500	£50,000	£100,000	£200,000
Mortgage	£28,000	35,000	60,000	120,000
Estate agent	–	–	–	–
Structural survey	150	150	250	300
Mortgage valuation	50	70	120	150
Your solicitor/ Land Registry	250	350	750	1250
Lender's solicitor	120	125	130	150
Stamp duty	–	500	1000	2000
Sub-total	570	1195	2250	3850
+ VAT (not on stamp duty)	85	105	190	280
Total	655	1300	2440	4130

As you will see, whether buying or selling, the costs involved represent a very small proportion of the overall price of the property. For this reason, we would stress the importance of employing a really good solicitor and if applicable, estate agent, to act for you, rather than scrimp and save for the sake of a few hundred pounds. A good estate agent will earn his fee in obtaining you the right price for your house – fast. A good solicitor will earn his fee in ensuring that you either sell your house with the minimum of fuss, or that as a buyer, you know precisely what you are getting for your money.

Scottish law

If you are contemplating buying a property in Scotland then we must stress the need for you to engage the services of a Scottish solicitor. You cannot use your English solicitor – he will not be sufficiently familiar with Scottish property law to handle the purchase of the property for you. To find a Scottish solicitor your own English solicitor may well have contacts, or alternatively you can contact the Law Society of Scotland:

PO Box 75,
26 Drumsheugh Gardens,
Edinburgh,
EH3 7YR.

Telephone 031 226 7411

The various stages of purchasing a property in Scotland are not dissimilar to those in England and Wales, except the terminology is different and the order in which things occur is not the same. Perhaps the main difference is that estate agents hardly figure at all. Property is generally offered for sale through solicitors' property centres, and although one or two estate agents have started opening up in Scotland, these are still very much in the minority and the movement of property remains very much in the hands of solicitors.

Properties are offered for sale with what is known as an *upset price*. This term means that the vendor is looking for offers above the figure quoted – in other words it is the equivalent of a reserve price at an auction. If you are interested in the property, then what you have to decide is how much more you have to offer above the upset price, in order to have your offer accepted. If a house, for example, is for sale at £45,000, you could try offering £45,500, only to find that someone has offered £46,000 and has had his offer accepted. Alternatively, you could put in a bid for £46,000 only to find that no one has bid over £45,000 in which case you could have saved yourself the best part of £1,000 and still have been successful. It really is rather a lottery.

The vendor, as well as setting the upset price, also specifies a closing date for bids. If you are interested in the property then,

unlike England, you must have it surveyed before you put in your offer. This means, of course, that if you make several unsuccessful bids, you may have to pay several survey fees.

So far as the offer is concerned, this is made through your solicitor – in other words you do not make the offer direct to the vendor. Your solicitor should be able to advise you where to pitch the price. He may well know the selling solicitor and will have discussions with him about the other bids. The trick is to put in your own bid at the eleventh hour, your solicitor having tipped you the wink as to what figure to bid.

winded process. If your offer is successful you should hear either on the closing date or the following day, and the moment your bid has been accepted then contracts move ahead.

Having had your offer accepted, as in England, you are still not legally bound to pursue the sale. At this stage local searches are carried out, which in Scotland will only take a few days, and if these are satisfactory then your solicitor will send the vendor a final contract letter, which is known in Scotland as *missives*. The sending of missives is the same as exchanging contracts in England and therefore is legally binding. The only difference is that, unlike England, there is no requirement to pay a 10% deposit which, of course, makes financing easier.

In Scotland completion is known as *settlement*. The procedure for settlement follows the same formula as for completion. Your solicitor will receive your mortgage funds, plus a cheque from you for the balance, and this he will hand over to the vendor's solicitors in return for the deeds, the conveyance and the keys to the property. Your transaction will then be registered in the Register of Sasines, which is the Scottish Titles Register. You will have to pay a fee for this registration and you will also have to pay stamp duty, as in England.

In some respects, the Scottish system is far more satisfactory than property transactions in England and Wales. The amount of preliminary work necessary before putting in a bid does tend to mean that the offers received are bona fide, whereas unfortunately, it has become a habit south of the border for rather cavalier, non-substantial offers to be made, just to hold a property in case the buyer can find nothing better. The other advantage is that the whole procedure tends to be considerably quicker than in England. Do take our advice, though, about employing a Scottish solicitor. It is not simply a question of his understanding the way round the legalities. He will also act as a negotiator on your behalf and ensure that your bid stands the best possible chance of being accepted.

Your offer document will be relatively detailed, more like a draft contract. You will have to stipulate not only how much you are prepared to pay but whether you want any of the contents, how much you are prepared to pay for them and the date on which you want to move in. Once your bid has been received, it will be compared with the other bids and the vendor is under no obligation to accept the highest offer. As in England, he will weigh up the offer price against other factors – such as whether you want to buy the contents, when you can move and also the likelihood of your being good for your money. It is not a long-

Why you may need a mortgage

While nothing is certain in this uncertain world, perhaps one of the few aspects of life upon which one can rely these days is the value of property. Clearly, if you buy a home which has a compulsory purchase order placed upon it, which has not been surveyed or is in a district which is obviously declining fast, then your investment could be in jeopardy. However, so far as most houses and flats are concerned, frankly your money could not be more safely invested.

As a result, banks and building societies are falling over themselves these days to lend money against a property purchase and certainly so far as we, the punters, are concerned, this has to be a good thing. We all have to live somewhere and wherever we live is going to cost us money. Paying rent is simply throwing money down the drain, whereas contributing towards a mortgage – even though you are paying a high interest rate for the use of someone else's money – is building a future. Our advice to anybody – regardless of age or circumstances – is if at all possible get onto the property ladder, even if it means taking a 100% mortgage.

There is just one main proviso however – never take on a mortgage which you cannot afford to service. In other words the size of your mortgage does not matter, provided you have the income to cope with the repayments each month. To take on too big a commitment is not only disastrous financially, but having your house sold over your head is a desperately disturbing and heartbreaking business.

So let us look at the various circumstances in which you would take up a mortgage loan:

◆ As a home purchase
The most common instance in which loans are taken out to purchase property are:
a) By the first time buyer, who usually has no existing relationship with either a bank or a building society and in many cases does not even have the cost of the deposit. In these circumstances, the first time buyer either borrows or receives a gift from relatives for the amount of the deposit or seeks a 100% mortgage.
b) On a change of home – where an existing property owner repays his mortgage and takes out a new one in its place. In most cases the new mortgage tends to be with the same lender, thus retaining the existing financing relationship. The exception to this sort of continuity occurs when there is a complete change of lifestyle – like moving abroad or retiring and purchasing an annuity.

◆ As an additional mortgage
Additional mortgages with the original lender are common. These fall into two separate categories:
a) An additional mortgage may be taken out to extend or improve the property in some way – build an extension, a swimming pool, put in central heating or conduct major repairs.
b) An additional mortgage may be sought to raise money for some use completely outside the home – in other words a straightforward loan using the house as security. This could be in order to buy a new car, take the holiday of a lifetime or perhaps rationalize existing borrowings, or set up a business.

◆ As a second mortgage
There is also the option of the second mortgage. As the name implies, a second mortgage is not a top-up facility from your existing lender but a new loan with an entirely new lender. The reason for this additional loan could be either to improve the property or as with additional mortgages, for some other purpose entirely. On the whole second mortgages normally fall into the latter category. If you are simply requiring a top-up mortgage to improve your property, you are far more likely to stay with the original lender than move elsewhere. In some instances people go on to obtain a third

or even fourth mortgage on their property. We would suggest that this is starting to enter the serious danger zone, despite the rapid and apparently consistent increase in property values. The security for a second mortgage follows that for the first mortgage.

Take a hypothetical example:

House value	£80,000
Mortgage	£60,000
Available security for second mortgage therefore	£20,000

Supposing, taking this example, you borrowed £15,000 on a second mortgage, to, say, start your own business and supposing that business went wrong leaving you with no income and a number of debts. As a result you would be forced to sell your house. If, because you had spent little time or money on the property in recent years it only fetched £70,000, the result would be that the first mortgage would be paid out in full from the proceeds of the sale, whereas the second mortgage lender would only receive £10,000. This would leave you with no house and still £5,000 owing on the second mortgage. In theory, you can say, this situation is very unlikely to happen, since your original £80,000 house is more likely to sell for £100,000 than £70,000. However we believe it is always dangerous to borrow speculatively right up to the hilt on the value of your property, just in case local or national trends cause an unexpected dip in property.

◆ **On a mortgage-free property**

A completely unmortgaged property can be used, of course, to finance either a property improvement or indeed a loan for any other purpose. It can also be used to buy an annuity. In the case of a retired couple whose income is rather low and who are reluctant to leave their family home, an annuity could be the answer, involving borrowing money against their home to buy an income for life. See page 159 for further details.

Your property is likely to be your biggest single asset and it is very tempting to borrow money against it, particularly when property prices are escalating. Take a situation where eight years ago you may have bought a house for, say, £60,000, with a £30,000 mortgage. In eight years that £60,000 house now could be worth £150,000 – not unreasonable figures in today's market. You might well be tempted to vastly increase your borrowing in order to improve your lifestyle. In a relatively modest way this is perfectly justified, but borrowing money costs money. It is very easy to find yourself in a position where you have borrowed more money than you can service and the only option left open for you is to sell your property.

GEORGE LIKES TO KEEP A VISUAL RECORD OF HOW MUCH OF THE HOUSE IS ACTUALLY OURS.

Various types of mortgage

There are three types of mortgage – the repayment mortgage, the endowment mortgage and the pension mortgage. Let us look at each of these in turn:

Repayment mortgage

With this type of mortgage you repay the loan by monthly instalments, over an agreed period, together with interest on the loan – again, usually on a monthly basis.

Repayments may be made by fixed monthly instalments of capital, with interest calculated on the reducing balance, and also paid monthly. On this type of mortgage loan the cash outlay is clearly very much greater in the early years, because each instalment will contain a fixed amount of capital, plus a variable amount of interest, which will be very high in the first few years. Take an example:

£25,000 loan, repayable over 25 years by flat monthly instalments of capital, with interest at 10% per annum:

First year payments
capital	£1,000
approximate interest, net of tax	1,840

Total in year	£2,840

Final year payments
capital	£1,000
approximate interest, net of tax	40

Total in year	£1,040

However, for most property buyers this heavy weighing of payments at the beginning of a loan is exactly what they do not want, and in fact represents a repayment schedule with which they are unable to cope. For this reason most repayment mortgages are repaid by level monthly instalments. They are calculated to settle the loan over the agreed mortgage period but initially the monthly repayments will contain a very small capital element. As the loan is gradually repaid and the monthly interest is thus reduced, so the capital element of each instalment increases. Here is the same example calculated in this way:

£25,000 loan, repayable over 25 years by fixed monthly instalments
(containing interest at 10% per annum, plus an increasing capital element).

Approximate first year payments –
capital	£340
interest net of tax	£1,860

Total in year	£2,200

Approximate final year payments –
capital	£2,120
interest net of tax	80

Total in year	£2,200

Whatever the repayment programme, the lender is likely to insist that the loan should be covered by some form of life policy, to the value of the outstanding amount. This is not an expensive policy – the typical premium being less than £100 per annum for borrowing £25,000, as in this example.

Endowment mortgage

With an endowment mortgage, the loan remains outstanding in full for the whole period of the mortgage and all you pay the

lender is the interest. However, at the same time you pay premiums on an endowment policy which is designed to produce a cash sum when it matures, which will repay the loan and – hopefully – produce a tax free surplus. The lender will require a legal charge on the endowment policy in order to guarantee that the proceeds will be used to repay the loan.

Endowment policies may be linked to specific investment funds – such as unit trusts – or may be written within the insurance company's general funds. One needs to recognize that the investment performance will vary from fund to fund, although the minimum maturity value will be guaranteed. Premiums, too, vary from fund to fund and company to company, and because they are life assurance policies, they are also influenced by the age and health of the policy holder. A typical example of an endowment mortgage, using the same basic figures as in the repayment mortgage illustrations, is as follows:

£25,000 loan – 25 year mortgage – interest at 10% per annum.

Annual interest, net of tax	£1,880
Endowment premium	430
Total payment each year	£2,310

This example would apply to a healthy, non-smoking male in his early thirties.

Pension mortgage

For anyone who is self-employed or entitled to arrange a personal pension policy, a pension linked mortgage can be very attractive. It works on the same basic principle as the endowment mortgage, with a fixed term loan and interest paid throughout the term of the loan. However, instead of an endowment policy, a personal pension policy is taken out, designed to cover the outstanding loan at retirement date. The Inland Revenue allows a certain proportion of a pension fund to be paid over in cash on retirement. This is used to pay off the mortgage, and the balance of the fund provides a pension.

The main attraction of a pension mortgage is that if the policy is written within the Inland Revenue rules, pension premiums can be offset against income tax. This means that you will receive tax relief on the whole of your 'mortgage payments' – both the interest (on a loan up to £30,000) and the capital.

One difference between a pension mortgage and an endowment mortgage is that the lender cannot take a legal charge on a pension policy. It has to be deposited informally, against an undertaking that the proceeds will be used to repay the loan.

It is extremely difficult to give a general example of the cost of a pension mortgage because pension premiums are closely linked both to age and the fund's investment policy. However, taking again the same example of a £25,000 loan, 25 year mortgage, interest at 10%, this is how the figure will tend to look:

Annual interest, net of tax, approximately	£1,880
Pension premium, net of tax	£680
Total payable in year	£2,560

As with repayment mortgages, a mortgage protection insurance will be required.

Building societies

Until a few years ago, building societies had a virtual monopoly on the mortgage market but recently banks have moved in aggressively – they are competitive and are prepared to be considerably more flexible. The result is that building societies now account for only about half of the home loan business.

People tend to save with building societies because they feel safe and comfortable to deal with and somehow less daunting than a bank. People go to building societies for mortgages because habit dictates that this is the natural, most obvious thing to do. The societies have responded to the inroads made by the banks into their traditional territory, by broadening the whole range of their services and they are becoming less rigid in their general approach.

You do not need to have an existing relationship with a building society in order to obtain a loan. The general view in the past was that even a few hundred pounds saved in the building society would give you an inside track when it came to applying for a mortgage. Now, shopping around for money is accepted as the norm – if the sums are right your application will be accepted on its merits, without the need for any previous association.

Virtually all building societies have established close links with life assurance companies and therefore are happy to become involved in the whole mortgage range – i.e. they deal with endowment and pension mortgages, as well as the traditional repayment mortgages. The two criteria upon which any application will succeed or fail are:

◆ The ability to pay
◆ The mortgage value of the property.

Ability to pay – income

It is your income which is the first concern of a building society rather than verifying the value of the property in which you are interested. In other words, the first criterion is to establish your buying power, for your income and prospects will determine the maximum mortgage you can obtain, and this in turn will determine the price range of property you can consider. These are the general rules applied:

You can normally borrow up to 3 × salary (gross earnings) plus 1 × partner/spouse's salary, or alternatively, 2½ × joint salary, whichever is the higher. However, this calculation is flexible at the local manager's discretion. If you are young, professional and have excellent prospects, it is likely that you can borrow upwards of this amount.

About 80% of building society mortgages are now on an endowment basis. There are schemes which incorporate quite low starting premiums on endowment policies with a gradual build-up over the first three or four years to full annual premium. This, of course, is excellent for the first time buyer and enables young people to take a bigger mortgage than would be strictly speaking appropriate for their income at the time of the initial purchase. Potentially, this could be a dangerous situation but in most instances the annual mortgage cost increases in line with the young couple's increase in pay.

Many building societies are prepared to provide an advance confirmation in writing, that a mortgage of up to £X,000 will be available. Obviously, it is very comforting to have this facility confirmed before you go house hunting but the advantages do not stop there. Such an offer is also valuable in a negotiation sense – having a piece of paper to show, which indicates that you really do have the finance available, may well give you the edge over someone else trying to buy the same property.

Value

The building society will arrange for your proposed property to be valued at your expense. However, it is very important to stress here that a property valuation is not a structural survey. The mortgage valuation is intended to be an assessment as to the worth of the property as security for the loan. Valuation, therefore, takes account of features such as central heating, the availability of all services, the location etc, etc. However, so far as the structure and maintenance of the building is concerned, the assessment will be very superficial. For this reason, you would be well advised with almost every property, to commission your own structural survey to make sure you know what you are getting.

Each building society has either a published or an unpublished in-house limit on the percentage of mortgage value up to which it will lend on standard terms. The limit is generally 75%. Having said that, virtually all societies will go up to nearer 100% – i.e. the full purchase price, *provided that the income cover is sufficient*. In these circumstances, where high borrowing is involved, the building society will only proceed provided there is a mortgage guarantee policy to cover the excess borrowing over and above the normal limit. This sort of guarantee policy is paid for by the purchaser, by way of a single premium. This represents another element of the cost of purchasing a property. The sort of cost involved in mortgage guarantee insurance is as follows:

◆ If your loan is up to 90% of mortgage value – 3½% of the amount over 75%
◆ If your loan is between 90 and 95% – 4½% of the amount over 75%
◆ If your loan is over 95% of mortgage value – 7% of the amount over 75%

Where a 100% mortgage is concerned, it is an important point to remember that the premium for this mortgage guarantee insurance cannot be included as part of the building society's lending. This is for obvious reasons – clearly they cannot lend more than the value of the property purchased.

Without doubt, there is something reassuring about dealing with a reputable and established building society. Their business is bricks and mortar. It has always been, and this does give them a unique feel and understanding of the market, which is perhaps not so evident with the banks, where property lending is just one of their many interests.

Banks

There was a time when banks would only lend short term money – usually in the form of an overdraft, reviewed every year but theoretically repayable on demand. Five years was usually the maximum period for a loan, though sometimes it was seven if you were lucky.

Not any more – '£100,000 for thirty years, certainly Sir!' This is the current attitude, for within the space of just a few years, the high street banks have moved into the home mortgage business with enormous success. They now have something approaching 50% of the market.

Banks offer the full range of repayment/endowment/pension mortgages. Some have their own life assurance or unit trust subsidiaries which enable them to offer the customer a complete 'in-house' package. Interest rates and general terms and conditions are broadly comparable as between the various banks. However there are slight variations so do shop around and compare what is being offered by the various banks with the building societies. If you have a good relationship with your own bank, start there, but before going to see your bank manager pick up a few of the competitors' brochures first, so you know what they are offering. Be confident in your approach and remember that you are the customer. Banks are very keen to attract custom and anxious to sell their mortgage facilities – they are not doing you a favour, it is the other way around.

Against a bank mortgage

You do need to consider whether you want your bank to know everything about you. It is sometimes useful to have two completely separate financial institutions in your life as it tends to give you more flexibility if you are something of an enigma! There is also the problem of causing resentment with your existing bank if you approach another because it is cheaper. Banks do not resent building societies, but they do resent other banks!

For a bank mortgage

Despite the growth of building society facilities, banks still offer a broader range of services. If you are buying and selling it is easier to arrange bridging facilities. If, at sometime in the future, you want to finance a new car, a holiday, your own business or school fees, your bank can be very flexible. They already have a charge on the property and the manager – especially if it is a local branch – will have a very good idea of the value of your property, enabling everything to be arranged quickly and easily.

---A personal case history---

We bought our own house two and a half years ago, since when there has been a great deal of movement on our mortgage. Shortly after purchasing the property, we had the chance of buying a piece of land adjacent to us, which was too good an opportunity to turn down. This meant really stretching our mortgage facilities to the hilt in order to make the purchase. About six months later we sold a business and suddenly had some spare cash, which we used to substantially reduce the mortgage again. Towards the end of this year we are building an extension which will push up the mortgage once more. Our mortgage is with a bank with whom we have had a long term relationship and each of these transactions has involved nothing more than a telephone call, followed by written confirmation. We doubt very much whether we would have received similar service with such speed and efficiency, from a building society. One reason, of course, is that we know our bank manager very well.

As with building societies, the governing factors for a loan from a bank are your gross annual salary and the value of your proposed property. Again, banks offer 2–2½ × the annual basic salary of yourself and your spouse, or 3 × the larger basic salary plus

1 × the smaller, whichever adds up to the greater amount. For properties over £100,000 in value, banks normally do not lend above 80% of the value of the property, although there may be some flexibility here if you are a very high earner with even higher prospects.

First time buyers

Most building societies advertise 100% mortgage facilities for the first time buyers, provided their salary and the valuation on their property warrants it. However, bank literature suggests that they are only prepared to offer first time buyers a 95% mortgage. While we suspect that there is a degree of flexibility based on background knowledge of the customer etc, etc, this does broadly speaking indicate the banks' feel on first time buyers – basically you are going to have to stump up some form of deposit.

As a young couple, starting out on your first home, one way round a rather tight mortgage position could be to ask your parents to guarantee the mortgage repayments, at any rate for the first few vulnerable years. As a general rule, asking one's family to take risks is not a clever idea – certainly asking a parent to guarantee an overdraft facility is almost certain to cause family strife! However, the guaranteeing of a mortgage is somewhat different. Most parents want to see their children settled in their own home and in any event they are not really at risk. If the young couple fail miserably to meet their mortgage repayments, the house can always be sold, and in today's property market, the likelihood of anyone losing money is slim – although not impossible.

Second homes

If brochures are anything to go by, banks seem far more interested in second homes and homes abroad, than building societies. Perhaps this is because building societies are in business to provide people with homes while banks are in business to provide funding for any viable proposition. Certainly if you are buying property abroad, the facilities offered by the banking system are likely to be a great deal more trouble free than operating through a building society.

Life assurance companies

Between them, banks and building societies account for the vast majority of mortgage loans, although the long established life assurance companies are still in the home loan market, offering mortgages linked to endowment and pension policies. There has been a tendency for the major life companies to concentrate their mortgage lending in the commercial and industrial market. However, they are still in a position to offer an attractive and economical combination of life/pension policy and mortgage loans. For instance, fixed interest loans are available from insurance companies which are not normally offered by banks or building societies. Again, as part of the re-structuring of the whole financial services industry, many large companies are offering package deals linked to specific banks. This type of deal provides an opportunity for small or overseas banks to get into the high street mortgage market. It would be well worth while thinking along these lines, particularly if you have some existing policies. The best method of shopping around is to operate through an insurance/pension broker, who can survey the market currently for you and come up with recommendations for the best deal.

The local authority

Another routine alternative source of finance for your property purchase is your local authority. In any event, if you are purchasing a council house, the local authority are under statutory obligation to offer you a mortgage, although, of course, you do not have to accept it from them if you can find a better deal. In addition, either from their own resources or by special links with a particular building society, local authorities are always in a position to offer mortgages – especially in difficult cases such as, say, single parents. It has to be said that, currently, the financial pressures on most local authorities make it unlikely that they will be either very willing or very competitive lenders. However, it is worthwhile giving them a try, particularly if you are having problems obtaining a mortgage elsewhere and have, in your view, a genuine social need for housing. Certainly they are very susceptible where children are involved and also where the only alternative is to seek council house accommodation. If you can demonstrate that you can service a mortgage, if private rented accommodation is very scarce in your area, if you have children and your only alternative housing is likely to be a council house, then you are in with a chance.

Vendor mortgages

A vendor mortgage is quite simply created by the person from whom you are buying your home leaving all or part of the sale price outstanding as a loan. On the face of it, this may seem a remote possibility, but a combination of circumstances could come your way which would make the whole concept feasible. Let us look at two examples:

◆ Perhaps you have known the vendor for many years. He and his wife are fairly elderly and their large garden has become too much for them. Planning indicates that they would be prepared for you to build a bungalow on the land. While your bank or building society may be prepared to advance you the money to build the bungalow, they may not be prepared to lend you sufficient to include the purchase of the land. In this instance, perhaps the vendor might be prepared to give you a ten year loan at, say, 8% per annum interest, which you start repaying in four years' time, when the main costs of your building have been completed. Maybe this is rather a euphemistic example, but from the elderly couple's point of view, they are immediately receiving an income from their land they would not otherwise have, the satisfaction of knowing they are giving someone they like a helping hand and ensuring they have the right type of neighbour.

◆ Perhaps a land owner has a tumble-down cottage – little more than a heap of rubble. A couple wishing to buy it can persuade their building society to lend them, say, 50% of the price being asked but no more, because basically the house is uninhabitable. The land owner would know that this is the kind of reaction that everyone will meet who wishes to borrow money against the property. He can either take the view that he will wait until somebody comes up with cash to spend or he could finance a couple whom he instinctively likes and trusts by granting them time to pay, by way of a second mortgage.

Finance companies

You would not go to a finance company for the normal purchase of bricks and mortar – this is not their business. However, for boats, caravans or mobile homes they are well worth considering. You might also consider them for alterations, extensions, a conservatory, a garage or perhaps central heating. Finance companies are not cheap and are fairly short term, but for the type of expenditure described, they sometimes can be competitive with banks and building societies, who do tend to charge higher interest rates for add-on loans.

Friends and family

Touching friends or family for a loan, in most circumstances, is not a clever idea. However, borrowing money to set up a home is somewhat different. A true friend or family member will want to help if he or she possibly can, and unlike a loan to keep you solvent, a loan to purchase a house or flat is a relatively safe investment from your family or friend's point of view. The degree of formality attached to it depends on how well you know the person concerned. Your parents might take the view that they will lend you a few thousand pounds now and leave you a little less in their will, while a friend might ask for the security of a second charge on the property.

Grants available from local authorities

To receive an outright gift of money, as opposed to having to take out a loan and repay it, plus interest, has to be very attractive. Let us look at the various types of grants which are available through the local authority network.

There are four basic grants available to the public – *intermediate grants, improvement grants, special grants* and *repair grants*. Let us look at each of these in turn:

Intermediate grants

Intermediate grants are mandatory – if you qualify, the local authority have to give you a grant. Essentially, intermediate grants are available towards the costs of installing missing amenities – such as an inside WC, hot and/or cold water, hand basin, bath or shower – in other words an intermediate grant is mostly available for missing items of sanitation. An important point – there is no rateable value limitation so far as intermediate grants are concerned. If you are missing the amenities then you are entitled to receive a grant to have them installed.

Improvement grants

Improvement grants are available to bring an old property up to a reasonable standard

The eligible expense limits (per dwelling provided) for these grants are:

	In Greater London £	Elsewhere £
For conversions of houses of three storeys or more:		
priority cases	16,000	11,800
non-priority cases	10,400	7,700
Other conversions:		
priority cases	13,800	10,200
non-priority cases	9,000	6,600

Higher limits apply to buildings which are listed as being of special architectural or historical interest.

of habitation. Improvement grants are discretionary and particularly today, when local authority money is scarce, it is not always easy to obtain an improvement grant. The property must have been built before 1961 to qualify, but other than that, the rules are extremely vague and much will depend on where you are and what other claims there are for the money. To qualify for an improvement grant, the rateable value of your house must be no more than £400 in Greater London or £225 elsewhere. It is unlikely that you will obtain a grant for more than half the cost of the total work taking place though, in some cases, where there is substantial structural work involved, you might receive up to 75%. Both tenant and landlord can apply for improvement grants – you do not have to be a home owner *and* occupier but there are some rules and regulations with regard to tenancy agreements which could preclude you from being eligible. Improvement grants are not intended to pander to the needs of your family. In other words, if you have four children and only three bedrooms, that is your hard luck. Improvement grants are more about items such as drainage, wiring, insulation, structural repair and basic standard amenities. An improvement grant, as the name suggests, is all about improving the standard of a property and bringing it up to an acceptable level.

Special grants

Special grants are not available to tenants. Essentially they are for improvements to houses in multiple occupancy, where there is no immediate prospect of conversion. Grants are commonly made to hostels or hotels and very often relate to improving fire escapes, as well as providing standard amenities. Special grants are discretionary and here again much depends on how much money your local council has available.

Repair grants

Repair grants are for houses built before 1919, needing substantial repair which must include structural work, as well as routine maintenance. In order to be eligible, the council must be satisfied that after the work has been carrried out, the house or flat will be in a state of reasonable repair and suitable for occupation. As with improvement grants, you will not qualify unless the rateable value of your home is less than £400 in Greater London or £225 elsewhere. The only exception to this is that if you live in a housing action area or a general improvement area, then there is no rateable value limitation.

If your house is in serious disrepair, it could be that the council serve you with a Repairs Notice, in which case they are under an obligation to offer you a grant at the maximum rate for your particular case. The normal total amount of eligible expenses for a repairs grant is £6,600 in Greater London and £4,800 elsewhere. However, if your building is of special architectural or historical interest, you may receive more – we will discuss this in more detail in the next section.

For further information on all these grants you would do well to acquire a helpful little booklet entitled *Home Improvement Grants – A Guide For Home Owners, Landlords And Tenants*. It is available from the HMSO or from your local authority.

Do bear in mind that if you sell your property shortly after receiving a grant you may have to repay all or part of it. Check this with your local authority at the time the grant is awarded.

Special help for the disabled

Over and above the normal grants system, there are certain special facilities aimed at helping people with disabilities, and normally such people are given priority when applying for assistance. Generally speaking, a grant will only be given if an occupational therapist confirms additional work is required to make a house suitable for a disabled person. This means that any grant application will involve the social services department and the environmental health department. These are the main areas of help available:

◆ Mandatory intermediate grants have an additional application for disabled people in that extra standard amenities will be covered by a grant if the existing amenities cannot be reached by the disabled occupant.

◆ Improvement grants are available to adapt a house or flat for a disabled person and where a disability is involved, the rateable value is no longer a limitation on being eligible for a grant. Improvement grants could involve putting in a downstairs bathroom, installing a stair lift and providing ramps for wheelchairs. Electrical work could also be included – such as putting switches and sockets at appropriate levels.

◆ Insulation grants. Elderly people, receiving supplementary benefit or housing benefit, can claim up to 90% of the cost of materials up to a maximum of £95 to have lofts insulated and hot water tanks and pipes lagged.

Generally speaking, it is the responsibility of the DHSS to give every assistance to the elderly or disabled person where it is clear they need their house or flat adapted to their use. This assistance should take the form both of assessing what work is needed and providing financial assistance where appropriate. If you are drawing social security then you will find that grants are readily available. If you have your own income or savings, it will be more of a struggle to obtain grants but some are still available, particularly where basic amenities are involved. For further information on help available, we would suggest you contact –

Age Concern,
Bernard Sunley Buildings,
60 Pitcairn Road,
Mitcham,
Surrey, CR4 3LL.

Telephone 01-640 5431

who will be able to give you facts on the grants which are available – not only for elderly people but also for people with disabilities.

Grants available for special property

English Heritage grants

English Heritage is now the body responsible for awarding grants for the structural repair of buildings of outstanding architectural or historical interest, or to houses which have been designated as being within a conservation area. Just because your house may be listed, it does not qualify you automatically for a grant from English Heritage, but of course it does help. Without doubt, it is far more difficult to obtain a grant from English Heritage than it is from your local authority, but if your building is deemed as really outstanding and you are able to demonstrate that you cannot undertake the necessary repairs from your own resources, then you may be lucky. Let us look at what help is available:

Ancient monuments

An ancient monument may be an archaeological site, buried or in evidence, or any type of ruin – a castle, a manor house, a monastery . . . Ancient monuments are not lived in, they are the remains of a former age and, as such, are very susceptible to the wear and tear caused by the passage of time. For this reason grants are sometimes available to protect and restore ancient monuments against the ravages of erosion. As far as English Heritage is concerned, the standard rate of grant is 40% but it could be higher in very special cases. Local authority grants are also available for ancient monuments but the total amount they will contribute is only 25%. For further information contact –

English Heritage,
Ancient Monuments Division,
Fortress House,
23 Savile Row,
London, W1X 2HE.

Telephone 01-734 6010, extension 414

Historic buildings

The vast majority of important historic buildings in this country are listed. There are three grades of listing – 1, 2* and 2. Of the total number of listed buildings most are grade 2, for grades 1 and 2* tend to be attributed only to buildings of national importance. It is these buildings – grade 1 and grade 2* – which generally attract grants, so it would not be wise to become over-excited about the possibility of a grant if your building is listed grade 2. As with ancient monuments, the standard rate of grant is 40% but a higher rate might be offered in special circumstances. Grants are only available to help with major repairs which are beyond the owner's means, and normally repairs of less than £10,000 in total would not be considered. In certain

alterations and conversions are not eligible. There are two types of conservation area grant – there is what is known as the *Town Scheme Grant*, which is made through the local authority, generally at the rate of 40% of costs. You need to check with your local authority if you are eligible for the Town Scheme Grant. The other type of grant is a *Section 10 Grant*, payable direct by English Heritage, but only 25% of the costs are available. For further information contact English Heritage, at the same address, but the telephone number is – 01-734 6010, extension 861.

Countryside conservation grants

These are available through your local district council and are aimed at land owners, farmers and smallholders. Grants up to 50% of the total approved cost are available, for such schemes as tree re-planting, woodland management and pond restoration. To be eligible for such a grant you must be able to demonstrate that the work would be of benefit to the public in a visual sense – i.e. you need to be close to a public right of way. Grants are not available for schemes of less than £50 in total, nor for areas of less than .25 hectares. Schemes greater than 30 metres wide and 100 metres long could be eligible for Forestry Commission grants if the species of tree is suitable. Contact your local district council for further information.

General notes on grants

In the case of English Heritage in particular, you are unlikely to obtain a grant shortly after the purchase of a property because they will take the view that you should have been aware of the problems with the property before you acquired it. This attitude does not apply to the local authority but, nonetheless, it would be extremely unwise to go ahead with the purchase of any property on the assumption that you will be eligible for a grant. Either check out the position very carefully in detail before going ahead with your purchase or press ahead on the assumption that it would be nice if you obtained a grant but it is not an essential part of your financial thinking.

circumstances the contents of a historic building might be eligible for grants – such as tapestries, sculptures and murals. For further information contact English Heritage, at the same address, but the telephone number is 01-734 6010, extension 882.

Conservation areas

There are over 6,000 conservation areas throughout England, mostly in the centre of historic towns. If your house is in such a locality, it is possible that you might be eligible for a grant if the work that needs doing is associated with the structure and appearance of the building. This could include re-roofing, treatment for dry rot, repairs to brickwork, windows or doors . . . However, routine maintenance,

Income tax

Buying and selling houses, renting flats, building extensions, investing in holiday homes, moving into sheltered accommodation – for most of us these kinds of decisions are dependent upon, and largely influenced by, our income – how much we are earning, how much we might be earning in a few years' time, how much we can afford now, how much we can afford in the future.

Clearly, income tax has a major impact on earnings and for this reason it is sensible to have some understanding of the tax system. An appreciation of the tax treatment applied to different aspects of the whole property scene is bound to assist you when it comes to making the basic decisions of where you are going to live at the various stages in your life.

Suppose we take a simple example:

Your monthly salary is		£1,200
From which you pay:		
National insurance	£108	
Income tax	£245	
Living expenses		
(fares, rent, food,		
clothes)	£700	£1,053
Free for luxuries		£147

This same example could be expressed another way:

Your monthly salary is		£1,200
National Insurance	£108	
Living expenses	£700	£808
Available for income tax		
and luxuries		£392

Looking at the second example, you will suddenly see that expressed in this way, income tax is taking over 60% of your available income. You may perhaps think this is a slightly unfair or unrealistic example but it is not dissimilar to how many people's income position looks. Now let us assume that of the £700 a month of living expenses, £400 is attributable to the rent you are paying, which is a realistic figure. Supposing instead of spending the £400 on rent, you spent £400 a month, gross, on the mortgage payment on a £30,000 loan. Because the interest content of your mortgage payment is subject to tax relief at source, your income tax will come down by £63 per month, increasing your spending money by over 40%. Quite apart from any other consideration, the advantages in a tax sense of paying off a mortgage, rather than renting, are very clear for all to see.

The basics

Let us look at the basic income tax structure. Everyone in this country is entitled to receive a level of income without having to pay any income tax. This tax free income is secured by the granting of personal allowances of one sort or another. This means that the first few thousand pounds we earn are exempt from any tax deduction. Income, of course, does not simply relate to wages. Income is the term used to describe virtually every form of money coming in – whether it is interest on savings deposited in a bank, a pension, unemployment benefit, dividend or investment earnings. All this, therefore, is totalled up and classified as income, and once the total exceeds your personal allowance and any further allowable costs, then it is subject to income tax.

For easy reference, the scale of personal allowances for 1988/89 is as follows:

Single person's allowance or wife's earnings allowance	= £2,605
Married person's allowance	= £4,095
Additional allowance for single parent families or widows	= £1,490
Age allowance (where either spouse is over 65)	
– single persons	= £3,180
– married couples	= £5,035
Age allowance (where either spouse is over 80)	
– single persons	= £3,310
– married couples	= £5,205

The age allowance is available if either spouse is over retirement age but it is an *alternative* to the normal personal allowance, not in addition to it.

In addition to personal allowances, a

number of other costs can be deducted from your gross income, to arrive at taxable income. The main allowances are as follows:

◆ Interest on mortgage or loans used to purchase your only or main residence. Tax relief is available on loans up to £30,000.

◆ Interest on mortgages or loans used to purchase or improve property that is available for letting throughout the year and is actually let for at least twenty-six weeks each year.

◆ Business expansion scheme investments of up to £40,000 each year.

◆ Premiums paid to approved pension schemes or for personal pension policies.

◆ Expenses necessary for you to carry out your work, such as travel and hotel costs.

◆ Professional fees and subscriptions linked to your work.

◆ If you run a business and are a sole trader or in partnership – all business overheads and expenses.

Having taken into account all the allowances, the rates of income tax payable on taxable income for 1988/89 are as follows:

◆ Basic rate on the first £19,300   25%
◆ Top rate on income over £19,300   40%

Tax relief on mortgage interest

Up until 1st August 1988, unmarried couples could make a joint purchase and each claim tax relief on a loan of up to £30,000. On new loans taken out from that date, relief is restricted to £30,000 per property. This change of ruling therefore has sorted out the anomalous situation where it was more tax effective to live together than to be married.

Relief is normally given under MIRAS (Mortgage Income Relief At Source). This means that if you have a £40,000 mortgage, at 10% per annum, you will pay net interest of £3,250 – i.e. £4,000 gross, less 25% tax relief on £3,000. Loans taken out before 1st August, 1988 will continue to be eligible for tax relief under the previous regulations, but if a couple subsequently marry, the

relief will then be restricted to £30,000.

Elderly people can benefit from tax relief on mortgage interest on borrowings up to £30,000 if they raise money on the security of their home to purchase a retirement annuity. Age, and therefore life expectancy, is a critical factor in calculating the benefits from this sort of transaction, but it can represent a useful addition to net income for the elderly – taking advantage of the value inherent in the home, without having to sell or move.

Pension policies

There are Inland Revenue restrictions on the amount of pension premiums allowable for tax. These restrictions limit the allowable premiums to a certain percentage of your income. If you are eligible to make your own personal pension arrangements, you can use the pension policy as a means of repaying your mortgage. The repayment in the form of pension payments is allowable for tax purposes by being offset against your income.

Business expenses

If you occupy part of your house for business purposes, you can claim part of the running costs as business expenses and thus offset them against your trading income.

Home improvements

One important change in the 1988 Budget is that mortgage interest relief is now restricted to loans taken out to purchase property. Interest on additional mortgages for improvements or extensions, are not now allowable even if you have not taken full advantage of the £30,000 relief available. This does not affect improvement loans actually in existence at 6th April, 1988.

What is not clear at the time of writing is how this will affect the purchase of a property where major renovation is planned. The Budget implies that there will be no relief on anything except the initial mortgage.

Capital gains tax

The 1988 Finance Act introduced some fundamental changes in the structure of capital gains tax (CGT) and has gone a long way towards removing the previous very clear distinction for tax purposes, between income and capital gain. Nevertheless, the longstanding freedom from CGT enjoyed by the home owner has been maintained.

As we have previously pointed out, the availability of finance and the income tax relief provided on at least part of the interest incurred, has enabled home ownership to develop. Inflation, coupled with these other factors, has ensured that the average home owner is now sitting on an appreciating capital asset for a comparatively low cost. What ensures that the value continues to be safeguarded is the lack of any form of taxation on any gains made.

In order to understand its effect, or lack of effect, on property, it is necessary to understand how CGT works. Capital gains are now taxable together with income each year. This means that CGT is payable at 25% or 40% depending upon the combined level of income and capital gain (see page 158 for income tax rates). Taxable gains may arise as a result of a disposal of any of your assets – including gifts – except for quite specific exempted items. The items which are exempt from CGT are as follows:

◆ The disposal of your only or main residence.
◆ Transfers between husband and wife.
◆ Sale of Government stocks and certain corporate fixed interest stocks.
◆ Disposal arising from death.
◆ Personal belongings worth £3,000 or less at the date of disposal, or having a useful life of less than 50 years when you acquired them.
◆ Gifts to charity.

In calculating capital gain, the element attributable to the effect of inflation is disregarded.

In addition to these exemptions, there is no CGT levied on the first £5,000 of capital gain in any one year. However this exemption cannot be carried forward. This means that if you made no profit on any disposal of assets last year, you cannot employ the unused exemption this year. This ruling does not apply to losses, for losses can be carried forward. If you sold some shares last year that raised £2,000 less than you paid for them, you can deduct that £2,000 of loss from any subsequent gain at any time in the future.

Do be careful about CGT if you are shortly getting married. In the year of marriage, both husband and wife are treated separately for CGT purposes, and are entitled to their full £5,000 CGT exemption *each*. In the year of marriage *only*, if they both own a home they can sell it and enjoy CGT exemption, which is obviously a tremendous advantage. Where CGT losses are brought forward, neither husband nor wife can offset these losses against each other's gains in the actual year of marriage, only against their own gains. Most important of all for couples contemplating marriage is to *Beware The 6th April*. If you marry on that date, which is the first day of the tax year, you will be treated as having been married the whole of the fiscal year, so that CGT exemption will not be available. So if you are determined on an early April wedding, make absolutely sure it is the 7th, 8th, 9th, 10th – anything but the 6th!

The 1988 Finance Act has introduced a new basis for the calculation of capital gains, so that only gains arising in the period since 1st April 1982 will now be taxable. There are some complex transition arrangements to cover this change in the rules, and if you are uncertain about your position, it would be sensible to seek the advice of your solicitor or accountant.

A note for the future

With the introduction of independent taxation, it is intended that from the 6th April 1990, a husband and wife should be treated as single persons so far as capital gains tax is concerned.

Specific points of importance on CGT and property

◆ Do bear in mind that the official use of part of your home for business makes that portion of your home no longer exempt from CGT. This means that if you set up offices in a couple of rooms of your house and for tax purposes claim all expenses you incur against the business – even perhaps charging the business a rental – the tax effectiveness of such a procedure is very questionable. Yes, you may be able to offset a few household expenses against your income but as and when you come to sell your home, the capital gain on the value of those rooms you have set aside for your business will be subject to CGT. In most instances, the CGT implications are likely to be far higher than the possible offsetting of a few expenses. For this reason, if it is not necessary for you to go 'official' so far as your business activities are concerned, so much the better.

◆ Only your sole or main residence is free from CGT. This means that all holiday homes and city pads – indeed any form of second home – will be clobbered for CGT as and when you come to sell it. However, the good news is that for those who have had a second home for many years, the 1988 Finance Act is a blessing as it takes out all pre-1982 gains from the CGT net.

For example, if you are retiring to your second home the position is this – you sell your main residence and it is completely free of CGT implication. You then move into your holiday home which you may have acquired some years ago. From the moment that holiday home becomes your main residence, any gain in value it achieves will be free from CGT. This means, therefore, that under the new ruling, if you bought a holiday home in 1970, for the express purpose of retiring to it one day, the gain made between 1970 and 1982 will be free from CGT implication. If you then moved into it as your main residence in 1988, the period of gain between 1982 and 1988 would be subject to CGT as and when you come to sell the property. However the gain from 1988 onwards would not be subject to tax.

Inheritance Tax

When considering your future and the future of your children, inevitably it is necessary to consider the question of inheritance tax. Since property tends to be most people's most valuable asset, it is important to thoroughly understand inheritance tax when planning your future living arrangements.

Inheritance tax was introduced in the 1986 Budget, to take the place of capital transfer tax. No inheritance tax is charged on an estate where the total value is less than £110,000. On the face of it, therefore, it appears that for many people this tax is simply not relevant. However, with the continuing spiral in house prices, it is relatively easy to see how an estate can be worth more than this figure – in which case it will attract inheritance tax.

Inheritance tax is chargeable at 40% on assets transferred, at death, and on gifts made within three years of death. Gifts made to individuals between three and seven years prior to death will suffer tax based on the value of the gift at the date it was given, but will be subject to a tapering percentage relief – more details of this in a moment. The affect of this is that lifetime gifts made to individuals more than seven years prior to the death of the person making that gift, will be free from inheritance tax, although of course they may be subject to capital gains tax. Where capital gains tax has been paid on a gift made within seven years prior to death, it does not safeguard the estate from having to pay inheritance tax as well. This fact alone does highlight the need to be very careful indeed in the transfer of assets as gifts.

The exemption of lifetime gifts to individuals can also be applied to the setting up of specific types of trust funds, for the exclusive benefit of, say, a child or perhaps a disabled member of the family. However, in order to attract tax exemption, it is imperative that the donor cannot benefit in any way from the trust.

Certain transfers on death, or made prior to death, are exempt from inheritance tax as follows:

◆ All transfers made between husband and wife.
◆ The first £3,000 of chargeable transfers made in the fiscal year.
◆ Outright gifts of up to £250 to any one person in a year of assessment.
◆ The amount by which the preceding financial year's gifts fell short of the permissible limit of £3,000.
◆ Normal expenditure out of income. The transfer must be normal or regular and leave the transferor with sufficient income, after tax, to maintain his or her usual standard of living.
◆ Gifts made in consideration of marriage to either of the parties of the marriage up to a limit of £5,000 from parents, £2,500 from grandparents and £1,000 from any other person.
◆ Transfers in the course of a trade, providing the transfer is an allowable deduction for tax purposes.
◆ Certain gifts to charity.
◆ Gifts to political parties.
◆ Gifts for national purposes to specific national institutions.
◆ Gifts for public benefit authorized by the Treasury.
◆ All assets that pass on the death of a person on active service.
◆ Death benefits payable to dependants under retirement annuity schemes and occupational pension schemes.

Relief from the full impact of inheritance tax is given on both lifetime and death transfers of business assets. Provided that the asset has been owned for at least two years before transfer, the value transferred will be reduced as follows:

◆ By 50% for an interest in an unincorporated business or partnership or a substantial (over 25%) interest of shares in an unquoted trading company.

◆ By 30% for the minority interest (not more than 25%) in an unquoted company.
◆ By 30% for land, building, machinery or plant in a partnership, in a controlled company or in a settlement.

Similar relief is normally available for agricultural property and forestry but the position is complex and each case needs to be considered in isolation. Certain business assets do not qualify for relief. These include:

◆ Investment companies or property dealing companies.
◆ Assets not wholly or mainly for the business.
◆ Shares in a company in liquidation.
◆ Assets where a binding contract for sale is in force at the date of transfer.

If exempt assets are owned by a company, relief given on transfer of its shares may be restricted.

From March 1988, the rates of inheritance tax for the value of an estate were simplified as follows:

On the first £110,000	nil
Over £110,000	40%

The relief applied to lifetime gifts is as follows:

Up to three years prior to death	nil
Three to four years prior to death	20%
Four to five years prior to death	40%
Five to six years prior to death	60%
Six or seven years prior to death	80%
Over seven years	100%

Gifts to trusts, other than the two already mentioned concerning children and disabled people, and also gifts involving companies, are subject to inheritance tax. These will be subject to tax at 50% of the full scale rates whenever they are made and then if the gift is made by an individual, it will be brought back into the estate on subsequent death and the tax re-computed.

As with any of the tax implications discussed in this book – but particularly in the case of inheritance tax – do seek the advice of your solicitor or accountant.

Other taxes which affect the property owner

The other taxes which affect the property owner are as follows:

VAT

It is prudent to work on the assumption that anything you buy for your home or spend on your home, is subject to VAT at 15%. However, there are some exceptions:

◆ The supplies for the construction of a new building are zero rated. This does not include conversion, reconstruction or enlargement of an existing building – it is purely for brand new building.

◆ Work on a listed building is zero rated, if you have obtained listed building consent for that work.

◆ Equipment for the handicapped in the home is zero rated, for such items as a bath, lavatory, lift, alarm system – in other words any specialist item which needs to be installed.

◆ Mobile homes and houseboats are zero rated.

◆ Building an additional flat or dwelling unit on to your existing house will be subject to VAT unless the new building is an entirely separate dwelling, either in the form of a flat or semi-detached house. By *separate dwelling* this means there must be no inter-connecting doors. If this is the case then it would be zero-rated. This is a particularly important point if you are thinking of building a granny flat for a very independently-minded granny!

◆ If you entirely demolish a house, leaving only the site and then rebuild from scratch, this will qualify for zero rating.

General rates

Rates are a tax, a local government property tax, which are levied to cover a whole range of local services, from education to road maintenance, to refuse collection. Every owner is responsible for the tax levied on his property and the only way to avoid paying rates is to let the property and pass responsibility for the rates on to the

tenant. Every person responsible for rates must pay them or run the risk of a fine or even imprisonment. Rates are calculated by the local council *fixing a rate* each year and this rate is then applied to the rateable value of your home. Say, for example, that your rateable value is £400 and that the rate fixed for the current year is £2.75. This means that you would simply multiply 400 × 2.75, so the actual rates payable for the year would be £1,100.

Clearly, the rateable value of any house you own or consider owning, is very important. In the case of property which has not been revalued for some years, the rateable value may well be out of date and comparatively low. Obviously, the longer that situation lasts the better. However, you do have to bear in mind that if at any stage you are planning an extension or major alteration, which involves planning permission and/or building regulations approval, the ultimate

with you are either minors, disabled or elderly, then this will accordingly increase your rate rebate. A rebate is part of what is known as *housing benefit*. It is paid by the local authority in the form of a reduced or nil rates demand.

Poll tax/community charge

Currently, the charge levied under the title of general rates is wholly a charge assessed on the property, the amount of that charge being based on the value of the property. It is proposed that instead of domestic general rates, a poll tax or community charge as it is to be known, should be introduced which will be wholly based on people, irrespective of the type of property in which they live. This poll tax will clearly be a good thing for people living in large, valuable houses but not so good for, say, a young couple struggling on a low income in a tiny flat.

Water charges

Water charges are another tax, entirely separate from general rates. Water charges are paid to your local water authority and cover the supply of water and sewage/drainage services. In some instances, water rates are not mandatory – you may have your own spring in the garden or a bore hole. You may possibly have a cesspool or septic tank instead of being on main drainage, in which case the costs involved will be paying a contractor to empty the tank for you every so often. If you have your own supply of water then the local authority will come and test it from time to time, to see that it is maintaining a standard which is suitable for human consumption.

spin-off will be that the district valuer will come and inspect the property with a view to re-assessing the rateable value in the light of the improvememts. It is at this stage that the true rating position will catch up with you.

Paying the rates is clearly a big item in any household budget and almost all local authorities are happy for you to pay quarterly or even monthly if you find this easier to cope with in a cash flow sense.

Rate rebates

You may well be entitled to rebate of rates if your income is very low and/or you are drawing supplementary benefit. Rebate is calculated on three basic issues – your income, the amount of your rates and the number of people living in your house. If the people living in your house are not dependent upon you then this will reduce the amount of your rebate. If the people living

Stamp duty

Stamp duty is the tax you pay when you buy a property for more than £30,000. Stamp duty is 1% on value and no allowance is made on the first £30,000 if the property you buy costs more than this amount. In other words if you buy a house for £32,000, you are not taxed on the £2,000 – you pay 1% of the £32,000.

Insurance brokers

Almost certainly, the most valuable asset you will own in your life will be your home and its contents. Insurance is something we like to brush under the carpet – a necessary evil to which we pay as little attention as possible. Yet accidents do happen, and whether they take the form of a burst pipe or a major theft, they are likely to have one thing in common – the damage and loss sustained is likely to be far more costly than you would ever have envisaged. We have a fairly modest home, containing precious few items of any real value – certainly no family heirlooms – yet we went through the exercise recently of adding up the total value of our home and its contents and the figure we reached was absolutely staggering. This, of course, was based on replacement value, and this is how you must always think – not the value of the goods at the time you bought them.

Insurance of your house or flat is not only about the tangible aspects of your home. There are other considerations, like what happens if the main family breadwinner loses his job, is seriously injured or dies. There is public liability insurance to consider, insurance against the enforcement of covenants or, in some instances, insurance to protect title where there is any uncertainty as to the validity of the deeds. Any job worth doing is worth doing well and insuring your house and home deserves your full attention.

If you have a mortgage with a building society or a bank, they will insist that you have insurance cover in order to protect their loan. In the mortgage documentation a specific insurance company may well be quoted, and unless you look carefully you are given the impression that you must insure your home with this particular company. This is not the case. In order to qualify for a loan you must be insured to an agreed sum, but no bank or building society can force you to insure with a particular company. With the proviso that the insurance company must be acceptable to the lender, you are free to shop around, and we would strongly recommend that you should do so, but rather than approach insurance companies direct, you should find yourself a good insurance broker.

The services of an insurance broker, so far as you are concerned, are entirely free since the broker receives a commission from whichever insurance company provides you with the necessary cover. A broker is not employed by any one insurance company, which means that he or she is free to go around the market. The cover obtained for you is unlikely to cost any more than you would pay if you approached an insurance company direct – indeed sometimes even less since the insurance broker has the experience and skill to do some interesting deals on your behalf. If you have never used an insurance broker before you may find that after an initial examination of your insurance requirements, he may be able to save you a considerable amount of money – certainly this is our experience.

In order to find a good broker, as with all professional people, it is best to seek personal recommendation. Your bank manager should be able to help you or your solicitor, or accountant if you have one. Unless you have a great deal of property, or wish your broker to handle your business affairs as well as your personal ones, look for a small broking firm or even an individual operating alone. The larger companies tend to be a little impersonal. For anyone who has tried to deal with an insurance company direct, has been passed round endless different extensions and given impersonal and often misleading advice, an insurance broker is like a breath of fresh air. Insurance can be made to measure – of course there are standard policies, but yours may not be a standard situation and even if it is, you want the best deal going.

Mortgages and insurance

Financing the purchase of your house or flat is something we have dealt with in detail under the finance section of this book. However, it is worth making the point here that besides a straightforward repayment mortgage, you can obtain a mortgage through an insurance company in the form

Some months ago my father died, and in trying to sort out his affairs, I discovered, to my horror, that the house he and my mother had been living in appeared not to be insured. I rang their insurance company, who confirmed that there was no current policy running. I was absolutely furious – my father was well into his eighties and had been dealing with this company for over fifty years. The company in question knew my parents were living at the same address for they were also insuring their car, yet such was the impersonal nature of their service that when my father failed to renew his premium, because of declining health, they did not even query the reason why. For nine months my parents lived in a house which was uninsured. If it had been the subject of a fire, their home and everything they owned would have been lost and they would have had absolutely no means of replacing it. This sort of situation would not have happened had they employed an insurance broker. Failure to renew would have had him ringing up, reminding them of the lapse and ensuring things would be put right.

of an endowment or pension mortgage. The different types of mortgage being offered, by a variety of companies, is confusing to say the least, but here again an insurance broker can shop around on your behalf. With a thorough understanding of the mortgage field, with no axe to grind other than acting in your best interests, his advice and help could prove invaluable.

Finally a word of warning on brokers. As with every industry, there is inevitably the odd dud in the pack. There are two professional insurance bodies who can provide you with a list of members if you are unable to make contact with a broker through personal recommendation. They are as follows:

British Insurance Brokers Association,
BIBA House,
14 Bevis Marks,
London EC3A 7NT.

Telephone: 01-623 9043

Corporation of Insurance and Financial Advisers,
6/7 Leapale Road,
Guildford,
Surrey GU1 4JX.

Telephone: 0483 39121

Insurance of buildings

When insuring your property, these are the main risks which you can and must cover:

◆ Fire, aircraft, explosions
◆ Special perils – storm, tempest, flood, burst pipes, earthquakes, impact, riots, strikes, civil commotion, malicious damage.

The vital point to bear in mind when considering your buildings insurance is to recognize that what you are insuring against is not the value of the property in the open market, nor the amount of your purchase, but what it would actually cost you to replace it. Supposing, for example, you purchased a house on a newly built estate. The builder's costings would have been based on the fact that he was building, say, twenty houses. This means that his building materials would have been bought in bulk and his workforce well utilized, because they would have been able to move freely from house to house. Contrast this with asking a local builder to re-build your house in the event of a major fire. Inevitably the costs would be much higher because it would be for a one-off job. Yet again, look at an old house partially destroyed by fire – think of the costs involved in matching period bricks and timbers. Bear in mind also the architect's fees, the delays, the disturbance . . . all adding to the cost. All these are what you should and must consider when it comes to insuring your building.

Buildings and mortgages

As mentioned in the previous section, if you have borrowed money to buy your house, you will have no alternative but to take out an insurance policy to protect the building because this will be a requirement of the lender. It is also clearly a requirement of you, the borrower, as well, for if your asset goes up in smoke, you need to have the means to repay your loan.

Flats

If you are buying a flat, you may well find that there is an overall insurance policy to cover the building as a whole, to which you must contribute. This policy will have been set up by the freeholder or head leaseholder or by the tenants' association, There will be little or nothing you can do to alter this policy if you do not agree with it, but this does not mean you should be complacent about it. The cover may be adequate for your requirements or it may not, in which case you may find it necessary to take out some top-up insurance to strengthen you security. An example of this could be if you work from home. Under the terms of your flat lease it may be acceptable for you to run your computer consultancy business from home, but what about insurance? If one of your computer terminals blows up and as a result the whole property burns down, the insurance company may well try to wriggle out of part of the claim if they have not been informed of your business activities.

INSURANCE SHOW HOUSE

annually but you can arrange for this to be paid quarterly or even monthly, if it suits your budget better. Each year your cover will be updated, since most buildings insurance policies are index linked, which means they rise automatically with the retail price index.

What do you get for your money?

We listed at the beginning of this section the main risks which are covered by a building insurance policy. What is not normally covered is anything which may be caused by lack of maintenance – i.e. damage by wet or dry rot, say. Genuine storm damage, as a result of excessive high winds, would be covered, so if your chimney falls through the roof and ends up in the downstairs bathroom, then you can be confident that your insurance company will meet the claim. However, if on a brilliant sunny afternoon, with not a breath of wind nor cloud in the sky, your chimney decides to do the same trick, you may well have your insurance company up in arms, saying this is a maintenance problem, not accidental damage. Do check the position with regard to fences and gates. When storms blew down our fences, we discovered they were not covered by our buildings insurance and this is not unusual. Particularly if you have a substantial amount of fencing, this could prove very expensive to replace, whereas an additional premium to cover it for insurance purposes is not expensive. A point worth remembering is that practically any risk *can* be covered – even though it may be excluded by the standard policy wording, your policy can be extended to cover special risks, or a separate policy can be taken out. Insurance against damage by dry rot or wet rot is, perhaps, a good example.

WARNING. Do remember that when buying a property, your responsibility to insure begins the moment you exchange contracts – not from the date of completion. If you have a mortgage, the lender should ensure that this is not forgotten, but if you are buying the property without a loan this is an easy point to overlook.

Tenants' cover

If you are leasing a house or a flat, much of what we have highlighted under *Flats* above applies to you. When renting a premises, either the landlord will have his own insurance cover – in which case he is likely to charge you for an appropriate portion of it – or, under the terms of the lease, you will be obliged to insure against specific perils. Either way, do not be influenced by the minimum requirements of your landlord/tenant relationship. Remember that the landlord purely will be looking at the buildings insurance from his point of view. If you feel the landlord's policy is inadequate then you will have to organize some top-up insurance yourself.

Costs

At today's rates, a typical buildings premium is going to be somewhere between £2.00–£3.00 per £1,000 insured, per annum. The premium is normally paid

Insurance of contents

There are two ways of insuring contents – *indemnity cover* and *replacement as new cover*.

◆ *Indemnity cover* provides insurance on the original value of the item, less depreciation.

◆ *Replacement as new cover* is as it suggests – the insurance company will pay you whatever amount is necessary to replace the item damaged or stolen.

Clearly, replacement as new is more expensive, but it is becoming the normal basis on which contents are covered, and we would recommend it – so that you don't find yourself hopelessly under-insured when it comes to a claim.

There is no obligation upon you to insure the contents of your home. Unlike buildings insurance, your mortgage company has no vested interest in your contents. However, you would be very foolish indeed not to cover your contents. While you may feel that most of the items you own are of little value, one is apt to forget that they have been collected over a number of years and the costs therefore have been spread. Try working out what it would cost you to re-equip your home today. The resultant figure will horrify you.

Contents insurance covers damage and theft. Take the example which we used in the previous section on buildings maintenance. Let us consider what happens if your chimney collapses and falls through the roof into the house below. Your buildings insurance will certainly cover the rebuilding of the chimney, repair of the roof and the making good of the walls and ceilings internally. However, what about the carpets and furnishings which may well have been damaged? You will not be insured for these under the buildings cover – these come under the heading of contents insurance.

You only have to open a newspaper to see that theft is a very real problem in our wicked world. Contents insurance will cover theft, but in some instances the insurance company may require you to fit additional locks or install a burglar alarm before they are prepared to cover you.

Personal case history

We live at the end of a single track road, on the edge of a farm and miles from anywhere. We feel the threat of a break-in fairly slender (fingers crossed!). When we re-assessed our contents insurance earlier this year, we found that we have been seriously under-valuing a number of items and therefore sent in an amended list of contents, through our broker, to the insurance company. This triggered off a visit from a representative, as a result of which we were told we had to have a burglar alarm fitted before they would cover us for the additional amount. Apart from the fact

How it works

Normally you, yourself establish the value of the items in your house and these usually fall into two categories – a general figure to cover the vast majority of your contents, plus a number of items of high value separately itemised by name and individual value. These individual items would tend to be jewellery, paintings and antiques. So far as these special items are concerned, it is possible that an insurance representative may want to see the valuation and certainly it is likely that a representative will call and inspect both the contents and the premises before agreeing insurance cover. It is at this point that it may be stipulated that additional security is required in order to provide cover.

The premium you can expect to pay for contents is somewhere between £60–£90

that fitting a burglar alarm would be expensive, it is also totally at odds with our lifestyle. The house is blessed with numerous cats and dogs, people come and go, and the back door is always open. We could see no way we could ever set the beastly apparatus without endless false alarms. As a result, we instructed our broker to shop around for a new insurance company, and sure enough he found the cover we wanted without the requirement for an alarm, thus saving us money and an enormous amount of potential hassle.

per year, for every £10,000 worth of contents – in other words it is not particularly cheap. In addition, most insurance companies tend to deduct the first £25 or even first £50 from each claim, to avoid having to deal with claims for trivial amounts.

You will have the option of extending the normal contents cover to include *accidental damage* risk – at an increased premium. You should also consider extending the cover on jewellery and such personal items onto an *all risks* basis.

As with all other forms of insurance, it is well worth while shopping around. Not only will you find there are considerable variations in the premium you will be charged, but the requirements of the insurance company will also differ. It is wise, if you can, to have both building and contents cover with the same insurance company – even though separate policies may be necessary. If you are unfortunate enough to have a claim, this will avoid any argument as to who has covered what.

Tenants' cover

If you are renting a house or flat, clearly you will be responsible for insuring your own contents. In this, you may experience a problem, for if the insurance company feel the security is insufficient you may have some difficulty in persuading your landlord to take the necessary steps to improve the position. Here again, it is a question of shopping around, trying to find a company which will adequately insure your contents without imposing unreasonable conditions. If all else fails, you will either have to settle for being under-insured, or if your lease is long enough, it may be worthwhile persuading your landlord to let you pay for the necessary security requirements.

Cash and credit cards

As part of your household insurance, you also can be covered for the loss or theft of money and credit cards, whether or not this occurs within the home. This is a particularly relevant insurance these days, especially where credit cards are concerned. Credit card companies are always plaguing us with insurance deals for individual cards – we would suggest that it is preferable to cover your cards under your general household policy, as it is likely to work out cheaper and is quite as effective.

Anything that threatens your home, whether it be damage or theft, can be a very unsettling and unpleasant experience. Home represents security and when that security is threatened, it can be very nerve-wracking. In these distressing circumstances, the last thing you need to discover is that you are inadequately insured so do take steps to make sure that at least if disaster hits you, you and your family will be able to make good your loss. Insurance companies will apply the rules of "average" in settling claims. This means that if you have £30,000 *worth* of assets insured for only £20,000 – a £3,000 claim will be settled at £2,000!

Additional insurance requirements

In addition to the actual insurance of your property and contents, there are other forms of insurance which are important to consider as a home owner or occupier. These are as follows:

◆ **On the move**

It is particularly important to consider your insurance position when you are moving house, for clearly your possessions are at some risk. In any event, you should choose a removal company which is a member of BAR (The British Association of Removers). BAR members will give you a good service and should have adequate insurance to cover your possessions in transit. However do check out the position very carefully. You may find that while items the removers have packed themselves are covered, any items you have packed are not. Similarly, you may not be compensated on a replacement value basis. Having studied the removal company's insurance, if in any doubt, it would be sensible to take out an additional policy to cover your belongings in transit. If your contents is already properly covered at home, this purely involves extending your existing policy on a temporary basis. In any event, it will need to be changed to your new adress.

◆ **Public liability insurance**

Generally speaking, public liability insurance is a standard, but optional extension of your buildings insurance, but it is important that you check this out and make sure you are covered, particularly if your building insurance is being organized by someone else – your mortgage company or perhaps your landlord. The normal amount of cover is £250,000 which extends protection to anyone who suffers injury or death while in your house, or as a result of being near your house. It is essential to have this insurance cover. If a slate from your roof fell on a passerby, who happened to be the well paid breadwinner of a family of five, you could find yourself the recipient of a hefty claim. It is simply not worth the risk. Incidentally, a particularly infuriating fact is that trespassers, or even burglars, can put in a claim against you if they are injured on your property – yes, truly.

◆ **Covenants**

Covenants, as we have discussed under the freehold section in this book, are conditions which sometimes are applied to a property regardless of who owns it. These covenants can stretch back over many years and may take the form of precluding the owner from building on any part of the property or altering the property or its land. In many instances these covenants are so out-of-date that they are no longer relevant. Nonetheless, you may be worried by the existence of a covenant and feel that in some way it could be detrimental to the value of your property, now or in the future. The simplest way to handle this situation is to insure against the covenant's ever being exercised. The insurance is not expensive and normally takes the form of a one-off premium. Certainly, if you have a covenant attached to your property, which in any circumstances could be troublesome, this seems a sensible precaution.

◆ **Insurance against faulty title**

As with covenants, sometimes the conveyance of a property, is not as clean as it should be, because of some confusion over title at some stage in the property's past. We ourselves had experience of this. We bought an old school from the Church and converted it into a house. In the deeds it was apparent that the land on which the school had been built had been originally gifted to the Church for church use only. This meant that at some stage in the future, a member of the family which had originally gifted the land might suddenly wake up to the fact that it was no longer being used for church purposes, and lay claim to it again. We, therefore, took out an insurance to cover this defect in our title. As with covenants, this took the form of a one-off payment, though we did have to contribute more over the years as the value of the property increased. As a rough indication of what this type of insurance is likely to cost, you are looking at a single premium of £1 per £1,000 of value – not a big sum.

◆ Mortgage protection policies

The mortgage company with which you deal will insist on the building's being insured, so that if anything happens to it, the asset backing their loan can be repaired or rebuilt, under the terms of the insurance policy. As a general rule, however, the mortgage company is not concerned with you. However, if you are responsible for re-paying the mortgage and you die, then your mortgage payments cease and your remaining family will either have to find the money or sell the property. The answer to this is a mortgage protection policy, which ensures that on the death of the person or persons responsible for paying the mortgage, the mortgage itself will be paid off.

In some instances, where the amount of money being borrowed is more than 75% or 80% of the value of the property, you may find that the mortgage company with whom you are dealing, insist on a mortgage indemnity policy. This gives the lender additional security on the top slice of the loan. There is a once only premium which is usually regarded as one of the costs of purchase (see page 149). Even if this is not a requirement of your mortgage company, it is a sensible thing to consider, particularly if you have a young, dependent family.

◆ Permanent health insurance/ personal accident

What happens if you are sufficiently badly injured or become so ill that you can no longer work and therefore pay the mortgage? To protect the family in these circumstances, you can either take out permanent health insurance – which will continue to pay you a percentage of your salary for the rest of your life – or you can have personal accident cover which will pay you out a lump sum in the event of serious injury. Either way, this is again a sensible insurance to consider, if you have a dependent family. It is not possible here to give you an indication as to what this will cost for there are so many facts to take into account – your age, your general health, whether or not you smoke, your occupation and your hobbies. However, in our view the premium is not high for peace of mind.

◆ Insurance of land and its use

If you are working the land, then there are various insurances you should consider:

★ Personal accident cover for yourself and any of your employees or family who may be involved in farm work.

★ Insurance of farm equipment, not only against accident or damage but against it breaking down at a crucial moment.

★ Public liability – in case your prize bull stampedes a passerby or your organic vegetables give everyone food poisoning!

★ Insurance of assets – i.e. stock and crops.

Working the land is a hazardous business and it is important to recognize the need for fully comprehensive insurance cover. The National Farmers Union will be able to give you guidance.

Making an insurance claim

Home Insurance proposal

Please complete white areas only in block capitals throughout

1 You the proposer

2 Your home/buildings

3 Your contents

4 Effective date of insurance

5 Paying by instalments

6 Insurance record

7 General questions

Declaration

If disaster strikes then the first thing you must do is to contact your broker, or if you have no broker, contact your insurance company direct. There are three stages for dealing with the damage sustained:

1 Under the terms of your insurance policy, you are under an obligation to lessen the damage so far as you are able. To take a facile example, if you return home from holiday to find you have a burst pipe, you are under an obligation to immediately call in a plumber to mend it. If your roof has caved in, then you need to get a builder to rig up a temporary tarpaulin to stop any more weather coming into the house.

2 Having taken steps to stop any further damage, you should then obtain permission to effect immediate emergency repairs. For example, supposing your house has been broken into and the back door virtually destroyed. You need to ask your broker if, on an immediate basis, you can replace the back door, to avoid there being any further burglaries. Although insurance companies have a reputation for being somewhat slow and ponderous over claims, in fairness they do respond quite well and quickly to this sort of request.

3 The final stage is to assess the extent of your claim. If your claim is for less than £1,000 and is in no way controversial, then it is likely your insurance company will meet the amount in question without argument and without coming to inspect the damage. If the damage is more than £1,000 then you may receive a visit from a loss assessor. In theory a loss assessor is supposed to be acting for both parties – i.e. you and the insurance company. In practice, however, most claimants would agree that the loss assessor seems to be very much on the side of the insurance company, since his objective appears to be to reduce the value of your claim if at all possible.

Claims for damage

As mentioned in earlier sections, if your property has been damaged and you wish to make a claim under your buildings insurance, what you have to be very careful to establish is that the damage is not a maintenance problem but the direct result of some trauma. Another controversial area at the moment is subsidence, where structural damage is caused to the building as a result of movement in the foundations. In theory, this is covered by your insurance policy but it is such a common problem that insurance companies tend to fight shy of claims, again using the alibi of its being a maintenance problem or a defect which was known about, and should have been disclosed when the policy was taken out.

If your damage is of a sufficiently substantial size to warrant the visit from a loss assessor, do prepare your ground carefully. If necessary obtain a letter from your builder confirming that the building was in good repair before the damage occurred. In other words, have your side of the argument well documented before the meeting.

In the case of damage to contents, you will usually experience no problems with standard pieces of furniture which, say, have been smoke damaged. Insurance companies will regularly accept this. Problems may arise, however, with regard to antique furniture or paintings of value, in which case you would be well advised to seek the advice of an antique dealer, who can look at the pieces in question and give you a written estimate as to what it would cost to repair them or confirm that basically they are irreparable. Here again, prepare your ground in advance of the arrival of the loss assessor, so that you can shoot down his arguments before he has thought them out!

Claims for burglary

The main loophole which your insurance company will be seeking, is to try and prove that you were negligent in your security arrangements. In other words, if you left the back door unbolted or the french windows open, then as far as the insurance company is concerned, you virtually invited the burglars to come into your home, and they will scale down the value of your claim accordingly. While obvious signs of a break-in may be very distressing at the time, nonetheless they do tend to prove that the burglary happened despite your efforts to secure your home.

As indicated at the beginning of this section, it may be necessary for you to take immediate steps to put right some of the damage in order to secure your home. Before doing so, however, take photographs of how it looked immediately after the burglary and make sure that both the police and your builder have noted the extent of the damage so they will be able to confirm the forced entry to the insurance company, if necessary.

The assessor may well query the value of the missing items. Bearing this in mind, it is terribly helpful if you have some proof as to the value of your more valuable items. If you have valuable jewellery then it would be sensible to have had this professionally valued by a jeweller, at the time of insuring it, so that you can produce written proof of its value. Of course it is very easy to be wise after the event, but if you do have any items of considerable value, then this is a useful precaution.

Another sensible precaution is to have a household inventory. This may seem unnecessary since you imagine you know precisely what you have and where it lives. Yet ask anyone who has been burgled and they will tell you of some items they did not realize were missing for weeks or even months after the burglary. A room-by-room inventory can solve this problem and it is not such an arduous job – do it on a wet Sunday afternoon.

Making the pay out

Insurance companies are not noted for their speed and you can expect it to be at least a couple of months before you receive compensation except in the case of emergency repair.

The above advice may make you feel that your insurance company is the enemy. This is not the case – provided you hold a sensible policy with a reputable company and have a genuine claim.

A broker will prove his worth when you have a claim, because he will be advising you, and negotiating for you with the insurance company.

Architects and draughtsmen

If you are planning to build a house, you will need an architect. If you are planning a new fitted kitchen, you will not need an architect. Between these two extremes there is any amount of conversion and improvement work, and it is in this middle ground that the need for a professional designer becomes less clear – a granny flat, an extra bedroom, a second bathroom, a utility room, play room, loft conversion, a new double garage, a swimming pool and sauna – do you need an architect's help for these, or not? The answer is, as always . . . it depends –

- It depends upon your own experience in building work, your inclination and your time.
- It depends upon your perception of what you want and how it can be achieved.
- It depends upon who is going to do the work for you.
- It depends upon who is going to draw up the plans, apply for planning consent and deal with the building regulations.

Before you can make such a decision, you need to understand fully what an architect does and how much he or she will charge.

- An architect will interpret what you want and translate it into a detailed set of plans, but this certainly is not all he should do. A good architect will guide you through all the alternatives and opportunities. In other words, the first part of his job is to be creative and it is this which sets him apart from a draughtsman.
Example: You have a building site and a requirement for a two reception/four bedroom/two bathroom house. A good architect might say – 'Why don't you take advantage of the sloping site and build a split level bungalow, with two bedrooms and a bathroom suite up here, running down the hill through an open living room area to kitchen and utility room, across, say a bridge into the guest wing, with two further bed-

rooms and a bathroom?' It probably would never have entered your head to think like this – like most of us you would be considering variations on a square box.
Example: You want to build a guest room and bathroom over the garage. A good architect might say – 'Why don't we move the airing cupboard into the bathroom, put some stairs where the cupboard is and go up into the roof space? I can give you a bedroom and bathroom, and a study for the children in the loft. It will cost less than building over the garage and look at the views!'

- An architect will give you an initial rough idea of building costs.
- An architect will draw up preliminary plans and discuss them with the local authority, with a view to obtaining planning and building regulations clearance.
- An architect will submit final detailed plans to the local authority.
- An architect will prepare specifications and invite builders to tender. He will recommend which builder should do the work, then place the contract with the builder and supervise the building work on your behalf.

For the kind of involvement mentioned above, you might expect to pay fees of up to 10½% for new building work and up to 15% for alterations to existing buildings. These are the recommended fees, but in practice the range is likely to be 8–13%. If you want to use the services of an architect for only some of these aspects, obviously the fee would be reduced, or an hourly rate charged. For smallish jobs, about £35 per hour would be typical.

Finding the right architect

If you were planning to commission an artist to, say, paint a portrait of your children, you would first examine the artist's other work to see if you liked his style. What applies to artists, applies to architects. You would be very foolish indeed to employ an architect

without first looking at a number of the jobs he has undertaken for other people.

As with any professional help, the best way to find a good architect is through personal recommendation and normally you can rely on the recommendation of your builder, if you already have one. The relationship between builder and architect is rarely an easy one. Now and again you may come across a successful partnership, but on the whole builders moan that architects do not know what they are talking about, and architects moan that builders never do as they are told. If you know of a good builder, whom you like and trust, and he in turn recommends an architect, then the recommendation has to be worth considering because it suggests that architect and builder will work together without strife, which is worth a lot. If you know neither a builder nor architect from personal experience, then it is a question of asking around. If you have seen a house or extension which particularly appeals to you, why not knock on the door and ask for the name of the architect. Imitation is the sincerest form of flattery and you are almost bound to receive helpful advice.

When you do not need an architect

You do not need an architect for small to medium-sized conversion or extension work if you know exactly what you want and have a good builder, known to you by experience or first hand recommendation. If you trust the work of your builder, he will know someone who can draw up some plans without incurring the costs of an architect. This could be a draughtsman, a local surveyor or structural engineer – retired or working part-time. Such people, if recommended to you direct, can be very useful both in terms of advice and practical assistance. However, they are not the right people to use if you want an artistic input and this also applies to your builder. A good builder has a wealth of experience of dealing with extensions and alterations, has the right contacts and plenty of practical knowledge and understanding. What you cannot expect is much imagination when it comes to design – but then that is an architect's job.

Builders and tradesmen

Builders tend to fall into three broad categories – the major contractors, the medium-sized building firms and the small local builders. If you are buying a new house on an estate, you may well find yourself discussing your problems with the developer, who is likely to be a major building contractor. However, for the purposes of the book, we are concerned with medium and small building firms, and the specialist tradesmen they employ or whom they appoint as sub-contractors, or, indeed, who work for you direct.

How to find a good builder

Once you find a reliable firm of builders, who charge sensible prices, who turn up when they say they are going to and whose work is of consistently good quality, then you will use the same firm again and again. Of course there are good building firms around but there are a fair number of con artists in the trade and you do have to be very careful.

If you are using a reputable architect whom you can trust, then his recommendation should be good enough. If you have lived in the neighbourhood for a number of years, then friends and neighbours should be able to advise you on whom to use. However, what happens if you move into a new neighbourhood, know no one and need major work carried out on your house urgently? Where do you start to look? The answer is a builders' merchant. Go to the biggest, busiest builders' merchant in your area, ask to speak to the manager and ask him to recommend a good builder. Builders' merchants really have their finger on the pulse. They know which builders are always in work and which are not. They also know which builders pay their bills. Builders who do not pay their bills usually have difficulty getting money out of their customers. Why? – because their work is incompetent. Builders' merchant representatives regularly visit building sites and they have a very good idea of who is a good builder and who is not.

What applies to builders applies to all trades. If you are seeking a good electrician, ask an electrical wholesaler. If you are buying a swimming pool, ask the supplier of the pool to recommend a plumber.

GOLDEN RULE. Do not employ a builder on any major piece of building work, without first seeing examples of his work elsewhere. As with architects, you need to see the work a builder is producing before committing yourself.

Builders are only as good as the people who employ them

Up to a point, bad relationships between builders and customers can be as much the fault of the customer as the builder. Here are some rules it is important that you follow:

◆ Be quite clear in your mind whether your prospective builder has given you an estimate or a quotation. There is a subtle, but quite definite difference, between the two. An estimate gives you a rough idea of what the total figure will be, but acknowledges that it is impossible to give a firm price at such an early stage. A quotation is a firm price to complete the work, whatever the circumstances. If you have instructed your builder to go ahead on the basis of an estimate, it is no good moaning if the price works out higher.

◆ Often during the process of building work it is necessary to carry out extra work. Problems arise – a rotten beam, a poor damp course . . . whatever. While it may be absolutely necessary for this additional work to be done, you should nonetheless ask for a quotation, so that you are aware at each stage how much will be added to the total bill.

◆ Completion time – one of the greatest complaints about builders is their inability to finish within the prescribed time. On a big job this can be overcome by inserting a penalty clause into the contract, to the effect that for every day, week or month the builder goes over the completion time, he pays compensation by means of a reduction in price.

This sounds an excellent idea but in practice it is difficult to make a builder accept these penalty clauses except where a big contract is involved. We have found the best method is straightforward bullying. Agree a completion date in advance and insist that the men are kept on site until the work is finished.

◆ As we mentioned in the previous section, do try and find a builder and architect who are compatible in their thinking. An architect whom the builders clearly despise and vice versa will have the two of them involved in some kind of power struggle – in which, without doubt, you will be the loser.

◆ Conflicting instructions – every builder's nightmare is the conflicting instructions so often received – mostly as between husband and wife. Do make sure that you and your partner are absolutely of one mind, so that the builder receives just one set of instructions.

◆ Always hold back part of the money on completion of work, whether or not your agreement with the builder entitles you to do so. The retention should be 10–20% of the total cost of the work, and you should hold onto it for a few weeks or a few months – until you are absolutely satisfied that everything has been done to your satisfaction. A retention is the only way to guarantee that you get the builder back to sort out any snags.

What can you do if things go wrong? You can sue, you can report the builders to the Building Trades Association, you can tell your local newspaper reporter about your experience and hope that a newspaper article will put the builder in question out of work for some time. All of these courses of action are possible but none of them begin to compensate for the drama, mess and general stress which will result if you fall out with your builder in the middle of a job. For this reason take great care with your choice of builder – indeed any specialist tradesman – you cannot afford to make a mistake.

Building your own house/major conversion work

It is a big step, building your own house or planning major conversion work and it is vital to consider carefully each stage – not rush headlong into decisions you will later regret.

◆ The site – it is possible you may receive permission to build your ideal home in the middle of a green field, but it is unlikely. More likely, you will receive planning permission to build a house on an in-fill plot of land or on the site of an existing house due for demolition. If you are to be involved in major conversion work, you could be building on a massive extension – bigger perhaps than the original house itself – or perhaps completely re-designing the house within its existing framework.

Whatever your plans, there are more considerations than whether the local authority will allow you to do what you want. Planning permission, building regulations clearance and highways approval are all vital, of course, but so is having enough money to do the job properly, and above all creating something with which you are pleased. While major building work is usually fraught with problems of one sort or another, the consoling factor should be that the end product reflects precisely what you want.

So, when looking at a site, consider it from every aspect – whether the house of your dreams will look right on it or whether the major conversion may solve all your internal problems, but completely wreck your otherwise lovely garden. Forget for a moment the practicalities, permissions and money. Concentrate on whether you can achieve your heart's desire, both practically and aesthetically, on the site of your choice. If it is a question of having to compromise, you might do better to buy an existing property without the hassle.

◆ Planning – it goes without saying that you should never buy a potential building plot without being sure that you can obtain planning permission. This can either be in the form of detailed planning consent – as the result of submitting precise plans of your proposed house – or outline planning permission where Planning agree that a house of a

certain size and type can be built on the proposed site. Either way, be careful that the tail is not wagging the dog. In other words, Planning may impose on you some very tight conditions which frankly make the whole scheme less than attractive. This can apply either with a new house or with major conversion. If this is the case, be careful not to get blinkered and press on regardless. If the planning authority's requirements do not suit, then find another site, or sell your existing house and buy a bigger one.

◆ Viability and price – building sites today are changing hands for unbelievable sums of money, as are collapsing barns and tiny workman's cottages. Indeed any piece of land where it is possible to extend, convert or build from scratch is at a premium. Add to this your building costs and you could find the money involved is way out of court. Typical building costs for new construction in the home counties is £36 per square foot currently. In London you can expect to pay double this figure, whereas the South West, Wales and the North of England are cheaper. For extension or conversion work you should think in terms of £46 per square foot, but if the work involves conversion on a listed building you can expect to pay much, much more.

◆ Architects – we have discussed architects in detail on page 176. Suffice to say here that for building your own home or for major conversion work, you do need an architect – if for no other reason than if things go wrong your architect will be covered by his indemnity insurance policy! Do make sure, particularly with the building of a new house, that the style is yours, not his. While it is important to benefit from an architect's artistic input *you* are going to have to live in the house and it is extremely important that you get what you want.

◆ The investment -
a)   If you are buying a plot of land and building a house on it, then you should spend no more, in total, on that house than can be recouped if, when completed, you decide to sell it – that is unless you intend to live in the house for a very long time.

b)   If you are undertaking major conversion work, seek advice from an estate agent as to what the conversion will do for the price of your house – in other words, will you get your money back, if and when you come to sell? If the answer is no, then here again you should not contemplate the conversion works unless you are intending to live in the house for a long time.

c)   Recognize that some properties cannot be improved beyond a certain point. Lavishing money on a property in an area which is 'going down', in a street of otherwise dilapidated houses, on a house with a poor aspect, no views and nothing special to commend it, is likely to be money down the drain.

d)   Practicalities are far more important an asset to a house than frills, which is why putting a second bathroom into your house will add to its value far more than installing a swimming pool.

◆ The contract – for any sort of major conversion work, with or without the help of an architect, you must have a firm contract with your builder. The contract should include penalty clauses, guarantees, insurance, payment terms, and a very clear indication of who does what. Normally, payments are made in stages, as the work is completed. The RIBA publishes a booklet entitled *Agreement for Minor Building Works*, which is a useful reference point and you should study this before signing any contract, to make sure all the necessary points are covered. The RIBA address is:

Royal Institute of British Architects,
66 Portland Place,
London, W1N 4AD.

Telephone: 01-580 5533

Roofs

It goes without saying that the roof is a very important structural element of a building – probably the most important. The quality of its design, construction, finish and subsequent maintenance will largely determine the soundness or otherwise of the whole of the building beneath it. If a roof's basic design is at fault, then even if it has been conscientiously constructed, it will give problems. Likewise a well-designed roof, badly constructed, will be no better. You need a good design, well built, and thereafter constant and diligent maintenance.

Types of roof

Shown here are the five main types of roof:

Roof construction

This illustration shows a typical roof construction and indicates the names given to the various parts of both roof and chimney structure.

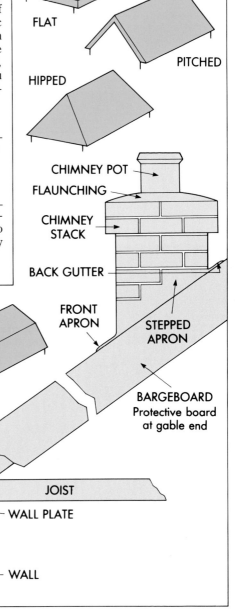

FLAT

PITCHED

HIPPED

CHIMNEY POT

FLAUNCHING

CHIMNEY STACK

BACK GUTTER

FRONT APRON

STEPPED APRON

MANSARD

LEAN-TO

BARGEBOARD
Protective board at gable end

NIB

BATTEN

TILE

GUTTER

RAFTER

JOIST

WALL PLATE

FASCIA   SOFFIT

WALL

Pitched roofs

Traditionally, in this country most roof constructions are pitched. It is a design suitable for our climate, has withstood the test of time and is still very much in use today. Hipped and Mansard roofs are really only a variation on the same basic pitched roof principle. There are three traditional types of pitched roof and one modern construction. These are as follows:

Traditional ridged

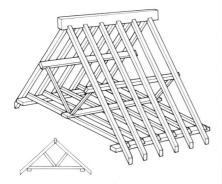

This roof is built with parallel rafters about 16" apart, between the ridge and the eaves. The rafters are supported by purlins, fixed at right angles and the ceiling joists are fixed to the feet of the rafters.

Trussed purlin

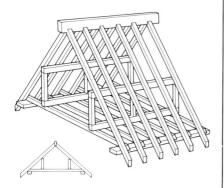

A trussed purlin roof is used if there are no walls to support the weight of the purlins. The truss runs the length of the roof and provides independent support. This type of roofing is obviously ideal for loft conversion, as there is plenty of central space.

Collared

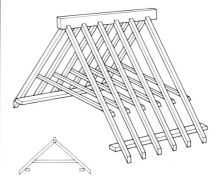

The collared roof is the old method of roofing which is mostly seen in halls or churches, and is usually exposed as open timbered roofing. The rafters are fixed together by horizontal cross beams and therefore the rafters do not require the support of internal walls or partitions.

Trussed rafter

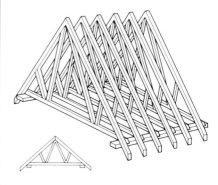

This is the modern construction most commonly used in new houses. The roof is supported by a series of rafter sections and the diagonal braces provide extra strength. You will see that unlike the traditional pitched roofs, the trussed rafter has no ridge along the top of the roof.

Roof coverings

◆ Pitched roof covering

Pitched roofs and their variations are designed mainly to take the following roof coverings:

Tiles –
    traditional slate or stone
    clay
    concrete
    shingles

Concrete is used now mostly, and shingles have only limited use in this country.

Thatch –
    skilled thatchers are an increasingly rare breed and good quality reeds are very costly. Thatched roofs are very attractive and still in demand because of their appearance. They have a relatively short life – 30–40 years but with modern roof construction and felting, they are snug and water-tight. Not favoured by insurance companies or building societies because of their high fire risk.

Various types of sheet material –
    Corrugated iron or asbestos, bitumen felt or bitumen tiling, glass or plastic.

◆ Flat roof covering

Flat roofs (which in practice must always have a very slight slope to facilitate drainage) can be constructed in a wide variety of ways – from timber to concrete. They are normally finished with a bitumen felt covered in stone chippings. Alternatively, flat roofs can be covered with copper, galvanised iron, aluminium, lead, mastic asphalt or corrugated glass reinforced plastic. Some roofs need to be supported, some are self-supporting between the rafters.

◆ Lean-to roof covering

Because lean-to's have a tendency to be the victim of DIY enthusiasm, roofs can be covered in almost anything. Corrugated reinforced plastic is favourite because it is easy to fix, light in weight and allows light through. This would certainly apply if your lean-to was to be used as a conservatory or a greenhouse. Lean-to sheds or garages tend to be either covered in asbestos cement or corrugated iron.

GOLDEN RULE FOR ROOF COVERING: Take care if you are considering re-covering a roof in anything other than its original material. If, for example, it was designed to take shingles or a corrugated sheet, you might find that the whole roof structure would give way under the weight of conventional tiles.

Roof problems

Minor

◆ Broken or missing tiles.
◆ Flashing lifting, splitting or breaking up.
◆ Chimney pointing or flashing missing.
◆ Guttering blocked, especially in the valley between roofs.

In themselves, the above problems are minor if *caught early*. However if they are left unattended, the constant impact of weather can quickly lead to major problems developing in the form of rotten timbers and ruined ceilings.

Major

◆ Bad design or construction causing structural failure.
◆ Age causing deterioration of timbers resulting in sagging and possible collapse.
◆ Damp/rot/infestation leading to collapse.
◆ Amateur tampering with roof timbers and structure, leading to sagging or collapse.
◆ Ageing of the slate/stone tiles or thatch, causing susceptibility to frost or storm damage.

You cannot mess about with roofs. If you ignore the minor problems they will become major problems. Therefore put things right as soon as they go wrong and do not be tempted to bodge the job. Much of your house can benefit hugely from your DIY asperations but do not, repeat, *do not* apply them to your roof. There are no short-cuts, you always need professional help, except for the most minor running repairs.

Roof and loft conversion

Roof conversion

Existing walls and foundations willing, it is sometimes possible to add one or even two floors onto a property. On face value, it seems a wonderful idea to be taking off the roof, adding another couple of floors and putting the roof back! In practice it needs to be recognized that this is a very expensive operation – indeed, as expensive as building a new house. Added to this, of course, are the problems of planning, neighbours and sensible access to the floors above. In cost terms, such an exercise can only really be justified in a town house, where there is a tremendous premium on the price of land. Certainly, at the time of writing this book, sites for residential development are now topping £1,000,000 per acre in the home counties. This being the case, it could make sense to move upwards rather than sideways.

Planning authorities are always difficult about altering a roof-line. If the houses around you are mostly tall buildings this may not be a problem, but a four-storey house surrounded by two-storey houses is not likely to be popular. The same goes for neighbours – plunging their former sunny little garden into a dismal, shadowy place is not going to endear you to them, and they would have every right to complain at such a proposal. Then there is the question of the look of your house – certain houses would completely lose their character if added to in height. Finally and most important of all, there are the structural problems. Before giving any serious thought to a major roof conversion, you need to seek the advice of a structural engineer who will be able to tell you, for a relatively small fee, whether in an engineering sense such a scheme would be feasible.

Loft conversion

Far simpler and much cheaper is the popular loft conversion. In many cases it is possible to convert your roof space for a comparatively small cost and in some instances, without the need for planning permission. Building regulations particularly as they apply to the staircase and to ceiling heights, are a normal requirement, though.

Quite apart from the fact that you may be fond of your home, buying and selling a house is very costly, both on the pocket and more particularly on the nerves. Creating extra space in your loft could be a cheap answer to your space problems. Loft conversion has the added bonus of not impinging on your garden or in any way affecting the outside of your house.

Let us look at the practicalities. You do not require planning permission unless your conversion is more than 70 cubic metres or 15% of the total volume of the house – whichever is the greater. (50 cubic metres or 10% if you live in a terraced house or in a national park or area of outstanding natural beauty or a conservation area.) If you require windows, then you will need planning permission though replacing existing windows with a slightly bigger and better design is unlikely to cause trouble, unless it directly overlooks your neighbours. Neighbours are an important point here, particularly if you are living in a semi-detached house. You do need to explain to them what is going on.

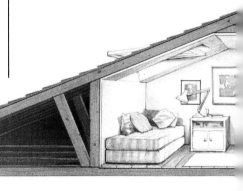

Roofs

The success or otherwise of your loft conversion depends enormously on your roof space. Modern roofs often have no ridge timber and are supported by prefabricated trussed rafters. If this is the case in your house, you must not start tampering with them or trying to remove some of the rafters to create more space – you could have the whole roof caving in on you. In fact what applies to new houses applies to all loft spaces – *do not start hacking away at any rafters or beams, without first seeking professional help*. The best type of roof for loft conversion is the trussed purlin, where the space is already created, but in many attics employing an RSJ or supporting beam at a strategic point could enable you to open up a great deal of space.

Windows

It has been our deliberate policy throughout this book not to quote branded products for fear of being accused of advertising. However, we simply cannot talk about loft conversion and windows in the same breath without referring you to Velux roof windows. They really are second to none – utterly weatherproof, easy to operate, good to look at and with their own range of fitted blinds. For further information you should write to:

Velux,
Telford Road,
Glenrothes,
East Fife,
KY7 4NX.

Staircases

Staircases should meet the requirements of building regulations, which dictate their height, their slope and their width. One of the problems with creating extra space in the roof is that you are going to lose space on the floor below, at the point where the staircase rises. Fire regulations can also be a problem, where staircases are concerned.

Re-rating

Do bear in mind that a loft conversion may involve the re-rating of your premises which, depending on the size of the loft, could be quite considerable. You should perhaps consider this point when looking at your overall costs.

Finance

You should have no problem in persuading your bank or building society to add on the costs of a loft conversion to your mortgage, provided, of course, you are not already over-borrowed. Most mortgage companies recognize that the work is likely to add value to your house and are happy to go along with your plans. It would be sensible to refer back to our section on grants, on page 154, for it is possible that you could be eligible for a local authority grant.

Builder

It is unlikely that you will require an architect for a loft conversion, unless you are planning very fancy use of the space. This being the case, you must be particularly careful in your choice of builder. There are a number of specialists in loft conversion but here, too, you do need to be careful, for there are a number of cowboys around. If you decide to use one of these firms, you will need several references and the opportunity to speak to satisfied customers and see the work that has been done.

Double glazing

Double glazing had its day about twenty years ago – no self-respecting house was without it. Otherwise charming rooms, with attractive windows, suffered the indignity of great unsightly panels of glass, set in cheap, metal frames. If the doorbell rang unexpectedly, it was as likely to be a salesman for double glazing as a friend calling for a chat.

Double glazing's day is over, in as much that it is now recognized to be nothing like as cost effective as we were led to believe. Yes, it is true that a single glazed house loses 20% of its heat through windows and cracks in the doors and that double glazing can reduce this by half. However the cost of installing double glazing cannot be recouped in fuel savings for many, many years – if ever.

There are two basic types of double glazing:

◆ Secondary glazing – this is the original form of double glazing which involves the installation of a 'second window'. In its crudest form, this can be a sheet of cling film fixed with self-adhesive tape, or acetate sheeting. In most instances it is a sliding panel of glass, fitted inside the window into an aluminium or plastic frame. Sometimes the secondary glass panels hinge outwards, as in the case of a French window, but more usually they slide. No secondary glazing can be described as attractive. If professionally and well fitted, it can be less obtrusive than a DIY job, but you certainly cannot pretend it is not there.

◆ Sealed units – a sealed unit, to the outside world, looks like an ordinary pane of glass. In fact it is two – the gap between the panes being between a 1/4" and 1/2" – and it is installed into the window frame as a single unit. Unlike secondary glazing, there is never any build up of condensation between the two panels and the glass can vary in thickness from 3 millimetres, through to 10 millimetres, according to the size of the windows and to your requirements and pocket.

There are standard sizes of sealed unit available or you can have them made to measure. Clearly this is the most acceptable form of double glazing aesthetically.

Advantages of double glazing

◆ Double glazing will reduce heat loss and considerably cut down on draughts.

◆ Close to the windows you will feel more comfortable, warmer and less vulnerable to the elements.

◆ Double glazing can be very useful in cutting down noise from outside,. If you live on a busy road this could be a big advantage but the glass does have to be thick and the gap between the panes must be between four and eight inches to be effective.

◆ Double glazing reduces window condensation.

◆ Double glazing does make it more difficult for a burglar to enter the premises.

Disadvantages of double glazing

◆ Double glazing is expensive and the expenditure will not be recouped in reduced heating bills – at least for many, many years.

◆ Secondary double glazing is unsightly.

◆ Secondary double glazing is a fiddle when it come to opening and closing windows. It is a potential fire risk, because of this difficulty.

While you cannot justify installing double glazing in fuel savings terms, if you need to change your windows anyway, the additional costs of having double rather than single glazed replacements will be most definitely worthwhile. Because sealed units look no different from ordinary glass, there is no reason why some of your glazing should not be single and some double, gradually replacing your windows over the years, as they need it.

Alternatives to double glazing

A point to consider – drawing the curtains is as effective as double glazing in terms of preventing heat loss. If your lifestyle is such that you are out at work all day and your house or flat does not need to be heated anyway, good thick curtains will soon help to build up a fug on your return from work in the evening.

However, by far the cheapest and most effective heat-saving device is the fitting of draught-proofing. Draught-proofing is simply the fixing of seals round the edges of your windows. Clearly your window frames have to be in reasonable condition to make this exercise worthwhile, but the difference draught-proofing will make in terms of heat loss, as against the cost involved, makes this a very attractive option.

Costs and savings

A leaflet published by the Department of the Environment in 1986, quoted comparative costs for restoring and replacing windows, against installing secondary glazing in two typical houses. The houses in question were –
a) a small terraced house, with 9 square metres of sash window, and
b) a semi-detached house with 13½ square metres of modern timber windows.

The survey also indicated the likely annual savings in heating costs which were likely to result from the various types of work carried out.

NB   If you are planning to install any form of double glazing, do make sure you choose a firm belonging to the Glass and Glazing Federation (GGF).

| | Terraced house | | Semi-detached | |
	£ cost	£ annual savings savings	£ cost	£ annual savings savings
Draught proof windows	85	20	125	24
Secondary double glazing	850	25	1300	33
Replace windows –				
as original	975	–	900	–
as original + sealed units	1350	34	1450	45
'High performance' timber with sealed glazing, draught proofing and ventilators	N/A	–	1850	45
UPVC replacement windows with sealed glazing, integral draught proofing	N/A	–	3700	45

Insulation

The problem is that most houses – even modern ones – have not been built with high enough insulation standards. Heating costs can be dramatically reduced in a highly insulated house. Although the largest single area of heat loss is the windows – for which draught proofing and double glazing are the answer – all other elements of the building can benefit enormously from insulation.

The comments we made about double glazing equally apply to insulation, in as much that increased awareness of insulation at the construction stage of a house is far more cost effective than trying to correct lack of insulation in an established house. What applies to a new building applies to conversion work as well. Whenever you lay a new floor or build a new wall, always incorporate high insulation values within the new work. Admittedly this may mean you do not have a completely insulated house but every little helps, and certainly if you are involved in any sort of major renovation, it pays to insulate walls, ceilings and floors while you are working on them. As with double glazing, however, it is important to recognize that many insulation measures – while improving the comfort of the house – cannot really be described as cost effective – i.e. the pay back period from fuel savings may see you reach your century before you move into profit!

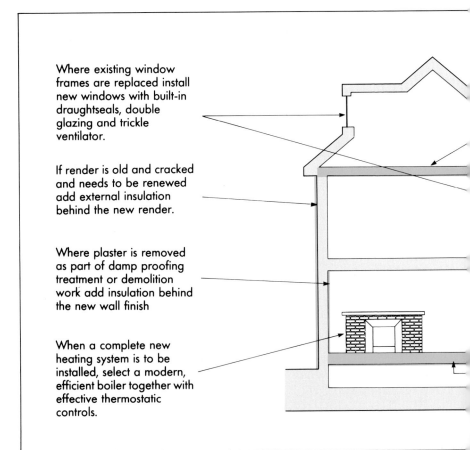

Where existing window frames are replaced install new windows with built-in draughtseals, double glazing and trickle ventilator.

If render is old and cracked and needs to be renewed add external insulation behind the new render.

Where plaster is removed as part of damp proofing treatment or demolition work add insulation behind the new wall finish

When a complete new heating system is to be installed, select a modern, efficient boiler together with effective thermostatic controls.

In Britain the object of insulation has to be to keep warmth within the house and stop the infiltration of cold from the outside. A well-insulated house will be cooler to live in during the hot summer months – but it is the heat retention in the winter which is the main objective.

Insulation is not just about air flow – an uninsulated concrete floor will be a very cold floor. The coldness seeping up from the ground will be shared by the floor slab and will be felt by the occupants – the result being that the house will be more difficult and more expensive to heat. If you put insulation on top of the concrete, although the slab will stay cold, the occupants will not notice it and the house will be appreciably warmer. Put insulation under the concrete (the preferred solution) and the floor slab becomes warm with the rest of the house.

What applies to floors, applies to walls, ceilings and roofs. Walls can be insulated by lining them inside or outside, or by infilling wall cavities. To stop warmth rising out of the roof, either the roof or the ceiling below can be insulated. See below the illustration which demonstrates the insulation points in a house.

NB Insulation should be accompanied by draught-proofing but do take great care to maintain proper ventilation and air circulation.

On the following pages are some examples of insulation, together with an indication as to their cost effectiveness. No prices

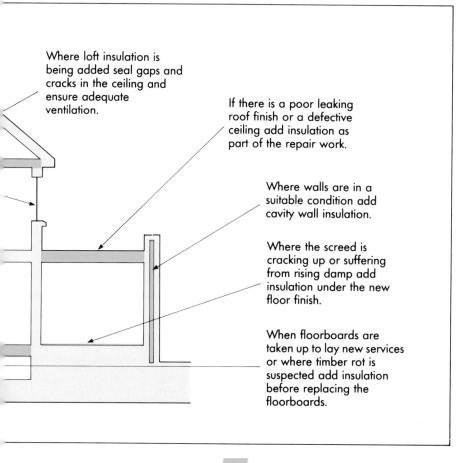

Where loft insulation is being added seal gaps and cracks in the ceiling and ensure adequate ventilation.

If there is a poor leaking roof finish or a defective ceiling add insulation as part of the repair work.

Where walls are in a suitable condition add cavity wall insulation.

Where the screed is cracking up or suffering from rising damp add insulation under the new floor finish.

When floorboards are taken up to lay new services or where timber rot is suspected add insulation before replacing the floorboards.

are quoted as obviously so much depends on the size of your house, but pay back figures will give you an indication as to how long it will take to recoup your money.

Pitched roofs – loft insulation

The most popular and widely used method of insulation. Minimum thickness of insulation quilt should be 100 mm but you should consider going up to 140 mm if you can afford it. Payback period on basic 100 mm approximately 3–5 years.

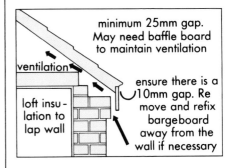

Flat roofs

As indicated in the illustration below, you can go for either a *cold* or *warm* roof technique – i.e. the insulation can be placed below or above the roof. Above the roof is best as it protects the whole roof area including the roof timbers. Payback period – warm roof 9–12 years, cold roof 7–10 years.

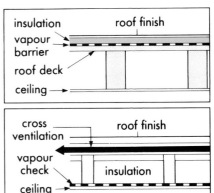

Cavity walls

Cavities need to be at least 40 mm wide to take insulation. They can be filled with foam polystyrene or polyurethane beads or granules, or blown mineral fibre. Beads have the fastest payback period at 3 years – the two other alternatives have a payback period of between 4–5 years.

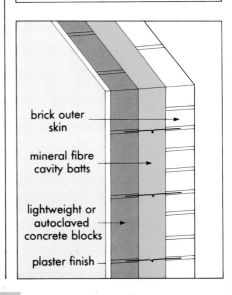

Solid walls

Insulation can be applied to solid walls, either externally or internally. External insulation is considerably more expensive unless, of course, your walls are in urgent need of repair in any event – in which case it is extremely cost effective to incorporate insulation at the same time.

External walls

There are various different types of insulation for external walls. The illustration below shows the metal carrier system which is one of the most popular, but in price terms there is very little difference between them all. Payback period – 11–13 years.

Internal walls

There are two methods for insulating walls, either by plasterboard laminates or timber battens infilled with insulation material. The timber battens method has a 5 year payback, plasterboard 9 years.

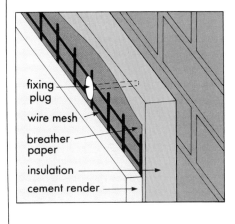

fixing plug
wire mesh
breather paper
insulation
cement render

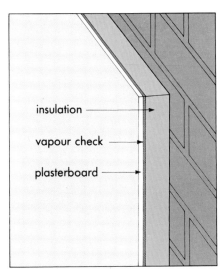

insulation
vapour check
plasterboard

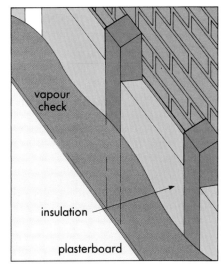

vapour check
insulation
plasterboard

NB There is a minimum building regulation requirement for insulation which you need to bear in mind, either if you are building a new house or indeed buying one. However, it is generally recognized that this minimum requirement is not over generous and if you are building your own house you would do better to increase your insulation over and above the building regulations standard.

The vast majority of us are living in, or about to buy, a property which already has some type of heating. This means we have to be thinking in terms of adding, altering or replacing an existing system, rather than starting from scratch.

Firstly, you need to chose the fuel source or indeed a combination of sources. The factors you have to consider are:

Personal preference
Availability
Convenience
Suitability
Flexibility
Compatibility with other systems
Installation costs
Running costs

WHO TURNED HIS THERMOSTAT UP TO TEN AGAIN?

A combination of these factors will decide for you what you should do and some of them will be greatly influenced by your personal circumstances. For example, if you are heating a weekend cottage, you will be looking for remote control flexibility. If you have reached retirement age, it would be sensible not to consider solid fuel because of the work involved.

Where running costs are your principal concern, you have a very real problem. If you pick up central heating information from your local gas show room and your local electricity board showroom, you will find leaflets comparing the annual running costs of a typical home - contrasting gas and electricity. The assumptions made in arriving at their respective figures are given in great detail and they each compare a very similar range of homes. The problem is that their conclusions are consistently different! The British Gas leaflet proves conclusively that gas is cheaper, followed by solid fuel with electricity the most expensive.

The leaflet from the Electricity Board – based on an independent assessment of running costs by the Energy Efficiency Office of the Department of Energy – proves equally conclusively that for a properly insulated home, electricity is always cheaper than gas! Not a great help, is it?

In addition to running costs there are also the very important considerations of the installation costs and the disruption caused by installation. The installation costs of a wet central heating system (boiler, radiators, header tank, circulating pump, thermostats, etc) will be far greater than putting in individual room heaters, and the disruption will be considerably more too. However, the end result may be less intrusive, give the degree of background heating you require and be more economical to run.

In order to assess your heating requirements, therefore, you need to:

◆ Know what is available.

◆ Know what the various systems and combination of appliances will cost to install.

◆ Understand the practical implications of having one rather than another system – i.e. the benefits and the drawbacks.

◆ Get some feel of the running costs of the various alternatives.

◆ Make sure that your chosen system is going to be installed properly, at the right price, to the right specifications and to the right standards.

◆ Make a choice based on everything you know but still reflecting your own personal preferences.

Let us look at what is available under each fuel source:-

Solid fuel

Solid fuel is splendid if you like the concept of having a real fire and can cope with the humping of fuel, the emptying of ash and the degree of mess involved. You also have to consider fuel storage space.

There is on the market an increasingly efficient range of room heaters, with back boilers for hot water and/or central heating. Log burning stoves certainly should be considered if you have ready access to a mountain of logs. They are very efficient at space heating, if you do not mind staring at a large lump of stove as the focal point of the room – few are truly attractive and contrary to much of the publicity, they cannot be opened up to display the fire while still operating efficiently. Some log burning stoves have back boilers but these are not as efficient as smokeless fuel heating, with water circulation.

Natural gas

Piped gas is one of the cleanest and most controllable fuels for heating. Boiler/radiator systems, individual room space heaters, individual radiant heaters and log or coal effect open fires – all these are available with a gas supply.

Ducted hot air heating from a gas boiler is an option which is available with newly constructed property, but running costs are high and you are lucky if it works really well, as design/efficiency problems are not uncommon. The major advantage of a gas central heating system using wet radiators, is the aspect of controllability – time clocks/thermostats mean you can have heat when you want it, where you want it. You can go away for the weekend and come back to a warm house, be at the office all day and come back to a warm house. Hot baths are always available when you need them.

Liquid gas

If you do not have mains gas connected but have space for gas cylinders or bulk storage, LPG can give all the advantages of mains gas with the same appliances. Your gas supplier can even arrange monthly top up of your bulk tank and quarterly billing. Running costs tend to be higher and there is a high installation cost because of the storage tanks.

Oil

More messy than LPG and prices have proved to be very susceptible to international politics. It is anyone's guess what the price of oil will be within the next five, ten or twenty years. Oil boilers need more servicing than gas boilers to keep them running efficiently. Large boilers are noisy and so need to be in an outbuilding, and oil is less flexible than gas, though it does come into its own in economic terms in very large properties.

Electricity

Electricity is quiet and clean, but reputed to be expensive for heating. However recently, big strides have been made towards economy and there are major benefits where appliances can utilize overnight low tariff supplies. Night storage heaters are now much slimmer in appearance and more efficient, with controllable input overnight and controllable output during the day. Individual radiant heaters, space heaters or electric radiators can be used in addition to night storage, or as an alternative. Under floor or in-ceiling heating has proved to be expensive and relatively inefficient. The same applies to ducted hot air supply.

There is a relatively new system – a super insulated electric water boiler which stores heat at overnight rates and is linked to a normal wet radiator system. The water circulates when needed during the daytime and you can give temperature boost at normal tariff rates during the day or evening if required. The system is very clean and very simple and claimed to be very economic. It is certainly worth looking at.

Solar heating

Expensive and inefficient in Britain. Do not even consider it. However if you have a villa on a Greek island then do not consider heating your water in any other way!

Bathrooms

It is reckoned in London today, that the installation of a decent additional bathroom can put between £20–£30,000 on the value of a house. Staggering, isn't it? The British have never been noted for their luxurious bathrooms and certainly have a reputation for being stingy with hot water. Times are changing, though. A house with more than two bedrooms is now almost expected to have two bathrooms, and a luxury flat automatically will have a bathroom en suite with each bedroom.

The range of bathroom suites, in terms of size, colour and design, is overwhelming and the prices can vary enormously, too. You can pay anything from £200–£250 for a basic bath, hand basin and lavatory, to well over £1,000.

Before you begin any serious measuring and planning of your bathroom, ask yourself what you actually want from it. Do not be hide-bound by the conventional view of a bathroom, look on it as what it should be – a very important area of relaxation. Where else can you have a little private time, where you can read, doze, plan the next business move or socialize with your partner away from the rest of the household? If you have a reasonable sized bathroom area, convention suggests that you should have a bath, a shower unit, a bidet, a wash basin and a WC, but you may hate showers and think a bidet unnecessary. What might be a great deal more fun would be an armchair and a shelf containing magazines and a stereo. Atmosphere is terribly important and much of it can be created by lighting, and carpeting is a must.

Do remember that a feeling of luxury and comfort can be created without spending a vast amount of money. A bath, basin and WC, at the bottom of the price range can look wonderful with some exotic taps and smart tiling. Add favourite pictures.

Planning your bathroom

Use the planner on the next page to enable you to play around with shapes in the space you have available. One square on our plan equals 100 millimetres. First draw your bathroom shape onto the planning grid and then cut out the shapes below and try fitting them in different positions. Do take particular note of the working space required for each unit, but recognize that the spaces can overlap each other. Whatever happens, do not overcrowd your bathroom – better to have one amenity less and be able to move around in comfort. Consider, too, a heated towel rail, mirrors, shaving socket, lights and storage space.

There is absolutely no need to employ the services of an architect. Having played around with the planning grid and decided, more or less, where everything should be placed, you can either use a small builder or go direct to a plumber. If you have no first hand experience of a good plumber we would suggest you talk to the manager of the bathroom centre from which you are buying your units. He should be able to advise on installation.

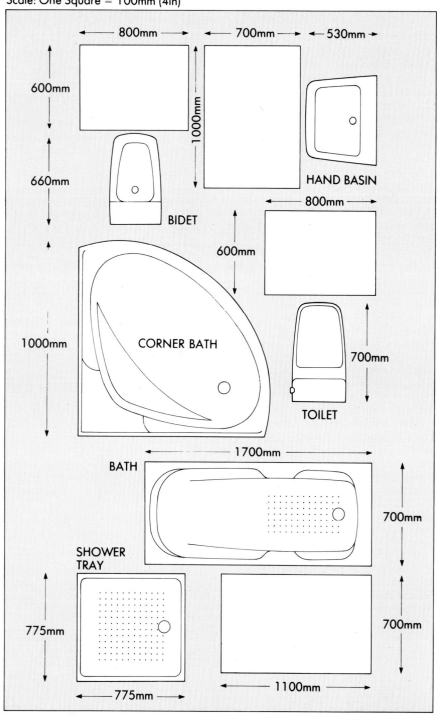

Scale: One Square = 100mm (4in)

800mm

600mm

660mm

BIDET

700mm

1000mm

530mm

HAND BASIN

800mm

600mm

700mm

TOILET

1000mm

CORNER BATH

1700mm

BATH

700mm

SHOWER
TRAY

700mm

775mm

1100mm

775mm

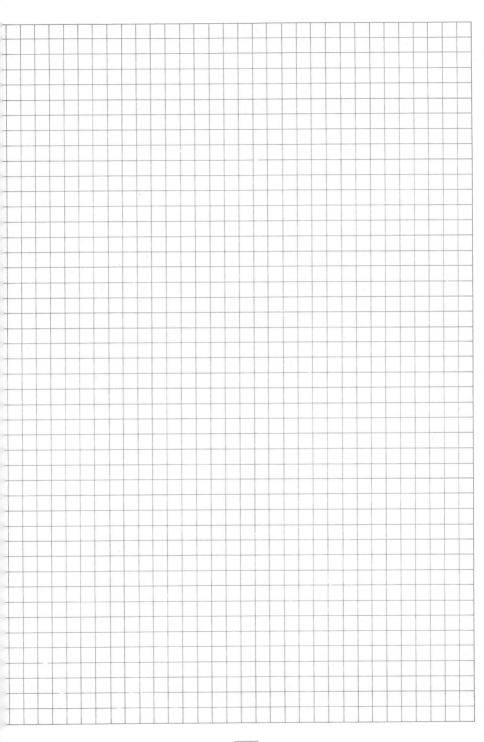

Kitchens

We live in our kitchen – we eat there, entertain there, relax there and work there. Even if your kitchen is confined to the preparation of food and you eat and socialize somewhere else, it will still be the busiest room in the house – the focal point of the home. A well designed kitchen, however small, is an enormous asset to a house – poor kitchens create stress and inefficiency and certainly earn a severe black mark if you come to sell your property.

Whether you are intending to design your kitchen from scratch or simply improve what is already there, you do have to be very careful not to become carried away. The range of kitchens available is absolutely amazing – bewilderingly so. We would suggest that before you go anywhere near a showroom, you should sit down with a pile of glossy magazines and decide on the look you want for your kitchen, so that you know what type of design you are seeking.

The starting point for any kitchen design or re-design, has to be the size of your budget and this is where you should stop and consider very carefully what you already have. Maybe you are not mad about the units that you have inherited with the house, but in our view, by far the most important feature of a kitchen is a good quality working surface. The uniform look of the whole working area covered in charming tiles can transform a kitchen. This is where the eye naturally falls and the units above and below pale into insignificance. A continuous work surface, spanning the odd gap between units, will give a feeling of cohesion to the whole kitchen. You can accentuate this feel by installing concealed strip lighting beneath the top units, which floods the work surfaces with lights and draws attention to them. If your units really do offend, or do not tie in with the tiles or work-top of your choice, there is an alternative to replacing them – why not buy new doors? It is possible to buy replacement doors as standard or if you would like to have non-standard wooden doors, you could have them made for you. Of course the problem with your kitchen may be so sev-ere in terms of design and layout that you feel you really do need to start from scratch, or you may have a new house requiring a kitchen design. If you are starting from scratch then it is probably best that you employ the services of a kitchen specialist, who will both plan and install the kitchen for you. **NB**. There is an organization called the Kitchen Specialists Association and, we would strongly recommend that you only use a firm who are members of the KSA.

Finance

So far as financing your kitchen is concerned, the best and cheapest method is to tack it on to your existing mortgage. Both banks and building societies are well aware that a nice-looking kitchen can only enhance the value of your house and assuming you are not over-borrowed already on your mortgage facilities, you should have no problem at all in raising the finance for such a project. The alternative could be to obtain credit from the supplier of your equipment, though here you do have to be very careful, for dealer finance tends to come expensive (usually 2% higher than bank or building society).

So . . . why not start designing your layout using the grid on the next page? Efficient kitchens have what is known as a work triangle when it comes to positioning the main appliances – i.e. the oven, the sink and the refrigerator. Try and have a walking distance between each of the three appliances of not more than six feet, it will save hours of time and shoe leather. Measure the size of your kitchen and transfer the measurements onto the grid – one square equals 100 millimetres. Mark in doors and windows, any units you intend to leave and electrical sockets and plumbing pipes. Once you have done this, using the cut-out units, start placing them around your kitchen plan until you achieve the effect you want.

Scale: One Square = 100mm (4in)

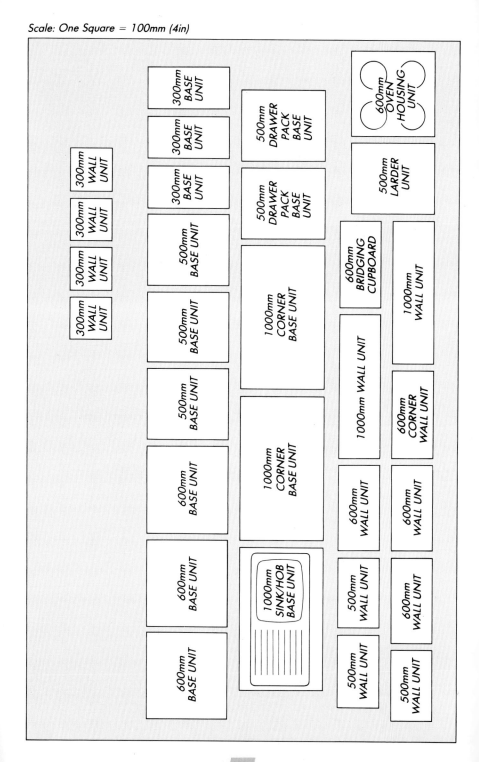

Interior decorating

Interior design and decoration of a house is a very personal thing. The combination of the decorations, the curtains and lighting can make a room come alive or turn it into a disaster. It can make one room pretty, another cheerless, one room warm and welcoming, another cold and hostile, one room masculine, another feminine . . . Yet it is difficult to look at the interior decorations of a room objectively, for what they should do is to reflect the lifestyle of the people whose home it is and provide the backdrop to their lives. The word *home* conjures up a feeling of peace, comfort and tranquillity – or at least, it should. Before rushing into a look-alike of the design interiors featured in the Sunday colour supplements, you need to be very certain that you can live with what are sometimes very theatrical effects. What you need to achieve are colour schemes which make each room an entity in itself, without contrasting too much in feel with the rest of the house. In other words, there needs to be a common theme but an individual look to each room – too much stark contrast is tiring. Of course there are exceptions – let your teenage daughter have a fling in her own room and pamper yourself with unashamed luxury in your own bedroom and bathroom. What you are trying to avoid is the hall contrasting too sharply with the kitchen, the kitchen with the dining-room and with the sitting room, and so on. One should flow into the other, picking up themes and colours and taking them on, with perhaps different but compatible effect.

Painting and decorating

Whether you are decorating yourself or employing a professional to do it for you, you and you alone must make the decisions as to what types of paints, finishes and colours you want. If you know little or nothing about paints, find a paint shop with a helpful manager willing to give advice. You need someone who knows what they are talking about, for there are so many different finishes that even knowledgeable householders are always learning something new.

Do remember that hard-wearing surfaces do not have to be high gloss – there are some very good satin finishes which are just as effective. However, if it is high gloss you want, there are some very easily appliable and effective paints available today. Most walls and ceilings around the house will look really good in emulsion paint – matt, satin or silk sheen. Few walls have to be papered – why not go for plain emulsion walls and add plenty of pictures. It is far easier to obtain exactly the tone you want with paint than paper. It is much less trouble to apply and so much easier to freshen up after a couple of years, or change the colour of a wall or the whole room if the mood takes you.

Do not be hidebound by fashion. Fashion in interior decorating is as fickle and short-lived as fashion in clothing. What is impor-

little Victorian commode which we have turned into a casing to house our television and stereo. Above the commode is a massive, stark painting, in the primitive style, beside it on the left is an enormous china harlequin great dane. On the right is a very comfortable armchair, covered in William Morris print, and above the chair hangs a warming pan, originating from the mid-eighteen hundreds. A crazy combination but it works for two reasons – each item is individual yet complements the other and each item is a well loved friend, which lends familiarity and comfort to the room.

So where to start with ideas? As you leaf through magazines, cut out the picture of any room which appeals to you and then try to analyse what elements attract you. When you visit friends' houses, consider your reaction to their rooms. If you like what you see, try and think why. Equally valuable is not liking a room and trying to decide where, in your view, your friends have gone wrong. With interior decorating you can learn a great deal from other people's mistakes.

Be practical, too – it is no good trying to realize your heart's desire if it just does not fit in with family activities. We made a hopeless mistake with our house when we moved in, by fitting it throughout with cream-coloured carpet, very similar to our old home. What we failed to recognize was that we are now living in the depths of the country and that our dogs and children are ten times muddier than they ever were before. Added to this, we acquired an extra dog because we had the space and allowed our cat to become pregnant! Feet marks, claw marks, dog hairs, sodden clothes from skirmishes in the river have all but finished our carpet – a darker, more hard-wearing quality would have lasted far longer and might easily have been cheaper.

If there is a message to this section it is this – do not let the search for interior decorative excellence submerge your individuality. If you are perhaps employing someone to design and decorate your house, or struggling alone with the help of magazines, always allow enough space for the room to develop and reflect the character of you and your family.

tant is that you feel comfortable and happy with what you create. The least successful rooms are often some of the most expensive, where people have slavishly followed some designer's suggestion, which leaves the room with no personality or character and no reflection of the day-to-day inhabitants.

Building a home cannot happen overnight – it is not an instant affair that appears from nowhere. To stare at a blank wall, decide it must be filled with pictures and so go out and buy some, is an appalling mistake. Pictures need to be built up over a number of years – to commemorate a well-remembered holiday, to celebrate a special birthday, a gift from a friend . . . Similarly it is a mistake to buy matching furniture for again it looks like a showroom. At this moment, we are in our sitting room facing a

DIY – a dangerous obsession

It is already a multi-million pound business, with enormous growth potential. The DIY superstores demonstrate this, as do the growing numbers of courses, magazines and sophisticated equipment now available. A controlled interest in DIY has to be an enormous advantage. It provides a relaxing yet worthwhile hobby, saves money and breeds satisfaction in seeing a good job well done. Taken to extremes, it becomes an obsession. Every weekend involves a new project, there is no longer time for family excursions, the house is in a constant state of upheaval and the strain takes its toll on all members of the family.

DIY, in the right place, is invaluable. For example, most people do their own decorating. In recent years the sophistication of paints, wallpapers and tools of the trade have developed to such a point that if you can read, you can decorate. It is a waste of money to have to call in a carpenter to erect some shelves, an electrician to mend a fuse, a glazier to replace a broken window or a plumber to replace a washer. However, beyond these simple tasks, the home owner has to decide to what extent he wishes to develop his skills. He should ask himself whether:

- He has the time
- He has the inclination
- He has the ability
- He does not have the ability but wishes to acquire it
- He genuinely believes that he can do a good job
- He can save money by doing it himself

So far as ability and inclination are concerned, this is something that only you can decide. Some people just do not have the patience for DIY, in which case they are likely to bodge any job they attempt, while others get a genuine kick out of achieving something for themselves. Time is a very serious commodity. If you are paid by the hour, freelance like us, or have your own business, you have to ask yourself how much money you could be earning at work, instead of spending the time on DIY. Add the cost of the lost working time to your raw materials and you will probably find it would be more economic to call in an expert, so you can get on with the job you know and understand.

For some people DIY is actually complementary to their work. Our job – writing – is a perfect example. There comes a point in the day where you feel you simply cannot write another word. However, because this can happen within what is technically the working day, it is very difficult to slope off and sit in front of the television, read a book or go to sleep, without feeling guilty. DIY offers the perfect outlet – the chance to do something relatively non-cerebral while at the same time useful, and allegedly, at any rate, cost effective.

Do's and don'ts of DIY

- Don't take on more than you can manage, either in terms of skill or in terms of time. Work up your DIY skills slowly, stage-by-stage – being too ambitious can lead to disaster.

- Do buy the best quality materials and tools for your DIY work. After all you will be saving money on labour, and good quality material will go a long way towards giving your work a professional look.

- Don't make a mess of jobs by hurrying and taking short cuts. A typical DIY carelessly completed job looks a lot worse than not doing it at all.

- Do recognize that if you develop your skills as a DIY enthusiast, you will probably spend more money on your home than if you relied on professional help. In other words, once you discover how much money you can 'save' by doing the work yourself, your aspirations and requirements will become increasingly exotic.

- Don't attempt any major work – either construction, electrical or plumbing. You must recognize your limitations and for big jobs call in a builder. However there is nothing to stop you offering your services as a labourer, if you have the time. This way the builder will be able to offer you a reduced quotation if you are undertaking all the unskilled work for him.

◆ Do recognize that DIY extensions and conversions will not inspire either bank or building society to lend you money. In some instances a sympathetic manager – perhaps knowing you personally and recognizing your skills – might be prepared to lend you at least part of the cost of materials. As a general rule, however, no bank is going to lend you money to do it yourself. If you need to finance your building work then either you are going to have to employ a professional builder or accept instant (and expensive) credit from your suppliers.

◆ Don't let DIY become an obsession. Your home should be a place where you can relax, which you can enjoy and where you spend time with family and friends. Just as there are people who cannot look round a room without searching for a cobweb or piece of dust, there is a growing band of DIY maniacs who begin twitching dangerously at the sound of a dripping tap or sight of a piece of cracked plaster or a badly fitting door. Keep your sense of proportion, try and adopt the 'mañana' attitude to life or you will find yourself in the position of having to go back to work for a rest.

Damp and decay

The tell-tale signs of chronic damp in a building are all too familiar – that cold, dank feeling, the musty smell, the stains on the wall and ceiling, turning in extreme cases to black mildew. What is sometimes not recognized, however, is that damp can be a major problem long before it starts to show itself in such obvious ways. The longer it goes undetected and untreated, the more it will take hold and the more difficult and expensive it will be to put it right.

Except in the cases of flooding and condensation, damp is always caused by a defect in the fabric of the building – either as a result of lack of maintenance, or faulty design or workmanship. This being the case, treatment is always twofold – finding and curing the cause and making good the damage.

Flooding

Provided the flooding of your home is a one-off disaster – caused perhaps by storm water or a water main bursting – although it

is very messy and traumatic, if you act quickly there will be no long term problems with which to cope. Your house insurance will cover you for flooding and obviously your priority has to be to rid the house of as much of the water as quickly as possible. You should remove carpets and wet upholstery, introduce plenty of ventilation and ultimately hire a de-humidifier to absorb the moisture residue. Problems arise when flooding becomes a regular occurrence – if you live on the edge of a river whose banks burst every January and February, for example. While an insurance company will be happy to pick up the bill once, they will become increasingly reluctant, until ultimately they may not be prepared to cover you at all. Your local authority will have on its staff an Emergency Planning Officer, who is there to cope with disasters. If you have a flood problem, we would suggest you contact him to see what he can do to help you.

Condensation

Condensation is a very common problem which can be caused by lack of proper ventilation, lack of proper or consistent heating, inadequate finish of the building or faulty roof, gutters or damp course. There is always some moisture in the air but condensation has become unacceptable when you start to find droplets of water running down the surfaces of your room and windows permanently misted over. There are various steps you can take to reduce condensation:

- Ventilate your house properly, particularly the kitchen and bathroom when they are being used.
- Heat your home a little more but not with paraffin or gas heaters which actually create moisture.
- Do not leave internal kitchen and bathroom doors open when in use – it spreads moist air round the whole house.
- When cooking, cover pans of water and do not leave kettles to boil for too long.
- Insulate and draughtproof. This in theory, sounds like a contradiction to ventilation but it is not so. Insulation

will ensure that your house stays warmer and draughtproofing will stop heat being lost.

♦ In extreme cases, rent or buy a dehumidifier to remove the condensation initially while you take steps to improve the situation long term.

Rising damp

Rising damp is a problem in this country. Moisture is absorbed from the ground into the very fabric of the building, which has wallpaper peeling off the walls, paint staining and bubbling, followed by mildew and smells. *It has to be said that there is no short-cut, cheap remedy to severe rising damp*, unless it is caused merely by a build-up of soil or debris over the top of an otherwise good damp course. Confronted with a real problem, you need to call in expert help, install a proper damp course and then have the affected area re-plastered with renovating plaster. Any patching up is a complete waste of time. A faulty damp course can be cut out and renewed, but the injection of a silicone barrier in the wall is a very satisfactory, long term (and less expensive) treatment.

Tanking

If a wall is constructed, partially or completely below ground level, it is particularly susceptible to dampness. We are thinking here of cellars or basements. Once damp takes a hold in these areas, there is no short cut. What you need is professional help to provide tanking. Tanking involves removing the existing plaster, making good the wall surface and then applying a waterproof membrane to completely seal the whole below-ground area. On the face of it, this sounds expensive but do not overlook the fact that it could provide you with another room – a play room, an office perhaps. Your damp basement which has housed nothing more than coal, logs and discarded bicycles could prove a very viable living area if properly treated.

Roofs, gutters and plumbing

Sorry – but there are so many possible causes of damp and decay in a house – blocked gutters, loose or missing tiles, faulty cladding, cracked downpipes, faulty flashing round the chimney, and so on and so on. It is not our practice to advertise any particular brand name but if you are faced with serious damp, without knowing why, the best possible solution is to call in a firm such as RENTOKIL and ask them to conduct their free survey, to find out precisely what is wrong with your house. This sounds potentially expensive, but judging by personal experience and taking their advertising literature at face value, often their survey reveals only a minor fault which can be put right at very little cost. If you cannot find the cause yourself, then you *must* call in expert help.

Timber decay

Timber decay takes two forms – dry rot and wet rot. In both instances the rot is caused by varieties of fungi and both fungi have the ability to cause the rapid decay and breakdown of timber, which in turn leads to loss of structural strength. Dry rot is the more serious of the two because it has the ability to spread more effectively – whereas wet rot is halted by the intervention of materials other than wood – i.e. bricks, water, plaster etc – dry rot can travel over these to find the next piece of wood to attack. Again, faced with timber decay, you really do have no alternative but to call in expert help – fast.

The message of this section is to take damp seriously and not pretend the problem will go away simply by covering it up. Do not over-react – a small patch of damp appearing on a wall may well be caused by a blocked gutter or some such problem which can be easily solved. However, persistent and increasing damp needs dealing with and you will not be saving money in the long term by looking for a cheap short term solution.

Dry rot, in particular, can prove to be a far more expensive problem than might be imagined when first located. A small patch detected in the corner of one room can easily lead to the replacement of the whole of the timbers on the ground floor, and the staircase!

Pests

While you may be happy to share your home with your beloved dog and cat, you need to recognize that there are many, many thousands of unwelcome living things also resident in your home – yes, really! An unpleasant subject maybe, but one which needs to be considered. We will deal with each particular pest in turn:

Timber infestation

There are three types of beetle which are likely to infest your timberwork –

The common furniture beetle

The deathwatch beetle

The house long horn beetle

The common furniture beetle is the most susceptible to insecticide whereas the house long horn and the deathwatch beetle are more difficult to eradicate. The areas most likely to be affected are the loft, the floor, the staircase and various pieces of joinery in your house, such as skirting boards, picture rails and architraves. While you can treat these areas yourself, we would strongly recommend that you call in experts who will strip and spray the affected areas and then replace floorboards, carpets etc, etc.

Vermin

If you have an infestation of rats, mice or cockroaches you should phone your local authority Environmental Health Department. They will send round a pest control officer, both to eliminate and advise and the good news is there is no charge for this service.

Ants

The common black ant is a familiar creature in this country. Most nests are situated outside – in flower beds or under the stones. Now and again, though, ants do make their nests in the foundations of a house and in any event often enter houses foraging for food. When dealing with ants, your primary concern should be finding the nest. Assuming you do so, you should pour boiling water on it and then use an insecticide dust or spray to cover the whole area. If it is impossible to find the nest then your only course of action is to spray all the access points i.e. window frames or skirting boards, where you see the ants are entering your house – this should deter them.

Bats

Carpet beetle

Bats are a protected species these days and contrary to popular belief, they are entirely harmless – they will *not* fly into your hair. Still, for many people sharing their home with a colony of bats is a far from happy prospect. Because of their endangered status, a well-established colony cannot be moved without permission. Certainly if you are buying a house where bats are resident, do not assume that they can be removed – you should assume that you may have to learn to live with them. For advice and help contact The Nature Conservancy Council in your area.

About the same size as bed bugs at about ⅛″ long, carpet beetles attack, besides carpets, any woollens or fur. They are now more serious a pest than ordinary clothes moths. Again, the Environmental Health Department will supply you with the necessary insecticide.

Bees

Bed bugs

These ghastly creatures are fortunately very rare these days. They are flat, round insects which feed on human blood, leaving itchy bites. They also have a strange odour which indicates their presence. Insecticide aerosols and advice are available from the Environmental Health Department.

Because bees are valuable pollinaters, they should not be killed. If you are having a serious problem, you should contact your local authority to see if they can help you, but essentially you should try and live with the bees in your garden. If you have to cope with a swarm of honeybees, contact your local police station. They will have a record of beekeepers in your immediate locality. This will enable you to find someone with the right equipment and attitude to remove your problem.

Moles

Most of the population of Great Britain have been brought up on *The Wind in the Willows* which gives them a soft spot for moles – that is until one morning when they gaze across their hitherto immaculate lawn and see large, brown lumps indicating a mole's progress during the night. The only effective way to cure the problem of moles is to insert poisoned bait deep into the run, to avoid it being dug up by your domestic pets. The poison should be added to a jam jar full of earth worms and the substance recommended is strychnine salt in a ratio of ⅛ of an ounce of salt to ½ lb of worms. Trapping is an alternative but not to be recommended as it is messy and time consuming.

Wasps

If you are having trouble with an abundance of wasps it means that somewhere near to you you have a nest or several nests. For nest removal you should contact The Environmental Health Department who, for a small fee, will send someone to help you.

Flies

You are most likely to be faced with the problems of the common house fly but an alternative is the bluebottle, which is shiny blue in colour, larger than a house fly and noisy in flight. The stable fly and horse fly, both brown in colour, can give a nasty bite. Flies can best be eliminated with a spray, unless you have caged birds or an aquarium of fish, in which case either use old fashioned flypaper or, an ultraviolet strip light, as found in catering kitchens.

Fleas

If you have dogs or cats you can be fairly sure that at some time you will have a flea problem. Fleas are small and red, jump about in an erratic manner and have an extremely itchy, unpleasant bite. Ordinary flea spray and shampoo works best. If one of your animals has the problem, bath all the animals, wash and spray all their bedding and all furniture likely to have been affected.

Mosquitoes

A number of midges, flies and gnats are often mistaken for mosquitoes in this country, because of the buzzing noise they make. In fact there are very few mosquitoes in Britain and these are mostly around water. Sprays are the most effective deterrent.

Silver fish

Silver fish are silvery grey and about ½″ long. They are most likely to be seen in baths and basins, indeed in any slightly damp area. They are not really a problem, even in large numbers. Spray if they are a nuisance.

Clothes moths

Contrary to popular belief moths do no harm – once they are flying around, they are not an enemy. It is the little white grub which eats wool, carpets, clothes etc. Spray your wardrobes with moth killer and store any precious clothing in plastic bags.

The best way to keep pests at bay is to concentrate on good hygiene. Never leave food scraps around – crumbs on the table, bags of rubbish or indeed anything which is going to attract them. Dealing with pests is a two tier problem – first you need to establish what is attracting the pest, and having removed the attraction, then you can deal with the infestation.

Landscaping

Since there are literally thousands of different gardening books currently in print on every conceivable aspect of horticulture, it would be quite wrong here, to try to emulate them. However there are a few points we feel worth mentioning and which apply whether your garden covers many acres or is no bigger than a postage stamp.

The first question you need to ask yourself is what you actually want to do in your garden and how often! Creating the perfect formal garden might be aesthetically very pleasing and will give you an immediate sense of satisfaction, but will you ever be able to maintain it? Are you prepared to become a slave to your garden? Surely its purpose is to provide a haven for relaxation in an otherwise stressful world. Creating a garden which needs endless work will mean you never relax in the sunshine, but are always busy in ceaseless toil to try and keep pace with the weeds. Of course none of this matters if you are a dedicated gardener with time on your hands, but for most of us we want a garden which gives us pleasure, without too much pain.

Planning a garden from scratch could be the result of your having moved into a new house, which is surrounded by nothing but a sea of mud. Alternatively you may have moved into a house with a well-established garden which simply does not appeal to you. Yet again, your circumstances may have changed. Perhaps your partner has died, or you and your spouse are simply getting too old to cope with the garden, or can no longer afford a gardener. In any one of these instances, your aim will be to greatly simplify the garden in order to make it as labour saving as possible.

Planning is the key, and of course much depends on the size of your pocket. If you have the money then clearly the most restful way to design and landscape your garden is to hand it over to the experts. A glance through the *Yellow Pages* will immediately demonstrate to you that there are any number of landscape gardeners offering their services. Ideally, as with almost everything, what you need is a personal recommendation but failing that, invite two or three different firms to come and see your garden and ask them to submit an outline proposal and give you an idea of the costs involved. Clearly, before you can take such a step, you need an idea of what you want, though much of your thinking undoubtedly will be stimulated by discussion with a garden expert. Once you have decided which firm you are going to use, always insist on a quotation in writing, but you will recognize that landscape gardening services do not come cheap since they are very labour intensive.

A good half-way house is to find somebody who will excavate and shift earth for you – which is the really hard work – leaving you to lay lawns, develop flower beds, build rockeries etc, etc. If you have bought a new house on an estate, you may well find that slipping the driver of a digger, still working on an adjoining site, a few fivers and a crate of beer, will have him shifting the earth around for you until you have the shape of garden you want. If you have an existing garden which displeases you, you can employ a landscape gardener to do this basic earth-shifting for you, including perhaps re-turfing where necessary.

Developing a garden plan

If you are going to design your own garden, you need a piece of graph paper on which you should draw, roughly to scale, the outline plan of your house and the boundaries of your garden. Then mark in north/south/east/west and shade into the garden area those parts which receive sun for the majority of the day, leaving unshaded the dark corners. The next step is to plot in existing flower beds, trees, shrubs, ponds, paths etc. Then mark in red any eyesores which you wish to hide, either in your garden or next-door's – an old shed, drain pipes, a glimpse of a factory chimney, pylon or telegraph pole. This finished, go inside your house and look at the view of your garden from each window. Do remember that for much of the year this is how you will see it. Particularly from the upstairs windows, do not restrict your viewing to your own garden but look beyond it. If you have a nice view beyond your boundary fence, then it is important that your garden

planning does not obstruct it – after all it is free and requires no maintenance! When this plan is completed you are ready to re-design your garden.

Within the confines of this book it is clearly impossible to give detailed advice on garden design but here are a few thoughts:

◆ The look of your garden will be greatly enhanced if you can create a mixture of heights. This can be done in two ways – by planting flowers and shrubs of different heights and by landscaping the garden in such a way as to create slopes and hollows, raised patios and rockeries. Try and create a three dimensional effect – a flat, level garden is boring.

◆ Aim for a balance in your garden. In other words create different areas – perhaps a vegetable garden, a greenhouse, a patio and barbecue area, a water garden and an area of lawn for the children. In a very small garden, obviously these areas are impractical – in which case you will have to rely on different heights to create the contrast.

◆ Many modern houses are not things of great beauty – certainly in their early years – and can be greatly improved by planting climbers against the house to soften the more severe lines and cover up unsightly pipework. Tubs, too, placed near the house can help in this respect.

◆ If you have a large garden, a smallholding or are a farmer or landowner of some substance, it may be possible that you can obtain a grant from your local council for a scheme to improve the look of your land. Most of the grant money available these days is for tree re-planting which is very understandable in view of the hurricane damage of 1987. However there is also help available for clearing ponds and restoring existing woodlands. To qualify for a grant you have to be able to demonstrate that the work will be of benefit to the public – so it must be visible from a public right of way.

Building in your garden

Generally, if you wish to build a conservatory, a greenhouse, a garden shed, an aviary, a poultry house or a garage in your garden, you may do so without planning permission. Needless to say, there are some inevitable provisos:

- The building must be for the benefit of the occupants of the house and connected with its residential use – so aviaries, rabbit hutches or poultry houses would come into this category if the animals are for domestic needs or for personal enjoyment – not if you are running a business.
- The building must not be placed closer to a public footpath or highway than the existing house.
- The building must not be more than four metres high, if it has a ridge roof, or three metres high otherwise.
- If your 'garden shed' is in truth a stable, it counts as an extension to the house – in which case you might require planning consent (see page 120).
- Garages are also treated as extensions if they are within five metres of the existing house or you live in a national park, a conservation area, or an area of outstanding natural beauty.
- If your proposed garage is intended to have a separate access, or will be used for business purposes, planning permission will be required.
- A sun lounge or conservatory will be regarded as an extension, if attached to the house, and may therefore require planning consent.

Before building in the garden, you should also study your conveyance if you have a freehold, or your lease if you have a leasehold property. Some freehold properties carry, in their conveyance, covenants which preclude the building of even the smallest garden shed, and if you are leasing a property, it is highly likely you will not be allowed to erect any sort of building – at any rate without the landlord's permission.

Of equal concern has to be the feelings of your neighbours. A greenhouse or garden shed placed in the wrong position, so far as your neighbours are concerned, could completely obscure their view or cast a shadow over their prize border. Yes, all right, it is your land and you should be able to do whatever you like with it. However, common courtesy should prevail to the extent that any building, however small, you intend erecting in your garden, should be preceded by a visit to your neighbours, to inform them of what you are doing and to make sure they have no reasonable objection. There is a practical, as well as a moral

reason for dealing with neighbours in this way. If they turn nasty and start complaining to the local council it could cause you a great deal of trouble.

Let us look at the different types of building which you are likely to erect on your land:

Conservatories

In Britain, a conservatory is a great boon, creating the link between the garden (often rain-swept and cold) and the house. It can be a glorified greenhouse or a very formal sitting room/dining room, and all stations in between. All the year round it offers protection to both plants and people, while giving one the feel of enjoying the garden in comfort. Conservatories vary enormously in style and can be virtually custom-built for very little more than the standard cost. It is important to match your conservatory to the style of your house. Some of the current Victorian style conservatories are charming but look very silly when attached to a modern house. Your *Yellow Pages* will head you in the direction of a suitable conservatory. Normally most conservatory manufacturers will erect but expect you to arrange for a local builder to prepare the foundations and floor slab. An alternative to double glazing are blinds, which are very effective in controlling excessive temperature variation, and also look attractive.

Greenhouses

Choose a sunny site, with the central pathway of the greenhouse running east/west. Make sure that there are no overhanging trees and keep your greenhouse away from both the road and the children's play areas, otherwise you will be always replacing broken glass. If you require a concrete floor then obviously a local builder can do this for you, though most greenhouses can be easily erected without the need for any professional skill. Aluminium is favoured these days. If you prefer the aesthetic look of wood, then go for cedar or oak. Most purists favour electric heating, in which case you need a power point. Paraffin and gas heaters are not considered good for plants. If the greenhouse is a lean-to, it might be possible to link the heating of it to your central heating. A greenhouse can be an endless source of pleasure and in the long run can save a great deal of money, providing you with flowers and vegetables.

Garden sheds

Garden sheds again come in all shapes and sizes and, of course, are vastly cheaper if you do not require a floor and windows. A shed is an absolute must for most homes, if the garage is not to be full of gardening clutter. Buy the best quality of wood you can afford and do treat it regularly with preservatives. Your local *Yellow Pages* will help you find a suitable shed.

Garages

Although a garage is quite substantial structure, you do not need planning permission provided you meet the requirements outlined at the beginning of this section, and provided that the garage is to be used for the benefit of the occupants of the existing house and not in any way let out or used as a separate dwelling. Some people build their own garage but usually a local builder is the best bet as you will require building regulations clearance. Sometimes there are problems with garages with regard to highways, particularly if you wish to create a new exit from your land. Check out if you need planning permission before starting work.

Odds and ends

Patios

A patio or terrace serves to create a focal point to the garden. In Britain it also serves a practical purpose – on showery days you can go in and out of the house without bringing mud and wet with you. A patio can be made by simply heaping gravel onto the ground surface but this is not very satisfactory. Paving stones are ideal, in real stone if you can afford it, or precast paving slabs, if not. What every patio needs is direct sun and an element of screening from the prevailing wind. Ideally you should provide some form of shading from extremely hot sun, particularly if you enjoy eating outside. This can either take the form of an awning or an umbrella. Tubs placed around the patio will give colour, and raised beds set into low brick walls will divide the patio from the rest of the garden. No patio should be less than 12′ × 12′ or there will not be enough room for table and chairs. A patio leading off from the kitchen is very convenient but in our experience it soon looks more like a backyard, for everyone leaves their wellington boots and discarded anoraks all over the place. A patio leading out of either the sitting or dining room stands a far better chance of retaining at least a degree of elegance!

If you are building a patio with any kind of dividing wall, why not consider building in your own barbecue as part of the wall structure? You can buy cooking grids, charcoal grills and trays in kit form from your local garden centre.

Driveways and hardstandings

The driveway, surprisingly, is an area which people tend to ignore, yet so far as most houses are concerned, the drive is the first feature any one approaching the house will see. More often than not, the driveway is made up of messy gravel or cracked, disintegrating paving stones, with a miserable border of neglected flowers or a piece of tatty lawn running up one or both sides. Driveways cause aggravation, too, with a small turning area and inadequate parking

for visitors and family cars. You would do well to re-appraise the front of your house. It might be better to do away with the flower beds and lawn and nicely pave the whole area with hardstanding for extra cars. You can break up the look of the paved area with a series of tubs and perhaps climbing shrubs up the side of the house to create the break between driveway and wall. There are a number of excellent products on the market in terms of long-lasting paving stones and, again, *Yellow Pages* should point you in the direction of your local suppliers.

Outside lighting

If you enjoy entertaining outside or in a conservatory, lighting your garden can prove a very attractive feature, but only if your garden is both well planned and well cared for! Highlighting the nettles is not clever. If you are planning a garden from scratch, then ideally this is the moment when you should consider the lighting, for it is then possible to bury cables below the paving stones or lawns. Strictly speaking the work should be left to a qualified electrician and it is vital that you use special-purpose cables and fittings intended for outdoor use. You really do have to be very careful with cable, for cutting through it accidentally when mowing the lawn is not a terrific idea. Remember that outside lighting should shine on objects, not into the eyes of people wandering in the garden. The idea is to create a number of features, which look attractive when illuminated, and then light them precisely rather than the garden as a whole.

Walls

A wall makes an excellent boundary. It provides privacy, it greatly reduces noise and is a far more permanent feature than a fence. However put a wall – particularly a high one – round a small garden, and it can feel extremely oppressive. Without planning approval, a wall must not be built more than two metres high, and where it runs along the boundary of your property adjoining a highway, it must not be more than one metre high. Again, you would do well to check your conveyance or lease – whichever is appropriate – to make sure there are no restrictions on the building of a wall. Clearly, too, you need to consult your neighbours to seek their approval.

Walls need a solid foundation and if you have no experience of laying bricks you should call in a professional, particularly if it is to be a high wall – they are very dangerous unless properly constructed and are responsible for a number of deaths and injuries every year. Walls can be made out of brick, stone or concrete and certainly if it is a natural stone wall you are building, you will need a professional – building stone walls is a very skilled business.

Fences

Like walls, a fence can provide privacy or can be made into a feature – such as a trellis or a picket fence. It all depends on what job you want your fence to do – whether you wish it to provide you with privacy or protection from the prevailing wind, or whether you want it to be child-proof or animal proof. Whatever type of fencing you choose, you will need posts at regular intervals, usually not more than six feet apart. Except where light fencing is concerned, ideally the posts should be set in concrete. Wooden fences should always be treated with preservative and galvanized nails should be used during erection. Always be on the lookout for any piece of fencing which is faulty and needs replacing. One piece of faulty fencing, caught by the wind, can bring the whole lot down.

Arches and pergolas

A pergola is a series of arches and whether you choose to erect one or a number, an archway can create an interesting break in a garden. Large garden centres sell kits and most archways are made of wood, although metal and occasionally brick can be used. Flowers such as wistaria, climbing roses, honeysuckle and clematis look charming draping their way round an archway and can create a very distinctive look to your garden.

Garden furniture

Gardens should be for sitting in as well as working in and attractive garden furniture can be a considerable feature. Undoubtedly, the most stylish and labour-saving garden furniture is made in plastic coated metal which requires virtually no maintenance, Alternatively, there is a lot of plastic and glass fibre furniture available. Traditional wood and cast iron looks very attractive but does require a degree of maintenance, and certainly in the case of cast iron, it is far from comfortable.

If you have a small garden you should perhaps consider buying folding tables and chairs which can be stored when not in use. There is a wonderful range of garden furniture available now at garden centres around the country, but do be careful not to overclutter a small garden.

Swimming pools

Without wishing to be too unenthusiastic, there are several negative points that you should consider before making a decision to install a swimming pool:

◆ A swimming pool is very unlikely to add anything to the value of your house, so do not labour under the belief that you will recoup your investment when you come to sell. You will not. In fact for some potential buyers, the pool will not be a plus point but a positive disadvantage.

◆ A swimming pool is certainly expensive to install and it is also very expensive to run. The authors' experience is that it can cost as much to heat a swimming pool during the summer as the whole house during winter – unless your family is very spartan.

◆ A swimming pool is enormously time-consuming in a maintenance sense. However much equipment and how-

ever efficient the covers you have for it, it is always needing attention. If you are wealthy enough to have a pool it may be that you are wealthy enough to employ somebody to look after it. Certainly this is the ideal answer, for otherwise you may find yourself spending more time cleaning your pool than actually swimming in it.

◆ The moment you have a pool you find you have friends you did not know existed, and it is very difficult to be firm with them, particularly in nice weather. If we are suddenly blessed with an all too infrequent heatwave, then clearly you and your family will want to spend as much time around the pool as possible. The trouble is, so will all your friends, particularly if they have small children. It leads to a tricky situation. While, in theory, you may say to your friends that you will tell them if it is inconvenient, in practice, on a blazing August day in the middle of the summer holidays, it is very difficult to deny close friends the pleasure of enjoying your pool. In temperament, therefore, ideally you either need to be a Scrooge or an extrovert.

Having done our best to dissuade you from having a pool, let us look at the sort of prices you will have to pay if you choose to ignore our advice! Firstly, the *Yellow Pages* will give you a list of swimming pool suppliers in your area and the magic word you are looking for is SPATA – the Swimming Pool and Allied Trades Association. If the firm with whom you intend to deal is a member of SPATA, then you can be sure of a fair degree of quality, and if there should be problems and the firm goes into liquidation while your pool is being built, then SPATA will see that it is completed for you without any further loss.

There are really four types of pool for you to consider. Let us look at the typical domestic size of pool, which is about 30′ × 15′, and compare the prices:

◆ Reinforced concrete block construction, with marbelite tiles, including filtration plant – cost aproximately £15,000. To this price you need to add approximately £1,000 for the immediate paved surrounds, plus £1,000 for gas heating or £2,000 for a heat pump. Fancy shapes and steps would be extra.

◆ Sprayed concrete construction which is both more rigid and has a longer life – cost £17,000–£20,000 with marbelite tiles and filtration plant. The extras would be the same as for the block construction.

◆ A liner pool – this involves a concrete block base with an internal polythene liner which has an approximate life of ten years – cost including filtration plant £9,000. The additional costs would be the same as above.

◆ Above ground pool – this is rather like a large, rigid paddling pool! Significantly cheaper, in a price range of between £1,000–£3,000.

Let us now look at the pros and cons of the various types of pool. The concrete block construction with tile finish is a nice looking pool but the problem is that the tiles tend to damage in the frost, and they need to be replaced fairly regularly to avoid the pool's looking tatty and causing injury. The sprayed concrete construction is without doubt the best and most long-lasting pool but is very expensive. The concrete block pool, with liner, is a very good answer for someone with a more restricted budget. Admittedly the liner does have to be replaced approximately every ten years – at a cost of about £1,000 – but this is not too much of an inhibiting factor. The above ground pools are, of course, the cheapest but they do look very unattractive and tend to have rust problems. Certainly in our experience, we have yet to see an above ground pool which even begins to blend in pleasantly with the garden. It is an eyesore any way you look at it.

Heating

As suggested above, the two methods of heating are either by gas or by an electric heat pump. If you have an existing supply of gas then the installation of gas heating for your pool is relatively inexpensive. If you have no gas supply then it is probably not worthwhile even considering this method of heating. A heat pump is more expensive to install but cheaper to run, although the difference in cost is not significant – the running costs for gas per season are approximately £300, and for a heat pump £200.

Additional facilities

If you are really going mad, then with your pool you need a chalet, a barbecue area, a sauna, a sunbed and a spa bath, not to mention changing rooms and attractive garden furniture. Certainly you can make a swimming pool the most marvellous focal point of your home but you still cannot escape the vagaries of the average British summer. We would strongly recommend that unless you have money to burn, you think very seriously indeed before installing a swimming pool.

Fall-out shelters

It began like this – the telephone rang and a voice, charged with emotion and high drama, said 'The name is Bond, David Bond. How can I help you?' An introduction like this stuns one into instant silence and it took some time to unravel the fact that David Bond was in fact the Emergency Planning Officer. Our immediate reaction was to panic. Had the garden shed we recently erected (with our neighbours' permission and full blessing) broken some horrendous planning rule, so horrendous that the emergency planning officer had been brought in to tear it from its foundations? No, the explanation was quite simple. At our request, our secretary had called in to the local district council and asked for any information they might have on fall-out shelters and this was the response!

Without in any way wishing to offend the charming and helpful Mr Bond, the degree of urgency and importance he attached to our request for information was somewhat out of proportion and we were tempted to wonder whether this was the first 'emergency' the Emergency Planning Officer had dealt with in some time. In any event, good as his word, through the post came a helpful little booklet entitled *Domestic Nuclear Shelters, a Home Office Guide*, which is available either from the HMSO or from your local district council for a cost of 50p.

The booklet is very comprehensive. It outlines three basic kinds of nuclear shelter:
- A simple shelter for short term indoor or outdoor use, which can be built from materials which you should already have to hand.
- Shelters which can be assembled from a do-it-yourself kit.
- Permanent custom-made shelters which are built into the ground and require professional help in both design and construction.

There is a list of suggested food and equipment and there is a highly unemotional, and informative, account of what to expect in terms of the immediate effects of a nuclear attack.

If you are intending to build a permanent shelter you may need planning permission and building regulations clearance. A permanent shelter may even affect the rateable value of your house, so it could prove quite an expensive operation.

World politics are not our field and it would be quite wrong of us to comment, one way or the other, on the validity of building a fall-out shelter. What one cannot ignore is the increasing use of nuclear power and in the light of the horrific experiences of Chernobyl, maybe some kind of shelter could be sensible. Certainly, if you live near, or are on the prevailing windward side, of a nuclear power station and envisage staying in your house for some years, then perhaps you might be justified in taking such a step. In the case of nuclear attack, of course, none of us know whether a shelter would be of any use, or even desirable. Most of us, when asked about nuclear war, say we prefer to have the bomb dropped right on top of us than to be a survivor. However, all of us recognize that this is bravado and we don't really know how we are likely to feel should such a dreadful thing occur.

Certainly, having read Mr Bond's little booklet, we came to the conclusion that, if nothing else, all home owners should have a copy for, strangely, it does bring a degree of comfort to know you have something to which to refer.

A properly constructed, professionally built outdoor shelter of course could have other uses – an excellent wine cellar for example, a good place to store bulbs, your apple crop and sacks of potatoes. If you have young children you can be confident that it will be turned into a secret camp.

It is interesting to note that Mr Bond's district council is in fact in the midst of building a fall-out shelter for the council officials, though why they should take precedence over the rest of us one cannot imagine. Perhaps our local district council knows something we do not. Certainly, it is a little unnerving how many fall-out shelters have been built around the country to house

– how shall we call them? – 'the bureaucrats'.

We cannot really imagine that a fall-out shelter will do anything to the value of your house. As with swimming pools, if you feel you would be happier with one, so be it, but do not try to justify the cost on commercial grounds. Most of us firmly reject the idea of nuclear war as a possibility, putting it out of our minds as much as we can. If you have a safe bunker sitting in your back garden, the grisly possibility of world destruction is constantly with you.

If you feel a fall-out shelter would be an advantage to your home, then we would suggest you contact the Mr Bond in your life – the Emergency Planning Officer at your local district council, who we are sure will be able to give you plenty of advice.

Authors' note

This may not seem a particularly optimistic note on which to end a book on property but at least you cannot accuse us of not covering every eventuality!